'This volume considers fast-evolving environments that present special challenges to businesses and entrepreneurs. It delivers a collection of carefully crafted micro studies and a general framework to understand successful business trajectories in turbulent environments. Recommended for entrepreneurship scholars, students and practitioners.'

Tomasz Mickiewicz, 50th Anniversary Professor of Economics, ABS, Aston University, Birmingham, UK

'Mets, Sauka and Purg offer a welcome, detailed study of the many facets and variants of the international path to entrepreneurship of firms in Central and Eastern Europe, while highlighting countries' similarities and differences. The reader finds in this welcome book a wealthy source of knowledge of the varied processes and strategies to internationalization in different firms which contributed to the varying degrees of success of countries in transition.'

Bruno Dallago, Department of Economics and Management, University of Trento, Italy

ENTREPRENEURSHIP IN CENTRAL AND EASTERN EUROPE

The process of the transition to a market-oriented economy for countries from Central and Eastern Europe (CEE) and the Commonwealth of Independent States (CIS) started some 25 years ago. A new technology base triggered the fast growth of new investments into intangible assets by global economic leaders at the beginning of the 1990s, providing the basis for a move towards a knowledge economy. During the past 25 years, entrepreneurs in CEE and the CIS have reshaped traditional industries and created new industries, combining innovative ideas with traditional competencies. Yet we still do not know very much about how and why companies led by entrepreneurs develop, how they expand globally and what the role of new knowledge and innovation is in the internationalization process. Understanding the pathways of entrepreneurial development, especially growth through internationalization, is important for the overall development of countries in transition and beyond.

Entrepreneurship in Central and Eastern Europe: Development through Internationalization provides an overview of entrepreneurship in a range of important emerging markets. This book aims to fill the gap in the literature by providing up-to-date data and case-based evidence.

With coverage of a range of national firms from countries including Belarus, Estonia, Hungary, Poland, Latvia, Lithuania, Serbia, Slovakia, Slovenia and Ukraine, this book will be vital supplementary reading around international entrepreneurship and essential reading for those studying the business environment in this vital emerging market.

Dr. Tõnis Mets is Professor of Entrepreneurship at the University of Tartu in Estonia.

Dr. Arnis Sauka is an Associate Professor and Director of the Centre for Sustainable Business at the Stockholm School of Economics in Riga, Latvia.

Professor Dr. Danica Purg is the President and Dean of IEDC-Bled School of Management, Postgraduate Studies (Slovenia), and the President of CEEMAN, International Association for Management Development in Dynamic Societies.

Global Entrepreneurship

Edited by Pawan Tamvada, *University of Southampton, UK*

Entrepreneurship has become a global byword for positivity in business and management. It is viewed almost universally as the key to developing a robust and growing economy. While most would agree that at its core entrepreneurship involves the identification of opportunities in the unmet, underserved and/or emerging needs of people through the marshalling of resources and the creation of enterprises or other entities to deliver need fulfilling products and services, the nature of the activity his highly context sensitive. What works in one place and for one group of people will not necessarily work elsewhere. Both the needs themselves and the methods and structures that can be acceptably developed differ from place to place and people to people

Global Entrepreneurship seeks to provide textbooks addressing entrepreneurship in the key geographic areas of the global socioeconomic system. The series provides a library of textbooks which give the student enough learning materials to gain a comprehensive understanding of entrepreneurship in general and how it is manifested in a variety of geographic and cultural settings.

Entrepreneurship in Central and Eastern Europe
Development through Internationalization
Edited by Tõnis Mets, Arnis Sauka and Danica Purg

ENTREPRENEURSHIP IN CENTRAL AND EASTERN EUROPE

Development through Internationalization

Edited by
Tõnis Mets, Arnis Sauka and Danica Purg

Routledge
Taylor & Francis Group
LONDON AND NEW YORK

First published 2018
by Routledge
2 Park Square, Milton Park, Abingdon, Oxon OX14 4RN

and by Routledge
711 Third Avenue, New York, NY 10017

Routledge is an imprint of the Taylor & Francis Group, an informa business

British Library Cataloguing in Publication Data
A catalogue record for this book is available from the British Library

Library of Congress Cataloging in Publication Data
A catalog record for this book has been requested

ISBN: 978-1-138-22850-4 (hbk)
ISBN: 978-1-138-22851-1 (pbk)
ISBN: 978-1-315-39238-7 (ebk)

Typeset in Bembo
by Wearset Ltd, Boldon, Tyne and Wear

CONTENTS

CONTRIBUTORS

Katalin Antalóczy is Professor at Budapest Business School/University of Applied Sciences, and Senior Research Fellow at the Financial Research Ltd, Budapest. She obtained her Ph.D. from the Hungarian Academy of Sciences in 1994. Her research topics include globalization, foreign direct investment, foreign trade and the pharmaceutical industry. She has published numerous articles in Hungarian and foreign journals and chapters in books in Hungarian and in English.

Alena Apiakun works as head of innovation centre "Innolab" and a methodologist in the research department at the Yanka Kupala State University of Grodno (YKSUG), Belarus. She graduated from the physics faculty of the YKSUG in 1990 and worked in YKSUG as a computer programmer and engineer. In 2005, she graduated from the Republican Institute of Innovative Technologies at the Belarusian National Technical University. Since then, she has been responsible for coordination of university–industry collaboration at the YKSUG. Since 2012, she has been working on her Ph.D. thesis. Her research interests are innovation, regional innovation system and entrepreneurship. She has published more than 40 papers. Since 2015, she has been participating in the implementation of the project "Promoting Internationalization of HEIs in Eastern Neighbourhood Countries through Cultural and Structural Adaptations".

Irena Bakanauskienė is a Professor at Vytautas Magnus University (Department of Management, Faculty of Economics and Management). She obtained her Ph.D. of Social Sciences (Management and Administration) in 1988 at State University of Management in Moscow. She accomplished habilitation procedure in Social Sciences (Management and Administration) in 2005 at Vytautas Magnus University. She obtained an Associate Professor academic title in 1994 and a Professor academic title in 2009. She has been working at Vytautas Magnus University from

1993 as a teacher, vice dean and head of department. She also has experience as a consultant, (JSC consulting company, Technology Transfer Center) and executive, as well as international training experience. During her professional life, she has been involved in more than 20 research and experimental (applied) projects on the European, national and regional level as head of the project, coordinator or team member. Since 2012, she has been a head of the research cluster "Managerial transformations for socially cohesive society and development of a competitive state" at Vytautas Magnus University. She has been a member of the Human Resource Management Professionals Association (Lithuania) since 2009 and a member of the Human Resource Commission at Lithuanian Business Confederation since 2014. She is a member of the international editorial boards of several scientific journals, registered in international databases. She is a member of the Joint Scientific Ph.D. Studies in Lithuania and advisor of Ph.D. theses (six are successfully defended). She has published around 50 scientific articles and is author or co-author of 11 textbooks.

Alenka Braček Lalić is the Vice Dean for Research and Co-Director of the Executive MBA study program at IEDC-Bled School of Management, Postgraduate Studies. She is also heavily engaged with CEEMAN, the International Association for Management Development in Dynamic Societies, where she acts as the International Quality Accreditation (IQA) Director.

Hang Do is a Post-doctoral Researcher at the Small Business Research Centre, Kingston Business School. She holds a doctoral degree in Business Administration from the University of St. Gallen, Switzerland. Previously, Hang was a Research Associate at the Swiss Research Institute of Small Business and Entrepreneurship. Her research project was funded by the MHV scholarship – Swiss National Science Foundation. Hang is currently working on several European and OECD funded projects on SME internationalization, born global enterprises, entrepreneurship and innovation, and contributes to the teaching of Entrepreneurship, Innovation and International Business at Kingston Business School. Her works have been presented in a number of international conferences on entrepreneurship and published in several international journals in innovation and small businesses.

Peter Džupka is an Associate Professor at the Faculty of Economics, Technical University of Košice. He has led the Department of Regional Science and Management since 2015. His research interest is in economic and financial valuation methods in the private and public sector. He is the author or co-author of more than 70 articles, studies or monographs. He has been involved in several research projects in the field of business development supported by the Slovak Research and Development Agency – for example, Analysis of business environment and limits of regional absorption capacity (2003–07) and Creative economy – national and regional incentives (2010–15). He works as an investment projects valuation expert for local and regional government in Slovakia and also for several national and international companies.

Nataliya Golovkina is Professor of Marketing, co-Editor-in-Chief of MIM-Kyiv multi-authored monographs and Academic Secretary of the International Management Institute (MIM-Kyiv). She has more than 40 years of research experience and has spent 20 years in teaching. Marketing and international trade and innovative teaching instruments are her main areas of research interest. Dr. Golovkina supervised MBA marketing and international business research projects for Group Pernod Ricard (France), Ukraine International Airlines (Ukraine-Ireland) and R.J. Reynolds Tobacco International (R.J. Reynolds Ukraine), to mention just a few. After receiving a Tacis ACE Program Fellowship, she conducted academic research in marketing communications regulations at Aston University in the UK. In 1996, she started using the Strategy Simulator Markstrat for teaching strategic marketing management to MBA students. Dr. Golovkina has authored more than 70 publications and spoken at many international conferences. She was awarded Certificates of Merit by the Academy of Science of Ukraine, Ministry of Education and Science of Ukraine and Ministry of Economy of Ukraine.

Milica Jovanović, MSc, works as a teaching assistant at the University of Belgrade, Faculty of Organizational Sciences, Department for Management of Technology, Innovation and Development. She is completing her Ph.D. studies at the Faculty of Organizational Sciences, University of Belgrade – Information Systems and Management. She has been involved in three consulting projects and one strategic project funded by the Ministry of Education, Science and Technological Development of the Republic of Serbia. Her primary research interests include technology and innovation management, quantitative management, sustainable development and performance management.

Ewa Lechman is an Assistant Professor of Economics at the Faculty of Management and Economics, Gdańsk University of Technology. Her extensive research interests concentrate on economic development, ICT and its role in reshaping social and economic systems and various aspects of poverty and economics in developing countries. She is author or co-author of multiple research papers and books issued by Elsevier, Springer and many others. She coordinates and participates in international research and educational projects and also works as an independent expert assisting with innovation assignments, including the evaluation of small and medium enterprise proposals, EU-financed programmes and policy design regarding innovativeness, digitalization, education and social exclusion. She was the 2013 winner of an Emerald Literati Network Award for Excellence and is a member of the editorial boards of international journals on technology diffusion, the digital economy and economic development. Currently she coordinates two international research projects: "Information and communication technologies for economic development. Special focus on intelligent knowledge grid information retrieval and diffusion" (Polish Ministry of Science and Hamdard University in India) and "Reshaping financial systems – identifying the role of ICT in diffusion of financial innovations. Recent evidence from European countries" (CERGE-Global Development Network).

Sanja Marinković, Ph.D., is an Associate Professor at the University of Belgrade, Faculty of Organizational Sciences, Department for Management of Technology, Innovation and Development. She is an author and co-author of several books (*Innovation Management in Services, Management of Technology and Development* and *Managing Sustainable Development*, all in Serbian) and more than 80 scientific papers published in Serbian and international proceedings, journals and book chapters. She is a lecturer at dual award master programme International Business and Management, validated by Middlesex University London (modules: Global Technology and Operations Management, Quantitative Methods in Technology Management). She has been involved in several research projects funded by the National Ministry of Science and the EU. Her research and teaching interests are in the fields of technology and innovation management, technology entrepreneurship and sustainable business models. Since 2015, she has been Vice-Dean for International Cooperation at the Faculty of Organizational Sciences.

Tõnis Mets is Professor of Entrepreneurship at the University of Tartu in Estonia. He was Marie Curie Research Fellow at the Australian Centre for Entrepreneurship Research at the Queensland University of Technology in Brisbane, Australia 2014–16. Also, Professor Mets has worked as a management consultant in his company (ALO OÜ), and as an entrepreneur, engineer and manager in various high-tech companies in Estonia. Tõnis graduated from the Tallinn University of Technology. He also holds a Ph.D. in Technical Sciences from St Petersburg Agrarian University. Professor Mets is author and co-author of 15 patents, and more than 50 chapters and articles with international publishers. His main research interests are in the fields of (technology) entrepreneurship, intellectual property, and knowledge and innovation management.

Jasna Petković, Ph.D., is an Assistant Professor at the University of Belgrade, Faculty of Organizational Sciences, Department for Management of Technology, Innovation and Development, where she received her MSc and Ph.D. degrees. She is author or co-author of several books and more than 60 scientific papers. Her research and teaching interests are in the fields of technology management, technology forecasting and SME development.

Danica Purg is the President and Dean of IEDC-Bled School of Management, Postgraduate Studies (Slovenia), and the President of CEEMAN, International Association for Management Development in Dynamic Societies, which brings together more than 220 management development institutions from 55 countries. She also leads the European Leadership Centre.

Mykola Radlinskyy is head of the Business Development Department for the APOLLONIA GROUP, a family-owned dental clinic and dentists' training centre in Poltava, Ukraine. He is also co-founder and CEO of the CompodenT.org retail firm that sells dental equipment and supplies. Before joining his family business,

Mr. Radlinskyy worked as a Colgate-Palmolive representative, assistant to the art director of Radioactivefilm Studio in Ukraine and even played pro basketball in Ukraine's National Basketball Super League. He graduated from the Interregional Academy of Personnel Management. He holds a degree in international trade and did research in management of healthcare institutions. Currently, Mr. Radlinskyy is a student of the MIM-Kyiv (Ukraine) DBA program.

Jovana Rakićević, MSc, works as a teaching assistant at the University of Belgrade, Faculty of Organizational Sciences, Department for Management of Technology, Innovation and Development. She is currently enrolled in Ph.D. studies – Information Systems and Management. She is author and co-author of about 30 scientific research papers and three book chapters. Her research and teaching area of interest includes technology and innovation management, performance measurement, SME development, sustainable development and technology entrepreneurship.

Magdolna Sass is a Senior Research Fellow at the Centre for Economic and Regional Studies, Hungarian Academy of Sciences, and she teaches at the Budapest Business School/University of Applied Sciences. She obtained her Ph.D. from the Hungarian Academy of Sciences in 1998. Between 1997 and 2000, she worked for the Organisation for Economic Cooperation and Development in Paris. Her main topics of research are foreign direct investments, internationalization of companies and related policies in the East-Central European countries, with special attention to developments in Hungary. She has been a member of the European Association for Comparative Economic Studies since 2008, a member of the executive board since 2012, Vice-President since 2014 and President since 2016. She is a member of the European Association of Development Training and Research Institutes and has been a co-convenor of the Working Group on Multinational Corporations and Development since 2014. She has published 150 papers, including in *Eastern European Economics*, *Post-Communist Economies*, *European Planning Studies*, *European Urban and Regional Studies*, *Review of Managerial Science* and *Acta Oeconomica*. She is a member of the editorial board of *Post-Communist Economies* and *Croatian Economic Survey*.

Arnis Sauka is an Associate Professor and Director of the Centre for Sustainable Business at the Stockholm School of Economics in Riga. Arnis has a Ph.D. from the University of Siegen (Germany) and has been a Visiting Scholar at Jönköping International Business School (Sweden) and University College London (UK). His academic research findings, which deal with the shadow economy, tax morale, competitiveness, social responsibility, internationalization of companies and entrepreneurship policies, have been published in a number of peer-reviewed journals and books. Arnis has also been extensively involved in applied research, including studies contracted by the OECD and various industry associations and NGOs in the Baltic countries.

Miriam Šebová works as an Associate Professor of Public Administration and Regional Economics at the Faculty of Economics, Technical University of Košice. She finished her Ph.D. at the University of Economics in Bratislava. Her main research areas are in the field of regional economics. She has been involved in several research projects focused on the development of innovative industries at the national and regional level supported by the EU (5th Framework project) and by the Slovak Research and Development Agency.

Iztok Seljak started his career at Rotomatika, Hidria's daughter company, in 1989. He has been the Vice President of Hidria since 2002. In 2004, he took over the responsibility for Hidria Automotive, one of the two core divisions in Hidria. Since January 2008, he has acted as the President of the Management Board of Hidria. In 2002, he was awarded the title "Young Manager of the Year" by the Managers' Association of Slovenia and, in 2012, with the title "Best Manager of South-East and Central Europe" by an international jury in Sarajevo. Under his leadership, Hidria in 2012/13 gained the title of the "Most Innovative Company in Europe" by EBA and in 2016 won the title of being the best Eco Innovation in the European automotive supply industry by CLEPA.

David Smallbone is Professor of Small Business and Entrepreneurship and Associate Director of the Small Business Research Centre. He is a past President of both the International Council for Small Business and Entrepreneurship (ICSB) and the ECSB. In addition, he is a Fellow of the ECSB and a Wilfred Whyte Fellow of ICSB. David is also an Associate Editor of the *Journal of Small Business Management*. He has been involved in research relating to SMEs and entrepreneurship since the late 1980s. One of his main research interests is entrepreneurship in transition economies. Indeed, in 2005 he received an Honorary Doctorate from the University of Lodz in recognition of his contribution to the study of entrepreneurship in transition economies. Much of his research has been conducted in partnership with researchers in other international centres; a good deal of it is policy oriented. Issues related to internationalization and SMEs has featured in his research since the mid-1990s.

Osvaldas Stripeikis is Director of Vytautas Magnus University Business Practice Centre, Head of "Entrepreneurship Academy" and Associated Professor at Vytautas Magnus University (Department of Management, Faculty of Economics and Management). He obtained his Ph.D. of Social Sciences (Management and Administration) in 2008 at Vytautas Magnus University. Since 2014, he has mainly been working on entrepreneurial competence development models by creating ecosystem university–business cooperation platforms. His main areas of scientific research are: the entrepreneurship process, entrepreneurial company ecosystem and commercialization process of social and business ideas. Since 2000, he has been coordinator and implementer of more than 100 national and international projects in the areas of social services, education and business development. Since 2004, he has been a certificated trainer on the following topics: team building, leadership, emotional intelligence development, development of entrepreneurial competencies, innovation management, business idea generation and business models in organization.

Iryna Tykhomyrova is President of the International Institute of Management (MIM-Kyiv), a leading business school in Ukraine. She has worked in the field of business education since 1997, contributing to the development of high-quality business education in Ukraine by participating in and initiating successful national and international MBA programmes, as well as developing projects for executives. Dr. Iryna Tykhomyrova served as an expert to the European Training Foundation on the assessment of management training needs in Central and Eastern Europe. Dr. Tykhomyrova is also the coordinator of the Working Group on Agricultural Policy and Innovation, a part of the international Reform Task Force on Agriculture of the National Reform Council for drafting and implementing a single and comprehensive strategy for agriculture and rural development in 2015–20. She has coordinated the IMD World Competitiveness Yearbook Ukrainian part of research since 2008. In 2014, she was awarded the title Merited Educator of Ukraine.

FOREWORD

Over recent decades, entrepreneurship and small businesses has been a hot topic and on the agenda for many governments – new, small and growing firms have been regarded as a "magic bullet" that create new jobs and economic development in the society, provide additional choices and variety to consumers, support local communities and act as agents of social change by integrating social and environmental concerns in their activities. For example, as far back as 1979, David Birch emphasized the importance of new and small firms for job creation, and over recent decades many structural changes have occurred in the economies around the world: technological advances, increased globalization, changes in consumer demands and so on; in many cases supporting the emergence of new and small firms in becoming an important mechanism in diffusing innovation, threatening existing inefficient businesses and creating new industries. Thus, the industry structure and globalization have changed considerably over time, making knowledge and internationalization play a more pivotal role in competition than before (Mason and Brown, 2013).

However, some of these assumptions can be challenged (Storey, 1994; Nightingale and Coad, 2014, 2016) – for example, it has been argued that many new firms exhibit a low survival rate, are less innovative and show low profitability and productivity, and while they create new jobs to some extent, these jobs tend to be of lower quality, more volatile and employees are typically paid less. Blanchflower (2004) goes so far that he concludes that there is no convincing evidence that a high level of self-employment in a society will produce positive macroeconomic effects, and Lerner (2010) poses the question of whether governments should be involved in the support of entrepreneurship and small businesses at all.

The conclusion will be that governmental interventions to support new and small firms are neither obvious nor simple. Many countries have introduced a range of governmental interventions to support both new and small firms. However, experiences have shown that:

- In many cases governments are focused more on the rhetoric than on the contents and the actual implementation of the policies.
- There is an overriding belief from politicians and policy-makers that they can govern ("pick-the-winner") of the future – the future is always uncertain and exhibits its own dynamics.
- Many mistakes are made when introducing policies for new and small businesses – for example, there is a risk that governmental interventions are driven by other considerations than stimulating the new and small firms, and sometimes governmental interventions tend to become more of an administrative solution than an incentive for the actors who will be affected by the interventions.
- There is a strong policy focus on searching for "best practice", i.e. searching for policies that have been successful in other contexts, and a mentality of "copy and paste", i.e. these successful interventions could be implemented in their own context. Obviously, it is valuable to compare economic policies in different countries and learn from each other; however, the notion that "one size fits all" could be questioned (Minniti, 2008) – context matters and policy instruments need to be tailored to the specific context.

What is needed for politicians and policy-makers to provide adequate interventions to stimulate new and small firms?

One obvious answer is: We need more knowledge! We need reliable information about the entrepreneurship and small business sector in different countries, an understanding of the globalization, and knowledge and evaluations of best practices, etc.

Since the opening of the markets almost 30 years ago, the countries in Central and Eastern Europe have shown incredible changes and developments. The opening of the market started in the new era of the knowledge economy and a strong development of the information technology sector, a development that to a large extent put entrepreneurship and small businesses at the forefront of politicians' and policy-makers' attention. It was also an era of increased globalization of the economies that also made the internationalization processes of entrepreneurial and small businesses a key issue for success. This book, *Entrepreneurship in Central and Eastern Europe – Development through Internationalization*, edited by Arnis Saukas, Danica Purg and Tõnis Mets, emphasizes the importance of both entrepreneurial and small businesses in the economies, and the internationalization processes of these firms. The book provides an important contribution to our knowledge – it includes well-developed knowledge about entrepreneurship and small firms in Central and Eastern Europe, particularly with regards to the internationalization processes of these firms. The case studies contextualize the development of entrepreneurship and small businesses in individual countries and critically review the policy interventions that have been introduced in order to stimulate the internationalization of entrepreneurship and small businesses in different countries. Thus, the book is an obvious choice of reading for politicians and policy-makers. The book also constitutes an important source of knowledge for researchers and students that want to know more about entrepreneurship and small businesses in Central and Eastern European countries.

Lund, Sweden, July 2017
Hans Landström
Sten K. Johnson Centre for Entrepreneurship
Lund University, Sweden

References

Birch, D., 1979, *The Job Generation Process, MIT Program on Neighborhood and Regional Change*, Cambridge, MA: Massachusetts Institute of Technology.

Blanchflower, D.G., 2004, "Self-employment: More may not be better", *Swedish Economic Policy Review*, 11, 15–73.

Lerner, J., 2010, "The future of public efforts to boost entrepreneurship and venture capital", *Small Business Economics*, 35, 255–64.

Mason, C.M. and R. Brown, 2013, "Creating good public policy to support high-growth firms", *Small Business Economics*, 40, 211–25.

Minniti, M., 2008, "The role of government policy on entrepreneurial activity: Productive, unproductive, or destructive", *Entrepreneurship Theory and Practice*, 32, 779–90.

Nightingale, P. and A. Coad, 2014, "Muppets and gazelles: Ideological and methodological biases in entrepreneurship research", *Industrial and Corporate Change*, 23, 113–43.

Nightingale, P. and A. Coad, 2016, "Challenging assumptions and bias in entrepreneurship research", in H. Landström, A. Parhankangas, A. Fayolle and P. Riot (eds.), *Challenging Entrepreneurship Research*, London: Routledge, pp. 100–28.

Storey, D.J., 1994, *Understanding the Small Business Sector*, London: Routledge.

PART I
Conceptual framework

1

INTRODUCTION

Entrepreneurship development and internationalization in Central and Eastern Europe, Ukraine and the Commonwealth of Independent States

Danica Purg, Arnis Sauka[1] *and Tõnis Mets*

This book is about the development of entrepreneurship in Central and Eastern Europe (CEE) and the Commonwealth of Independent States (CIS) as well as Ukraine – countries that only 25 years ago were operating in different political and economic systems. The disappearance of restrictions from the Soviet Union opened up the global world and created a new situation for these reborn states. The start of the transition to a market economy took place at the same time as the inception of a new era of information and communication technology (ICT) and the Internet. A new technology base triggered the fast growth of new investments into intangible assets by global economic leaders at the beginning of the 1990s. That was the basis for moving towards a knowledge economy. Entrepreneurs, a new rising class in CEE and CIS society, faced the great challenge of reshaping the economic framework in an open world context. Entrepreneurship is seen as the process leading to growth and improved welfare in these countries.

During the past 25 years, entrepreneurs in CEE and the CIS have reshaped traditional industries and created new industries, combining innovative ideas with traditional competencies. We still do not know very much about how and why companies led by entrepreneurs develop, in particular how they expand globally, and what the role of new knowledge and innovation is in the internationalization process. This knowledge, however, could be important for other entrepreneurial firms (i.e., those who seek development strategies, also through internationalization processes) from these regions as well as other regions of the world in different development stages. Understanding the pathways of entrepreneurial development, especially growth through internationalization, is also important for the overall development of countries in transition. Considering the specific environment these companies come from, however, strategies as to how CEE and CIS companies "go global" may be different – compared with companies from more developed market economies, where various support schemes are established, but also among CEE and CIS countries.

The book has five parts. The first part introduces theory and development patterns with an introduction to the volume by the editors and a conceptual discussion by David Smallbone and Hang Do, which provides an overview of internationalization in European SMEs, with a particular focus on Central and Eastern Europe. This chapter looks at the theoretical perspectives of internationalization of SMEs and the challenges faced by SMEs in CEE and CIS countries while their economies are in transition from state to market focused.

Smallbone and Do identify three primary routes to internationalization for SMEs in the CEE and CIS regions: the incremental approach, the network theory approach and the resources-based theory approach. Each one takes advantage of competencies in the SME to expand beyond its home country borders. They also identify the main challenges that SMEs in the region face, primarily a shortage of capital and human resources, a lack of adequate and high-quality information and, very importantly, a lack of public and governmental support. The authors also include a discussion on the "born global" phenomenon and the need for public policy support for SMEs as they internationalize.

Considering the potential impact of the contextual influences on entrepreneurship processes, this volume aims to provide an in-depth picture concerning the development of entrepreneurship through internationalization pathways of companies from Central and Eastern Europe, Ukraine and the Commonwealth of Independent States. Thus, the second, third and fourth parts of the volume present case studies showing key aspects of entrepreneurial processes leading to internationalization, compiled by entrepreneurship scholars from Ukraine, CEE and the CIS.

Both single and multiple cases are included in Parts II–IV and various types of internationalization are addressed, ranging from exploring companies that have started exporting at a later stage after establishment to "born globals," thus revealing the complexity of the internationalization process. Namely, country case studies are "classified" drawing on the type of internationalization, while the second part concentrates on case studies of entrepreneurs reshaping industries: markets, products and services. Part III focuses on companies that are born to be global and Part IV looks at entrepreneur-innovators going international.

Part II of the book looks at three companies that have transformed themselves and their products and services to meet the needs of evolving markets in their home countries and beyond. Each company has taken advantage of evolving market forces to expand and grow into successful international businesses.

More specifically, Part II starts with a chapter by Arnis Sauka from Latvia exploring a food manufacturing company that is more than 100 years old. The case study is about Laima, a producer of a product that people in many countries enjoy: chocolate. While relatively old, the company can still be labeled as a "born global." Yet, one of the keys to this long-term success, as exemplified by the case study, is not merely in the product the company is offering. As a representative of Laima put it: "It is often more of a packaging business that comes together with appropriate distribution." To maintain their positions and expand in markets where the brand name "Laima" has been known for many years (such as Russia) and to further penetrate new markets globally, including Asia and the US, the company constantly seeks better ways to adjust to the frequently changing requirements and preferences of their customers.

A chapter by Osvaldas Stripeikis and Irena Bakanauskienė from Lithuania follows, looking at a much younger company, also in the food industry. The authors look at how this company started and developed in the post-Soviet era, initially as an import company, taking advantage of the opening of Lithuania's market to Western products and then transitioning into a production company with significant overseas interests. To do this, they continued to develop the logistics system they established in their early days to expand the reach of their products to the far corners of Europe. While they have had some distractions along the way (expansion into the footwear industry for one), the company has recently refocused its efforts towards its core business and continues to be successful.

Finally, Part II concludes with a chapter written by Alena Apiakun and Tõnis Mets about a logistics SME which formed after the fall of the Soviet Union. This company quickly realized that their location in Belarus provided an ideal conduit between Asia, Russia and the rest of Europe. However, they continue to struggle with international transportation and legislative issues that are often holdovers from the Soviet era. The company has been very successful in building its own fleet of transportation equipment and developing a freight forwarding business, essentially reshaping logistics in Belarus. However, it still has trouble competing successfully against logistics companies from Western Europe.

Part III takes a closer look at companies that were "born global." Many "born global" companies embrace ICT. After the fall of the Soviet Union, countries in CEE and the CIS were quick to embrace new technologies. These countries often leapfrogged over older technologies that were absent or underdeveloped in their countries and quickly became some of the most technologically advanced countries in the world. This naturally led to entrepreneurial ICT startups in this part of the world that quickly, if not immediately, went international.

The first chapter in Part III, by Tõnis Mets, is about a business in Estonia that was "founded to be sold." The author discusses the development of Estonia as an innovation-driven economy where tech startups such as Skype and Fit.me (the company in this chapter) were developed. The entrepreneurial founders worked through public-private partnerships to develop the concepts, only to go international immediately and ultimately sell their creations to companies in Western countries. As the author notes, Estonia did not have the market to support the company in this case, so if it had not been "born global," it would have gone out of business.

The second chapter in Part III, by Ewa Lechman, examines the success factors of an ICT company in Poland. While the company in this chapter did not enter other countries from the very beginning, that was always the plan. First, the founders wanted to find their footing in Poland and then look outward. They knew that their company would be international in short order and started the planning process very early on. They recognized that their technology was in demand not just in Poland but also in the rest of the world. Through partnerships in Romania and the United States, the company has been able to expand into many other countries.

In the third chapter of Part III, Sanja Marinković, Jovana Rakićević, Milica Janović and Jasna Petković examine the ICT industry in Serbia. The authors note in particular that, while Serbia lags behind its neighbors in many areas, the ICT industry is a shining star. Serbia has become one of the leading exporters of ICT, increasing the value of ICT exports from $139 million in 2010 to $437 million in 2015. The two companies discussed in this chapter are prime examples of this trend. One company exports software and hardware for businesses and the other creates social games; however, both were "born global" and are enjoying tremendous success in the global marketplace.

The last chapter in Part III looks at internationalization trends in Slovakia. This chapter, by Peter Džupka and Miriam Šebová, includes a case study about a high-tech company that differs from the companies in the previous chapters in that it has used technology to create a product that is not always associated with high tech: early warning systems. Slovakia's accession to the EU in 2004 played a significant role in its internationalization. Many companies in Slovakia did not have any international interests until after Slovakia entered the EU. The company discussed in this chapter was no exception. Although, it is the oldest company in the section, tracing its roots back to the early nineteenth century, its current form started with five entrepreneurial founders right as the Soviet Union was collapsing. However, it did not pursue an active internationalization strategy until the twenty-first century, calling itself a "born-again" global. Today it operates in over 50 countries.

Part IV of the book looks at some highly innovative companies and the impact they have had on entrepreneurship and/or internationalization in their home countries. In particular, it looks at companies that saw a specific need or niche in the market and, through innovation and entrepreneurship, evolved (or are evolving) into some of the most successful international companies in Europe.

The first chapter in Part IV looks at a non-traditional entrepreneurial company with significant international interests. Katalin Antalóczy and Magdolna Sass examine the case of a pharmaceutical company with a long history in Hungary, first established in 1901. However, due to significant political and market upheavals, it has had to be entrepreneurial over the years to survive. This company's most recent entrepreneurial accomplishment was to move into a new niche market, "specialty pharma," where it could avoid direct competition with so-called Big Pharma. According to the authors, the company's innovative management team spearheaded this move. The authors further argue that this company's international position and prominence in the Hungarian economy has an influence on internationalization trends in Hungary as a whole.

In the following chapter, Danica Purg, Iztok Seljak and Alenka Braček Lalić explore trends in entrepreneurship and internationalization in Slovenia through one of the top innovative and international companies in the country. Slovenia started to develop an entrepreneurship-based and internationalized economy prior to the breakup of Yugoslavia, but the temporary loss of the rest of the Yugoslavian market accelerated the process. One example that illustrates this point is the case study: The company in question already generated about 50 percent of its sales from exports prior to 1991; however, afterwards that number jumped to almost 90 percent as they sought to replace the lost business from former Yugoslavian countries. In the subsequent decades, the company reinvented itself to become one of the most innovative companies in Europe, focusing not just on technology but also on how to monetize it.

The final chapter in Part IV looks at entrepreneurship and internationalization through a business not normally thought of as international: the dental industry. Authors Iryna Tykhomyrova, Nataliya Golovkina and Mykola Radlinskyy examine the internationalization challenges of a dental clinic and training center in Ukraine. This particular clinic, founded as the Soviet Union fell apart, had active international business, primarily in Russia, prior to 2014. However, after the crisis started, business from Russia dropped to almost nothing. Combined with a drop in Ukrainians seeking dental care because of economic concerns, the clinic found itself in need of a new direction. Using technology such as e-learning, the clinic decided to focus on expanding its training program primarily to the CEE region but also into the EU, Asia and the Americas. The clinic had pioneered an innovative way to repair and replace teeth and was now looking to share that innovation with the world.

The book concludes in Part V with a chapter written by Tõnis Mets. This contribution discusses the findings from case studies included in this volume from the viewpoint of an existing conceptual framework on the internationalization process and development of companies in a transition context. Using Porter's stages of evolution of national competitiveness development, Mets puts the countries in this book into a framework that illustrates how different countries evolved concerning entrepreneurial development and internationalization of companies, in part based on where they started their transition in the early 1990s. By grouping the countries according to their stage of economic development, the author is able to examine the factors that influence the level and sophistication of entrepreneurial activity in each country as well as the role of internationalization in that process.

The author's analysis shows that a more open and international entrepreneurial system greatly benefited the economic and competitive development in each county. This subsequently led to greater internationalization as the level of economic development increased. Furthermore, how quickly the entrepreneurial ecosystem developed within each country is at least in part dependent on the stage of economic development as well as the political choices made in each country. As the countries in this region of the world are far from homogenous, it is important to recognize that the needs for and progress of entrepreneurial and international development vary from country to country.

The primary focus of the book is development of entrepreneurship in CEE, Ukraine and the CIS, with a focus on how internationalization has helped or can help in this process. For this reason, even though case studies of particular companies are included in Parts II–IV, all cases also incorporate a broader discussion, i.e., link the discussion with development of entrepreneurship in a particular country. Namely, each case study presents a brief introduction to the context where entrepreneurs and their companies originate, such as the economic environment and entrepreneurial ecosystem, export levels, support for companies hoping to go global and the like. Furthermore, while highlighting the main challenges and success factors for internationalization, strategy and pathways of the selected case company, all case studies were selected to represent major aspects of entrepreneurship development – through internationalization – of a particular country. Finally, cases identify successes and challenges during the internationalization process and capture context-specific implications – the direct or indirect impact of the environment where these companies originate.

Altogether, this volume aims to contribute to the ongoing debate on the internationalization process of companies from transition economies. The aim is to provide a fresh, in-depth view of the complexity and specific features of the internationalization process as influenced by the "transition context" in various stages of development. Instead of focusing on cases that can be used solely for teaching purposes, this book includes academic cases that can be used as supplementary material in courses on international entrepreneurship or more general entrepreneurship courses and may be a useful and inspiring resource for both junior and advanced entrepreneurship scholars. The book also looks to foster policy discussion to advance further internationalization of entrepreneurship in CEE, Ukraine and the CIS.

Note

1 Contribution of Arnis Sauka to this volume has been supported by the National Research Program 5.2. EKOSOC-LV.

2

INTERNATIONALISATION AND EUROPEAN SMALL- AND MEDIUM-SIZED ENTERPRISES

David Smallbone and Hang Do

Introduction

The aim of this chapter is to consider the implications of increasing internationalisation for Europe's SMEs, paying particular attention to Central and Eastern European economies. Since the last quarter of the twentieth century, there has been a rapid increase in the level of internationalisation, as a growing number of businesses are engaged in entrepreneurial activities across national borders. The process has been facilitated by developments in communications and transportation technology, which in combination have contributed to a reduction in the barrier effects of distance (European Commission, 2010). Alongside this, increased competition has resulted in a growing number of businesses actively seeking to reduce their costs. As a consequence, internationalisation processes involve firms identifying and exploiting new markets as well as contributing to lower production costs. Although internationalisation processes are affecting businesses of all sizes, there are particular implications for SMEs because of a range of size-related characteristics.

The term internationalisation describes a process of increasing involvement in international operations. Globalisation is another commonly used term, which at the micro level is characterised by the establishment of manufacturing plants and marketing affiliates across international boundaries. It can also involve the extensive use of outsourcing inputs and the marketing of outputs across national boundaries. Although sometimes used interchangeably, the terms internationalisation and globalisation involve differences in scale. Another definitional issue is the relationship between internationalisation and exporting. Although sometimes mistakenly used as substitutes for one another, exporting and internationalisation do not describe the same thing. Exporting is one form of internationalisation but other forms include licensing, franchising and international contracting amongst others. Moreover, internationalisation can involve joint ventures, strategic alliances, mergers and acquisitions at an international scale.

The rest of the chapter is divided into four main sections plus some conclusions. The next section describes the main theoretical approaches to the study of internationalisation and SME together with some of the key concepts. This is followed by a discussion of opportunities and challenges facing SMEs in Europe with respect to internationalisation. Whilst the focus is on Central and Eastern European countries, this is necessarily placed in the wider context of SME development in Europe. The third main section discusses so-called born global companies which epitomise the increasingly internationalised nature of SME development. The fourth section focuses on some of the public policy issues reflecting the growing interest in internationalisation as a topic.

Some theoretical perspectives

A brief review of the literature reveals three main approaches to the explanation of SME internationalisation, although in some cases there are variants within these categories. The first group comprises stages models, which essentially describe an incremental approach to internationalisation. There are many different versions of the stages model but what is common to all of them is the view of the firm's international market development as a sequential, i.e. stage, process. According to the stage theorists, firms adopt an incremental approach to foreign markets, gradually deepening their commitment and investment as they gain international market knowledge and experience. In this approach firms are also believed to target neighbouring countries initially because of the short psychic distance between them. This is likely to mean they believe that they have a greater understanding of the culture, business practices and so on, of neighbouring countries. A good example of this is a country like Poland, where Russia is seen as a potential market particularly in the medium and longer term. The incremental nature of the process that is emphasised in this view is the idea that the internationalisation process, as far as an individual firm is concerned, involves a series of incremental decisions over time rather than a spectacular foreign market entry.

Four different stages have been identified based on a firm's international involvement: first, firms with no regular exports; second, firms exporting via independent agents; third, firms that are selling into foreign markets through sales subsidiaries; and fourth, firms selling into foreign markets through production facilities they have established abroad. So we may conclude that the incremental internationalisation approach has some merit as a framework for classification purposes, although it may be argued that its contribution to understanding the process of internationalisation is limited. At the same time, one aspect that is relatively common is the reporting of evidence which supports the psychic distance concept. Indeed, more prescriptive studies have suggested that concentration on foreign markets that have a short psychic distance makes good business sense.

The second type of theoretical framework identifiable in the literature draws on network theory and has its roots in international industrial marketing. The essential proposition of this approach is that internationalisation proceeds as the firm's knowledge and experience of foreign markets increases. So, as in the case of a stages approach, some change can be seen over time although, unlike the stages approach, in a network-based framework there is an emphasis on learning processes. These processes have their roots in the interactions that develop between the key actors in the foreign markets and the businesses that are looking to internationalise. A network approach results from a dynamic interaction between the firm and a variety of external actors. It may be argued that, whilst a stages framework is more relevant in the case of large firms than it is in SMEs, a network-based approach is much closer to the approach that is used in small businesses. As the innovation literature demonstrates, innovative activity in small businesses is typically generated from an interaction between a small business supplier and the buyers in the purchasing organisations.

In network theory, markets are seen as a source of relationships, and it is the nurturing and development of these relationships that lies at the heart of successful exporting. As Kevin Ibeh (2012) has stated there is no doubt that a network-based approach has brought immense value to the understanding of the internationalisation processes, particularly among SMEs. There is a considerable body of evidence to support the proposition that network relationships are important in SME internationalisation (Coviello and Munro, 1995). Working with foreign companies on a supply basis is not easy but, rather, a challenge for many domestic market oriented businesses.

The third main source of theory is resource-based theory. Such an approach is superficially attractive, not least because of the limited internal resource base that small companies are typically faced with in comparison with their large firm counterparts. It is also attractive because it can be linked to a wider theory of the firm. This means that export or foreign market internationalisation focused processes can be put into the context of the growth of a business more generally. A growing number of authors have drawn attention to the potential integrative approach of resource-based theory, since a resource-based perspective is based on a holistic view of the firm, emphasising that firms will have a different set of capabilities associated with a particular resource competitiveness mix.

In a resource-based view, key internationalisation decisions are viewed as being made within a coordinated framework of resources and capabilities as well as environmental realities. Theories coming from this starting point emphasise that firms that are internationally active will have a different mix of resources and competencies than firms that are not. Typically there are also sectoral variations in the level of internationalisation. Those sectors which show the highest levels include trade, manufacturing, transport and communications and research. One of the concerns identified in the EIM study is that, with the exception of imports from China, the BRICs were generally under-developed as markets for European Union (EU) SMEs.

Opportunities and challenges within internationalising SMEs

Internationalising SMEs are forced to deal with a variety of challenges as well as positively responding to opportunities. In terms of the barriers that SMEs reported, respondents appeared to be more concerned with internal barriers such as those associated with resource constraints than external barriers. In terms of internal barriers, a shortage of capital was a particular concern as was a lack of adequate and high-quality information and what they perceived to be a lack of business support more generally (Cernat *et al.*, 2014; European Commission, 2010; Baum *et al.*, 2013). In addition, other barriers mentioned included the difficulties associated with paperwork and human resource deficiencies in terms of management skills. Interestingly reputational resources were a particular concern, reflecting their lack of credibility in the market and a low level of market knowledge.

Rather surprisingly a shortage of capital and adequate public support scored higher, with reference to the EU markets (European Commission, 2010), than in the case of non-EU markets such as the BRICs, which at first sight seems counter-intuitive. However, it most probably reflects the fact that it's the larger firms and those more experienced in exporting that felt less concerned about finance and business support in the most distant markets. As in many other cases, the awareness shown of public support programmes amongst SMEs was typically low. SMEs were not generally well aware of the existence of public support programmes for internationalisation that they could make use of, although, once again and not surprisingly perhaps, this did tend to vary with size of firm – lowest awareness in the smallest firms, highest level of awareness in the larger companies. Given this, it is perhaps not surprising also that only a small number of SMEs were actually using public support measures to help them to access foreign markets. The difficulties faced by European SMEs both in entering foreign markets and in exploiting them profitably did vary between countries, and also in terms of the types of businesses involved.

In the case of China (Smallbone and Elk, 2011), for example, the main obstacles identified related to the business environment, which included an unstable legislative framework, poor access to skilled labour, cultural differences, trade barriers, problems of accessing finance in the form of credit, an insufficient IPR framework and enforcement, differences in the application of regulations in different provinces of the country, limited transparency and poor access to information. These are not necessarily in rank order.

However, business opportunities for EU SMEs exist in a variety of sectors in China. Some of these are associated with China's need to modernise and upgrade its technology base; others relate to the rapidly growing consumer markets; whilst others are related to the ongoing processes of structural change within the Chinese economy. The most commonly mentioned sectors with opportunities for EU SMEs are machine tools, which reflect China's current strengths in manufacturing. Opportunities also exist in business services such as public relations, advertising and specialist financial services; this includes factoring, private equity to access to management consultancy. On the consumer side opportunities exist in personal services such as hairdressing and medical services, education, environmental products and services, energy, particularly renewable energy, and low carbon technologies. A growing consumer market in China is also creating opportunities for luxury products. It needs to be kept in mind that, as well as being the world's leading exporter, China is also the third largest importer in the world. However, China and the BRICs generally are under-developed as markets for EU SMEs.

Exporting can be a challenge for SMEs in any country, but for those in central European countries there are additional barriers associated with their recent development path. This requires substantial modernisation and understanding of what constitutes innovation in a market-based system and how the innovative performance of SMEs in these countries needs to be more market oriented.

Table 2.1 summarises the strengths and weaknesses of Polish SMEs operating at the time Poland entered the European market. The table clearly shows that the weaknesses outnumber the strengths, which is of considerable importance as, in the first decade of the transition process, SMEs were one of the few sources of dynamism in the Polish economy. The assessment contained within the table may be viewed as an agenda for Polish policymakers to address with the help of EU Structural Funds. At the same time, the table summarises the status quo with regards to existing businesses, operating mainly in traditional sectors. Another development priority for the Polish economy is to raise the level of innovation and harness the entrepreneurial spirit which is a characteristic of Polish people.

The challenges that are summarised in the table are not confined to Poland, but are commonly repeated in other new member states of the EU that, only 25 years ago, were operating under central planning and a socialist model of development. Raising the level of innovation is a particular challenge because the innovation systems that developed in these countries were typically focused on supporting the Soviet military machine. As a consequence, it is necessary to undertake a major restructuring of their innovation support systems, which involves a reduction in

TABLE 2.1 Strengths and weaknesses of Polish SMEs in 2004

Strong points	*Weak points*
High development priorities	Poor financial liquidity
Relatively well-developed forms of cooperation based on vertical integration (i.e. a supply chain)	Low investment activity Outdated technology Weak supply chains Export activity below EU average; a low level of cooperation with foreign enterprises High level of dependence on the domestic market Weak management Human resource deficiencies Low level of innovation

Source: Piasecki and Rogut (2004).

expenditure on research and development in state agencies and significantly increasing the R&D spend by individual businesses. This is part of the transformation into market-based economies which represents a quantum leap for many firms as well as for higher education institutions expected to play a different role than they were during Soviet times.

Nevertheless, the nationwide survey of over 1500 SMEs in Poland within 2010–2012 as reported by Starczewska-Krzysztoszek (2011) suggested several changes of Polish SMEs after Poland joined the EU. As described in Table 2.2, the main concerns are related to the firms' inclination to growth, competitive standing, innovation, human resource and financial resource. First, Polish SMEs tend to target growth based on increasing sales, market shares and lifting up the firm's value. However, this orientation is more popular amongst medium-sized firms rather than micro and small firms who still mainly rely on their domestic market or the regions where their firms are based. Second, there has been a change in the SMEs' perceived competitive standing of an enterprise. Instead of focusing on 'price' as the success factor, many SMEs perceive 'quality' of product as the key to compete in the European market. The combination of quality, price, innovation, promotion and distribution has significantly lifted up the competitiveness of Polish firms. This philosophy has dramatically changed the way SMEs built their images, particularly since Poland joined the EU by the end of 2008.

TABLE 2.2 Strengths and weaknesses of Polish SMEs in 2011

Strengths	*Weaknesses*
Polish SMEs are more concerned about firm growth by enhancing sales, market shares and the company's value	The majority of SMEs operating on shrinking markets are more concerned by survival rather than improving their business profiles
High self-esteem on competing on EU markets using quality, innovation, price, promotion and distribution. Product quality is prioritised over price regardless of size and is central to business success	
The significance of human resource is emphasised as the core element to develop the firm's competitiveness, particularly amongst small firms	Low inclination to foreign expansion except for those SMEs operating in the industry, information and communication sectors
Investment in innovation is highly oriented in SMEs. Medium-sized firms are more susceptible to innovation and firm expansion than small firms	Low inclination to innovations amongst micro and small-sized firms
More willingness to utilise external funding than in the time of economic recession	Unproductive utilisation of the Common Market potential

Source: Starczewska-Krzysztoszek (2011).

This change has been driven by the increase of customer demands and the improving of living standards, rather than the effect from the previous low economy. This has consequently resulted in SMEs' tendency of increasing their expenditure on innovation investments and human resource, which play a key role in improving the quality of products/services and enhancing their competitiveness in the market. Nevertheless, micro and small firms have low inclination to innovation, particularly amongst firms who have no access to EU funds or when their subsidies come to an end. This can be attributed to their ignorance, misperception, or low capabilities and resources that enabled them to engage in innovation. It also resulted in the low inclination to foreign expansion amongst micro and small firms, which remains a significant weakness due to their limited cooperation with foreign partners. Finally, another important change is related to SMEs' willingness to utilise external funding, which helps to improve the firms' existing pool of financial resource. However, SMEs were criticised for their lack of capabilities to exploit the Common Market potential, which lengthens the weakness list of Polish SMEs.

One of the key themes emerging in the paper is that the influence of internationalisation on SME development varies according to the stage of development reached by the country and, in particular, the extent to which it has taken on the characteristics of an emerging market economy. Clearly, SMEs in central European countries have needed to cope with, and positively respond to, the effects of internationalisation on their business environment at a time when their economic structures were going through a process of radical transformation. The ability of SMEs in central European countries to compete in foreign and domestic markets varies between sectors. For example, one study undertaken in the 1990s found that in the food processing sector some SMEs were been able to penetrate foreign markets.

In this case, the main effect of internationalisation has been to increase the level of competition in domestic markets. The survey evidence showed that foreign market penetration by food processing SMEs is often focused on markets in other transition countries rather than in Western markets. However, in contrast with the food industry, in clothing the effects of internationalisation are quite different. This is because of the highly internationalised nature of the clothing market and the production system that supplies it. It is worth pointing out, however, that SMEs in countries such as Poland and Estonia (Smallbone, 2008) were able to attract subcontract work from firms in Western countries based on their low production costs. Of course there is always a risk with this type of work, which can be very volatile, disappearing almost as quickly as it is secured. Northern Greece and Macedonia are good examples of this. At the same time, the relationship which subcontractors have with their main contractors can be managed. In Estonia, for example, there are businesses which have evolved from sub-contractors to firms with a portfolio that includes some products of their own.

It is also the case that one would expect some change over time in the nature and force of internationalisation processes. Using the Estonian example again (Smallbone and Welter, 2009), when business owners were asked in a survey about the main constraints that they face in developing and running their businesses, the most commonly mentioned factor tended to change over time. Specifically, this involved less emphasis on regulatory barriers and changes in the taxation system and more emphasis on market-related factors, including the effects of increased competition from foreign firms. In other words, as transformation proceeded, the effect of internationalisation on Estonian SMEs increased.

Born global companies

The past decade has seen born globals (BGs) attract considerable attention from academics and public policymakers, which needs to be seen in the wider context of a focus on growth companies which born globals would seem to epitomise. Moreover, in the context of a discussion of internationalisation, born globals would seem to have a particular role because they will engage in internationalisation in the very first years after their foundation (Rialp *et al.*, 2005; Weerawardena, 2007; OECD, 2009; European Commission, 2010; Cavusgil and Knight, 2015; Hitt *et al.*, 2016; Gulanowski *et al.*, 2016). More specifically, BGs are often characterised by their internationalisation orientation, targeting foreign markets from the outset instead of moving from domestic to overseas markets (Cavusgil and Knight, 2009), which is what a stages approach would predict. Recent evidence has shown that at least 20 per cent of young internationalising enterprises are born globals in Europe (Eurofound, 2015), indicating an increasingly significant role for this segment. Prior research has found that BGs' export behaviour turned out to be more entrepreneurial than traditional exporters (Rialp *et al.*, 2005). In addition, existing literature indicates that the concept of born globals is not simply a feature in countries with small domestic markets but has in fact been spread worldwide, particularly by firms aiming to reduce production costs and enrich their resource pools in internationalisation (Cavusgil and Knight, 2009; Eurofound, 2015).

The speed and growth of internationalisation by born globals is mainly driven by the founders or owner-managers' 'entrepreneurial prowess', which are typically generated from their previous international experience (Hewerdine and Welch, 2013). Founders or owner-managers often view the international market as their target destination to enhance sales, hence embarking on a development path in which the speed of their internationalisation is much greater than that of traditional exporting firms (Cavusgil and Knight, 2015). In a similar vein, Moen (2002) has emphasised the role of financial and human capital (i.e. the number of founders, their educational background and their prior international experience) as being the key factors driving the BG's growth. In addition, Neubert (2016) has suggested that the business model, market entry and market development, technological capabilities, foreign market opportunities and the size of their home market are the keys to the speed of their internationalisation and overall rate of growth. This is confirmed by Karra *et al.* (2008)'s study, which revealed the three most significant entrepreneurial capabilities contributing to a BG's success as international 'opportunity identification', 'institutional bridging' and 'cross-cultural collaboration'.

The BGs' foreign market entry modes and speed of internationalisation are dependent on their existing international market knowledge, which is typically obtained from their network before their initial foreign market entry (Sharma and Blomstermo, 2003). SME internationalisation is known to involve not only export and import but also other forms of international activities such as foreign direct investment (FDI), international sub-contracting and international technical cooperation (European Commission, 2010). However, BGs are more likely to engage in import and export activity and sub-contracting due to their small size and focus (Majocchi *et al.*, 2005; Hollender *et al.*, 2017). As in the case of other SMEs, FDI is the least preferred mode of internationalisation entry to born globals due to their higher risks and costs involved (European Commission, 2010; Taylor and Jack, 2016).

Despite their limited resource constraints, BGs often possess distinctive intangible resource capabilities, such as skills, networking and international experience, that enable them to sustain in the international market (Rialp *et al.*, 2005; Freeman *et al.*, 2006; Jantunen *et al.*, 2008; Cavusgil and Knight, 2009; Zander *et al.*, 2015). Recent evidence has also indicated a positive relationship between the level of internationalisation and the firm's innovation (European Commission, 2010). Hence, born globals tend to be more oriented towards innovation as a source of their competitiveness in the international market than other firms. For example, recent statistics of European internationalising SMEs showed that over 50 per cent of internationally active SMEs are more likely to introduce new innovation than SMEs which are less active in internationalisation (European Commission, 2010).

The degree of SME internationalisation is, therefore, influenced by the level and type of innovation. Statistics from a survey of internationalisation amongst European SMEs shows that for those firms introducing new products/services for their sector in their countries, the proportion of internationally active firms is three times more than that of domestically orientated SMEs (European Commission, 2015).

Internationalising SMEs in Central and Eastern Europe typically face a number of international barriers, particularly those relating to their weak financial, human and social capital (ACCA, 2012; Stoian *et al.*, 2016). Even though they are more likely to offer competitive prices in international markets, BGs in these countries are typically weak in promotion and distribution, compared to Western internationalising SMEs (ACCA, 2012). Weerawardena *et al.* (2007) stressed the significant role of dynamic capabilities, one of which is an internationally oriented mindset of entrepreneurs, in determining their rapid internationalisation. Early internationalisation is also dependent on the capability of entrepreneurs to undertake multiple tasks, managerial commitment and vision, entrepreneurial and learning orientation.

BGs in Central and Eastern Europe tend to be 'pushed and pulled' towards international markets, mainly relating to their domestic barriers to market entry (Nowiński and Rialp, 2013). These BGs not only have to deal with their poor resource endowments but also intangible constraints, such as restricted international experience and limited social capital. Consequently, the principles of effectuation and bricolage (Baker and Nelson, 2005) tend to be effective for BGs in controlling their resource constraints, enabling them to exploit foreign market opportunities (Sarasvathy, 2001; Nowiński and Rialp, 2013). Nevertheless, like other internationalising SMEs, BGs encounter the liabilities of newness, which imposes a burden for them to survive in the international market (Nummela, 2011). External challenges to BGs are related to their ability to identify and penetrate new markets while extending existing ones. Other external challenges include government regulations, network, cultural and geographic locations, administration, technology, exchange rate, high costs, payment issues and foreign market competition (OECD, 2009; European Commission, 2010). Besides, industrial factors such as the internationalisation of the sector, the competitiveness and size of the domestic market and the heterogeneity of international markets are also identified as external drivers of the BGs' speed of internationalisation (Thai and Chong, 2008; Taylor and Jack, 2016).

The public policy dimension

In general there are two main justifications for public policy intervention with respect to the SMEs. The first is to do with the contribution of enterprising SMEs to competitiveness, keeping in mind that the competitiveness of an economy depends on the competitiveness of individual firms. The second is with regard to the potential role of entrepreneurship in relation to social inclusion. As far as internationalisation is concerned, it is clearly the first of these two justifications that would seem to be the most relevant. As a result, the key question becomes: how can the EU member states collectively and individually assist European SMEs in their desire to internationalise on the basis that internationalisation represents one of the routes to competitiveness? This is an area where there is considerable help available, although a recurrent problem is often that business owners are not fully familiar with what is available.

Surveys that have been undertaken of entrepreneurs and business managers in SMEs seeking to internationalise consistently point to a shortage of finance, and specifically a shortage of working capital, as one of the main constraints facing SMEs seeking to internationalise their operations. At the same time, it needs to be recognised that not all these financial constraints may be necessarily related directly to internationalisation, since finance is one of the most commonly reported challenges for small business owners and managers across the board. At the same time, it has been shown that the nature and extent of financial constraints typically varies between sectors, which not surprisingly, tends to be more prominent in the case of manufacturing enterprises than service sector ones.

The funding required for internationalisation may be divided into financial assistance for exporters in the form of export credits and guarantees; and finance to support longer term international collaboration and/or to assist firms seeking to invest abroad, in order to ensure that the experience is a profitable one. Clearly financing is essential for international trade and the official export agencies, particularly in the more advanced countries, play a key role in providing, guaranteeing and insuring such finance. Most European countries have some form of finance available to businesses interested in entering, or increasing, their activity in export markets. This reflects the fact that there are economic benefits and potential welfare gains to the economy as a whole from export activity as the income earned from export activity has a multiplier effect on employment as well as income.

In giving credit to its buyer, an exporter faces two particular problems. One is that typically they have to wait for their money, which affects the suppliers' cash flow; and second, the exporter is exposed to the risk that the buyer can't or won't pay for the exports. In order to deal with these issues, an exporter can get help from a bank or specialist finance institution. Because there is a greater risk of not being paid for exported goods, most countries have an export credit guarantee scheme, which acts as an insurance policy for the exporting firm. The risk of not getting paid can represent a bigger problem for small companies than for large firms because of their more limited internal resource base. This means that, unlike large firms, they are likely to be in a less resilient position should, for example, a buyer go bankrupt. At a detailed level, the share and type of export credits that are extended to SME exporters varies across countries. At the same time, export credits are generally divided between short term – those under two years; medium term – usually 2–5 years; and long term – more than five years. However, in the European Union it has been reported that short-term credits have been mainly privatised (OECD, 2017).

In new member states of the EU, there has been significant institutional change to adapt to the fundamental restructuring that has been necessary as part of their adjustment of the role of the state in business activity. Referring to the Czech Republic, for example, an export credit bank was established in 1995 which is the main institution through which state support for exporting is channelled. Its offer includes the provision and financing of export credits and other services connected with exporting. There is also an export credit agency (EGAP), which is the national organisation insuring credits connected with exports from the Czech Republic against political and commercial risks that are normally uninsurable by commercial insurers. This agency was formed in 1992 as a joint stock company completely owned by the Czech state. The agency provides guarantees, mainly for credits, to the countries in Eastern Europe and the former Soviet Union, where the Czech firms traditionally hold a strong position. This emphasis is in line with the national export strategy. It may be argued that the provision of export credit coverage is one of the main tools that the government has at its disposal to stimulate national exports.

A comparison, of the Czech Republic with Germany, for example, suggests that in the Czech Republic foreign or private insurers are conservative by comparison with those of more advanced countries. Detailed investigation suggests that credit insurance is much more readily available, and to a higher level, in Germany than it is in the Czech Republic (Picha, 2014) and, as a consequence, it contributes to the competitive advantage of German exporters. Taking a longer term of view of internationalisation processes, the extent to which the country is investing in innovation and knowledge-based activities is likely to have some bearing on its medium and longer term pattern of internationalisation. In the Czech Republic, the R&D funding is administered by a series of national institutions, including the Academy of Science of the Czech Republic, the Grant Agency, the Technology Agency and seven government ministries (Picha, 2014).

The export support programmes tend to focus on the finance question and also reducing the risk for exporters, since it is recognised that the chances of not being paid are greater in the case of export to other countries than it is in the case of a sale within the domestic economy, but, in addition to these programmes, there are also other measures which can impact on export activity, even though this may not be their prime focus. Most notable of these are growth programmes, such as in Denmark. These growth programmes are particularly close to export support in the case of small economies such as Ireland or Finland because it is well established that in such environments growth-oriented firms will need to look to foreign markets almost from day one. As a result there are definitional issues surrounding what constitutes policy to support exporting.

We can make a distinction between those policies which are explicitly focused on supporting export activity and those which can have an effect. One of the policy issues with respect to foreign inward investment is how best to maximise the benefits for the national economy from this type of investment. Until recently the mainstream view was that inward investing companies (i.e. FDI) typically bring little benefit to host economies other than the jobs that they create directly. In addition, because much of the FDI involves simple assembly-type activity, it can be easy for foreign companies to withdraw their investment, at short notice. What this means is that the investment doesn't have the same kind of multiplier effect as a domestic firm might well result in. However, the world is changing with respect to FDI in two important respects (Smallbone, 2008).

One is the new sources of investment finance that are emerging which traditionally have been dominated by the United States but which now include FDI originating from countries such as India and China. The second new feature is that the market is not completely dominated by large firms in the way that it has been in recent years. The significance of this is that when a medium-sized company invests abroad, the investment is likely to represent a much higher percentage of that firm's asset base than in the case of a large enterprise. As a consequence, medium-sized companies are much more likely to be interested in some form of collaboration with local businesses in order to acquire local knowledge of markets, for example, or simply to just 'hedge their bets'. These features present some new opportunities for transition and developing countries because, if it is possible to produce more of the supply of parts, components and services to these inward investing companies in local SMEs, then the potential economic benefits of FDI to the destination economies will be much greater. In this context, it needs to be recognised that FDI is potentially a source of upgrading and a source of potential growth as far as this domestic SME sector is concerned.

Although the changes described in the pattern of FDI are market driven in order to stimulate more of the better potential benefits for the local economy, it is necessary to have appropriate programmes and policies in place. In recent times, promoting FDI–SME linkages has been an emerging policy theme in the OECD amongst others. Good examples of what can be achieved through this type of intervention can be seen in the case of both Malaysia and Singapore. More recently the OECD themselves have been working in Kazakhstan to try to harness more of the potential supply base for the oil industry for domestic firms, rather than being imported.

In most countries it is a minority of SMEs that make a disproportionate contribution to economic development and employment generation. In some transition and developing countries there is evidence of a missing middle, reflecting the lack of a core of medium-sized, growth-orientated SMEs, between large firms on the one hand and micro enterprises, and small firms operating mainly in the informal economy, on the other. In this context, policies to promote FDI–SME linkages would seem to offer a mechanism for addressing this issue.

This leads to the question of what kinds of policies are necessary in order to help to facilitate stronger multiplier benefits for a local economy. First, there is a need for policymakers to engage with inward investing companies in order to ensure that they are fully aware of the potential supply opportunities within the economy in which they are investing. Second, there is a need to make the local SME sector fully aware of the potential that exists around these inward investing companies and, more specifically, what exactly they are looking to purchase in terms of goods and services that may be potentially supplied from within the local economy. In addition to providing some 'marriage guidance' facility between the inward investors and the local SMEs to perform this supply function, it is also likely to be necessary to develop programmes which are aimed at building the capacity of domestic SMEs to perform this supply function. In principle at least, if business owners can see the potential for gaining new business, they are more likely to be willing to invest some time and resource into quality assurance programmes, for example, than they are to do this in situations where it is a more abstract concept.

The potential benefits of FDI to host economies are summarised in a framework developed by Dunning back in 1992. Dunning (1992) identified five main types of linkages and spill-over effects through which the presence of multi-national companies can affect the development of businesses in the host economy. This refers to the extent to which components, materials and services are sourced from within the host economy; in other words backward linkages. Since, if they can, then new market opportunities are created for the domestic SME sector. Such linkages can range from a market-based transaction to deep, long-term inter-firm supply relationships. The second method presented by Dunning involves forward linkages with customers. This can include the marketing function which may be outsourced alongside linkages with industrial buyers. The third method is linkages with competitors. Foreign investors may set new standards in a host economy which local firms may seek to compete with. Maybe the term 'linkage' is somewhat misleading in this case, in that it is an effect, not merely a direct linkage. The fourth method is through linkages with technology partners. This may include joint ventures, licensing agreements and strategic alliances. Lastly, there are other spill-over events which include demonstration events – as inward investors demonstrate new and better ways of doing things, so local firms' managers will hopefully pick up on these.

Conclusions

It may be more accurate to refer to emerging themes rather than conclusions per se, in view of the introductory role of this chapter in the book. In this context, a number of broad themes may be drawn from the paper. The first is the growing influence of internationalisation which is affecting businesses of all sizes, creating opportunities as well as challenges. Opportunities exist for entrepreneurial firms to respond positively to the effect of increasing integration of markets facilitated by the revolution in communications and transportation technology.

At the same time, it is important to stress that internationalisation can take many forms and it is a mistake to define it simply in terms of exporting. Certainly, when broadly defined, internationalisation cannot be ignored by any firm because, at the very least, it is likely to contribute to increasing competition within the domestic market which some firms will be threatening. For others, it represents an opportunity to upgrade themselves.

Another important theme is the heterogeneity of experience and contexts within the SME group. There are few serious research publications in the SME field that do not recognise this heterogeneity, which in policy terms means the sector mix, the age of businesses and, arguably most important of all, the aspirations of the owner of the business for its future development. This heterogeneity is by no means a new finding but the rest of this paper certainly illustrates its importance in terms of relevant theories to explain this increasing internationalisation. The SME dimension makes a network-based approach arguably the most useful but, at the same time, some SMEs show some evidence of a staged approach, particularly where there are strong cultural ties with neighbouring countries on the basis that this can help them to understand the market better. However, it must be recognised that the field of international entrepreneurship is a relatively recent one and the development of theory to explain internationalisation is still evolving.

Turning to the European dimension, it is evident that the international aspirations of European SMEs are typically focused on other countries within the internal market rather than countries outside the European Union. In terms of public policy, it seems that various attempts at the national and supranational levels to assist Europe's SMEs to internationalise have had varying degrees of success. This is partly because of the ongoing problem of entrepreneurs not knowing about the help that is available to them. In addition, the extension of the European Union to take in countries that until recently have been operating under the rules of central planning is having a major impact on the nature of European SMEs' experience.

The main problem for SMEs in these new member countries is that there is typically a lack of underlying competitiveness, which is affected by a variety of internal and external factors but, in essence, it is about more than simply SMEs. There is a desperate need to raise the innovative capacity of individual firms, which may require a upgrading of workforce and leadership skills but for SMEs it also requires a strengthening of innovation systems.

As the world's economies become increasingly interrelated, the need for global perspectives is increased. In this context, the concept of born global, which is briefly reviewed in the paper, is very relevant to the development priorities of these new member countries. Exporting is an important source of innovation and innovative ideas which can result from their cooperation with buyers and suppliers. This reflects the long-standing experience in mature market economies where the supply chain is typically the most common source of innovation for SMEs. As a result, in terms of public policy, this suggests there is a need to focus on supply chain development rather than just on individual firms.

Although public policy is important in providing and facilitating a framework, ultimately entrepreneurship and competitive business development depend on the motivation, skills and commitment of entrepreneurs. In this context it should be noted that, whilst inward investment offers potential business opportunities to aspiring suppliers in host countries, it can also be a major challenge for them. This is because multi-national companies are typically a demanding customer group. As a result, domestic entrepreneurs must be willing to commit themselves to providing high-quality products and services, as well as understanding the needs of multinational clients by recognising the improvements that they may be required to undertake in their production systems. This type of work will almost certainly involve investment of capital as well as time and skills.

Finally, it is important to recognise that SMEs may not necessarily come in at the top of the supply chain. In other words they may be much lower down, which means that their dealings may not necessarily be directly with the multi-national but, rather, with other local firms that may be higher up in the supply chain. In such circumstances, public policy should be targeted at supply chains rather than at individual businesses.

References

ACCA, 2012, SMEs Internationalisation in Centre and Eastern Europe. Available at www.accaglobal.com/content/dam/acca/global/PDF-technical/small-business/pol-tp-sicee.pdf. Accessed 6 June 2017.

Baker, T. and Nelson, R.E., 2005, 'Creating something from nothing: Resource construction through entrepreneurial bricolage', *Administrative Science Quarterly*, 50 (3), pp. 329–366.

Baum, M., Schwens, C. and Kabst, R., 2013, 'International as opposed to domestic new venturing: The moderating role of perceived barriers to internationalization', *International Small Business Journal*, 31 (5), pp. 536–562.

Cavusgil, S.T. and Knight, G., 2009, *Born global firms: A new international enterprise*, New York: Business Expert Press.

Cavusgil, S.T. and Knight, G., 2015, 'The born global firm: An entrepreneurial and capabilities perspective on early and rapid internationalization', *Journal of International Business Studies*, 46 (11), pp. 3–16.

Cernat, L., Ana, N.L. and Ana, D.T., 2014, *SMEs are more important than you think! Challenges and opportunities for EU exporting SMEs (No. 2014–3)*, Directorate General for Trade, European Commission.

Coviello, N. and Munro, H., 1995, 'Growing the entrepreneurial firm: Networking for international marketing development', *European Journal of Marketing*, 29 (7), pp. 49–61.

Dunning, J., 1992, *Multi-national enterprises and the global economy*, Reading, MA: Addison-Wesley.

Eurofound, 2015, *Born global – young firms that internationalise rapidly*. Available at www.eurofound.europa.eu/printpdf/born-globals-young-firms-that-internationalise-rapidly. Accessed 2 September 2017.

European Commission, 2010, *Internationalisation of European SMEs*, final report, Brussels: EIM Business and Policy Research. Available at www.ec.europa.eu/enterprise/e_i/index_en.htm. Accessed 2 September 2017.

European Commission, 2015, *Internationalisation of small and medium-sized enterprises*, Flash Eurobarometer 421, doi: 10.2873/886211.

Freeman, S., Edwards, R. and Schroder, B., 2006, 'How smaller born-global firms use networks and alliances to overcome constraints to rapid internationalisation', *Journal of International Marketing*, 14 (3), pp. 33–63.

Gulanowski, D., Plante, L. and Papadopoulos, N., 2016, 'A knowledge perspective on the Uppsala and born global internationalization models', in L. Petruzzellis and R. Winer, eds., *Rediscovering the essentiality of marketing*, Proceedings of the Academy of Marketing Science, Cham: Springer, pp. 503–504.

Hewerdine, L. and Welch, C., 2013, 'Are international new ventures really new? A process study of organizational emergence and internationalization', *Journal of World Business*, 48 (4), pp. 466–477.

Hitt, M.A., Li, D. and Xu, K., 2016, 'International strategy: From local to global and beyond', *Journal of World Business*, 51 (1), pp. 58–73.

Hollender, L., Zapkau, F.B. and Schwens, C., 2017, 'SME foreign market entry mode choice and foreign venture performance: The moderating effect of international experience and product adaptation', *International Business Review*, 26 (2), pp. 250–263.

Ibeh, K. 2012, 'Internationalisation and entrepreneurial businesses', in S. Carter and D. Jones-Evans, eds., *Enterprise and small business: Principles, practice and policy*, Harlow: Pearson, pp. 430–449.

Jantunen, A., Nummela, N., Puumalainen, K. and Saarenketo, S., 2008, 'Strategic orientations of born globals-Do they really matter?', *Journal of World Business*, 43 (2), pp. 158–170.

Karra, N., Phillips, N. and Karra, N., 2008, 'Building the born global firm: Developing entrepreneurial capabilities for international new venture success', *Long Range Planning* 41 (4), pp. 440–458.

Majocchi, A., Bacchiocchi, E. and Mayrhofer, U., 2005, 'Firm size, business experience and export intensity in SMEs: A longitudinal approach to complex relationships', *International Business Review*, 14 (6), pp. 719–738.

Moen, O., 2002, 'The born globals: A new generation of small European exporters', *International Marketing Review*, 19 (2), pp. 156–175.

Neubert, M., 2016, 'How and why born global firms differ in their speed of internationalisation – a multiple case study approach', *International Journal of Teaching and Case Studies*, 7 (2), pp. 118–134.

Nowiński, W. and Rialp, A., 2013, 'Drivers and strategies of international new ventures from a Central European transition economy', *Journal for East European Management Studies*, 18 (2), pp. 191–231.

Nummela, N. 2011, *International growth of small and medium enterprises*, New York: Routledge.

OECD, 2009, *Top barriers and drivers to SME internationalisation*. Available at www.oecd.org/dataoecd/16/26/43357832.pdf. Accessed 1 July 2017.

OECD, 2017, Officially-supported export credits and small exporters. Available at www.oecd.org/tad/xcred/2634848.pdf. Accessed 10 September 2017.

Piasecki, B. and Rogut, A., 2004, 'Poland: the Zary and Bialystock regions', in L. Labrianidis, ed., *The future of Europe's rural peripheries*, Aldershot and Burlington, VT: Ashgate, pp. 271–297.

Picha, J., 2014, *Comparison of export financing programmes in the Czech Republic and Germany*, Paper presented to the Construction Macro-Economics Conference.

Rialp, A., Rialp, J., Urbano, D. and Vaillant, Y., 2005, 'The born-global phenomenon: A comparative case study research', *Journal of International Entrepreneurship*, 3 (2), pp. 133–171.

Sarasvathy, S.D., 2001, 'Causation and effectuation: Toward a theoretical shift from economic inevitability to entrepreneurial contingency', *Academy of Management Review*, 26 (2), pp. 243–263.

Sharma, D.D. and Blomstermo, A., 2003, 'The internationalization process of born globals: A network view', *International Business Review*, 12 (6), pp. 739–753.

Smallbone D., 2008, 'Foreign direct investment and SME development: Some policy issues for transition and developing countries', in K. Todorov and D. Smallbone, eds., *Entrepreneurship in a united Europe: Challenges and opportunities*, Sofia: Bulgarian Association for Management Development and Entrepreneurship, pp. 96–115.

Smallbone, D. and Koos van Elk, T., 2011, *Market access for European SMEs in China: Results of interviews January 2011 in Beijing, Shanghai, Wuxi & Nanjing*, Brussels: DG Enterprise and Industry, European Commission.

Smallbone, D. and Welter, F., 2009, *Entrepreneurship and small business development in post-socialist economies*, Oxon: Routledge.

Starczewska-Krzysztoszek, M., 2011, *Advantages and disadvantages of micro, small and medium companies*, European Social Fund. Available at http://konfederacjalewiatan.pl/en/_files/publications/RaportMSP_EN_30_03.pdf. Accessed 30 August 2017.

Stoian, M.C., Rialp, A., Rialp, J. and Jarvis, R., 2016, 'Internationalisation of Central and Eastern European small firms: Institutions, resources and networks', *Journal of Small Business and Enterprise Development*, 23 (1), pp. 105–121.

Taylor, M. and Jack, R., 2016, 'Born global firm internationalisation: The influence of industry factors', *Contemporary Management Research*, 12(3), pp. 289–308.

Thai, M.T.T. and Chong, L.C., 2008, 'Born-global: The case of four Vietnamese SMEs', *Journal of International Entrepreneurship*, 6 (2), pp. 72–100.

Weerawardena, J., Mort, G.S., Liesch, P.W. and Knight, G., 2007, 'Conceptualizing accelerated internationalization in the born global firm: A dynamic capabilities perspective', *Journal of World Business*, 42 (3), pp. 294–306.

Zander, I., McDougall-Covin, P. and Rose, E.L., 2015, 'Born globals and international business: Evolution of a field of research', *Journal of International Business Studies*, 46 (1), pp. 27–35.

PART II

Entrepreneurs re-shaping industries

Markets, products and services

3

ENTREPRENEURSHIP DEVELOPMENT THROUGH INTERNATIONALISATION IN LATVIA

The case of Laima: born sweet and global

Arnis Sauka

This chapter presents key development trends in the economy and entrepreneurship in Latvia and presents a case study of chocolate producer Laima. The chapter covers the period prior to 1991, while providing more in-depth insights into entrepreneurship development after 1991, when Latvia regained independence from the Soviet Union. Particular attention is paid to the export orientation of Latvian companies as well as the inflow of foreign direct capital into the country. In the context of development trends in entrepreneurship, the chapter proceeds with a case study of Laima, in particular, the company's distinct strategies for entering the US, Russian and Asian markets during 2008–2013.

Introduction

A brief overview of the history and development of the entrepreneurship climate in Latvia until 1991

Latvia is a relatively small country with approximately 2.3 million inhabitants extending over an area of 64,589 square kilometres. The country is bordered by the other two Baltic States – Estonia and Lithuania – as well as Russia and Belarus and is located on the shores of the Baltic Sea. Due to its favourable location, Latvia has a very rich history that has also shaped the development of the economy within the country. For instance, in the nineteenth century, Riga, the capital city of Latvia, was among the most industrialised cities of the Russian Empire (Švābe, 1990; Bleiere *et al.*, 2005).

After the end of the First World War, on 18 November 1918, Latvia was proclaimed an independent state for the first time in its history. This period is remembered in Latvia as marking a shift from industrialisation to agriculture, yet with remarkable success in both areas. Namely, the export of agricultural products such as butter, meat, linen and wood material – mainly to Western Europe (Jansone *et al.*, 2008) – was developed and a number of manufacturing companies, including VEF, a producer of a wide range of products (from radio receivers to airplanes), were established. As a result of such developments, by 1937 Latvia had already repaid all its external debts and raised some six tons of gold in various banks in the United Kingdom, Switzerland and the United States (Avots, 2004).

In 1939, however, the Second World War started and, following the Molotov-Ribbentrop Pact, Latvia fell into the zone of impact of the Soviet Union. This eventually led to the occupation of Latvia in 1940 and the resulting 'Year of Terror'. Namely, during 1941 approximately 65,000 members of the German intelligentsia – Baltic Germans – left the country, creating heavy losses for the economy, culture and educational system of Latvia (Jansone *et al.*, 2008; Bleiere *et al.*, 2005). This year is also marked in history by the Holocaust on the territory of Latvia, with some 70,000 Jews murdered. In between two large countries at war, Latvians were recruited into both the Soviet army and the German SS. Approximately 200,000 Latvians perished on both sides. Unfortunately, the situation did not improve much after the war. For example, to decrease the resistance to 'collectivism' among the local intelligentsia, the largest deportation in the history of the country was implemented in March 1949, with as many as 42,125 Latvians deported to Siberia and the Far East overnight (Jansone *et al.*, 2008).

On the bright side, the economic situation of the country progressed somewhat even within the Soviet Union, with the chemical industry, machinery, textiles, building material production, pharmaceuticals and electronics represented in the relatively small territory of Latvia. As a result, Latvia became one of the most highly industrialised regions of the Soviet Union, yet not without costs, such as the inflow of people from other parts of the Soviet Union (Jansone *et al.*, 2008; Bleiere *et al.*, 2005). Eventually, with the collapse of the Soviet Union, on 21 August 1991, Latvia regained its independence and the transition from socialism to a market economy started.

Transition to a market economy after 1991: key development trends in the economy and entrepreneurship

As in other Central and Eastern European countries, in Latvia transition was not an easy process. For example, the real GDP growth of Latvia fell to –34.0 per cent in 1992 and almost all factories were closed during the early 1990s. Adjustment to a market system did indeed take some time as both politicians and entrepreneurs – a newly developed private sector that had not existed for more than 40 years – simply lacked skills and knowledge. Furthermore, some events, such as the bank crisis in Latvia in 1994 and the crisis in Russia in 1998, negatively influenced the process of development, which was not easy as such. Yet Latvia continued along its development path and joined NATO and the European Union in 2004, which, among other things, fostered the inflow of foreign capital into the country, further strengthening the economy. The key development patterns of Latvia are reflected in Figure 3.1 and Table 3.1.

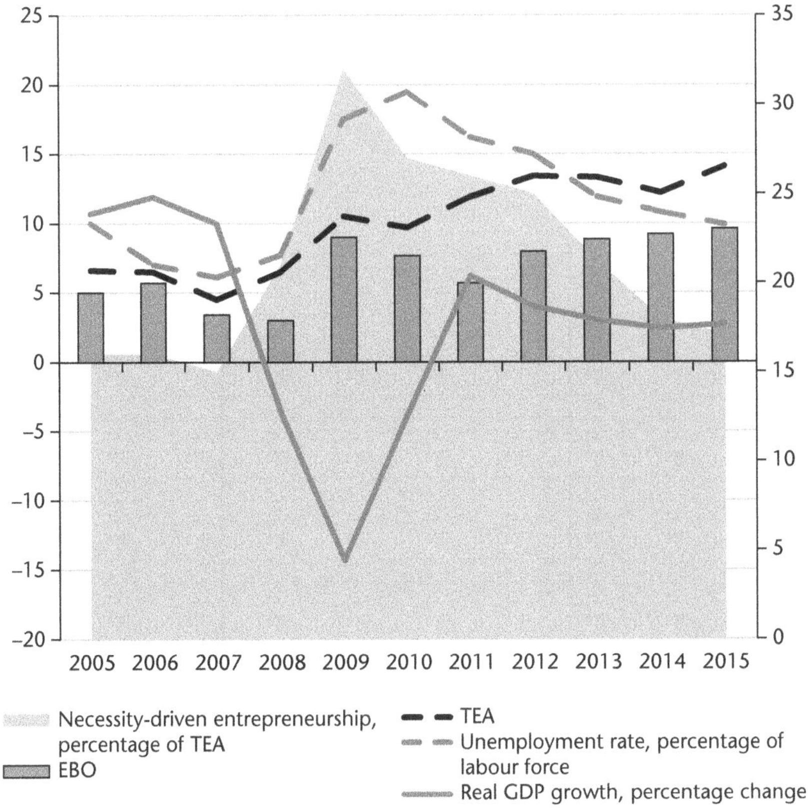

FIGURE 3.1 Dynamics of entrepreneurship in Latvia, 2005–2015.

Source: GEM Latvian adult population surveys and EUROSTAT.

As exemplified in Figure 3.1 (see real GDP growth, per cent change), Latvia experienced a fast growth rate, reaching GDP growth of +12 per cent in 2006. At that time, it was the highest growth rate in the European Union, and thus Latvia and the other two Baltic countries were often referred to as the 'Baltic Tigers'. Steady growth, however, was followed by a sharp downturn in early 2008; as a result of the world financial crisis as well as increased consumption driven by easy access to cheap bank loans, GDP fell by approximately 18 per cent in 2009. Furthermore, data from the Global Entrepreneurship Latvia study show a variation in entrepreneurship rates in Latvia as a result of major changes in the economic development patterns.

For example, the prevalence rate of nascent entrepreneurship was about 6.6 per cent in 2005 and 2006; it decreased to 4.4 per cent in 2007 and increased sharply in 2009. Here, GEM data clearly show that necessity-driven entrepreneurship activity during the economic downturn accounts for most of the growth in nascent entrepreneurship activity in Latvia. Another explanation for the increase, however, is the

TABLE 3.1 Key indicators of economic development in Latvia

	2008	*2009*	*2010*	*2011*	*2012*	*2013*	*2014*	*2015*	*2016*
GDP (real prices, billion EUR)	24.4	18.8	17.9	20.3	21.8	22.8	23.6	24.4	25.0
	Growth compared to previous year, %								
GDP	–3.6	–14.3	–3.8	6.4	4.0	2.6	2.1	2.7	2.0
Private consumption	–7.9	–16.0	2.8	3.0	3.1	5.0	1.3	3.5	3.4
State consumption	2.4	–10.7	–8.1	3.0	0.3	1.6	2.1	3.1	2.7
Exports	2.4	–12.9	13.4	12.0	9.8	1.1	3.9	2.6	2.6
Imports	–10.7	–31.7	12.4	22.0	5.4	–0.2	0.5	2.1	4.4
Export–import balance, % of GDP	–12.9	–1.6	–1.5	–5.0	–4.4	–3.2	–1.9	–1.1	0.6
Changes in employee numbers (15–74 years, % compared to previous year)	–0.2	–13.9	–6.4	1.3	1.6	2.1	–1.0	1.3	–0.3
Employment, %	62.0	54.3	52.0	54.0	56.1	58.2	59.1	60.8	61.6
Unemployment (in search of a job % of economically active inhabitants. 15–74 years)	7.7	17.5	19.5	16.2	15.0	11.9	10.8	9.9	9.5

Source: Official Statistics, CSB (2017).

lower opportunity cost for entering entrepreneurship during the crisis. Namely, the level of salaries during economic growth was rising steadily; thus, professionals working as employees had a high opportunity cost in moving from a well-paid job to private business. This, however, changed with the economic crisis, when salary levels decreased sharply in a short period of time (Krumina and Paalzow, 2017).

How to overcome the economic recession and how to pay off a 7.5 billion EUR loan taken from the European Commission and the World Bank as well as other organisations and governments to stabilise the financial sector in Latvia – this became a topic of very hot debate in Latvia after 2008. Several reforms were undertaken that resulted in the recovery of the economy as early as 2011, with GDP growth of 6.4 per cent (see Table 3.1). Latvia also experienced a decrease in unemployment starting in 2011 and some positive dynamics in export figures (see Figure 3.1).[1]

Soon after, the indicators also improved with regard to the quality of nascent entrepreneurship activity in Latvia. As shown by Figure 3.2, since 2009 Latvia has enjoyed a decrease in necessity-driven entrepreneurship.

Furthermore, according to the 2013–2014 GEM Latvia report, overall in 2013 people in Latvia saw more business opportunities compared to 2012 (2013 – 35 per cent; 2012 – 33 per cent). The population has also become more confident when it comes to their entrepreneurial capacity, yet also more afraid of failure. According to the GEM 2013–2014 report, Latvia ranks first out of the 28 countries examined in the GEM project in involvement in early stage entrepreneurial activity (13.3 per cent of Latvia's population is involved). It should also be emphasised that females in Latvia (9.8 per cent in 2015) are most actively involved in TEA compared to other European

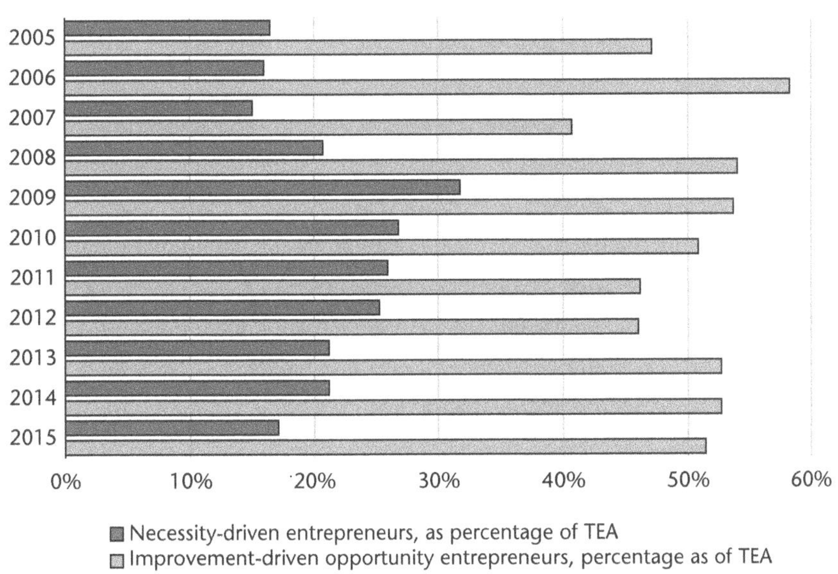

FIGURE 3.2 Motivation for entrepreneurship, Latvia, 2005–2015.

Source: GEM Latvian adult population surveys, 2005–2015.

countries. The number of economically active companies as well as the dynamics of registered and liquidated companies are provided in Table 3.2 and Figure 3.3.

It should also be noted that the development of entrepreneurship activity differed significantly in Riga (and the Riga region) compared with other regions of Latvia. That is, there were as many as 58 active companies per 1,000 inhabitants in the Riga region in 2005 (the most recent data available on these indicators) (41 in Riga City and 17 in other parts of the Riga region), whereas the number of entrepreneurs in provincial regions reached only 11–15 enterprises per 1,000 inhabitants. Altogether, this pattern reveals the important role of Riga and the Riga region and highlights the comparably low economic activity in other regions of Latvia, which also has implications for designing business startup and self-employment development policies targeted at underrepresented and disadvantaged groups.

Internationalisation of Latvian companies, export and import

From a macroeconomic point of view, business internationalisation is shown through the intensity of foreign trade. Indeed, a steady internationalisation of

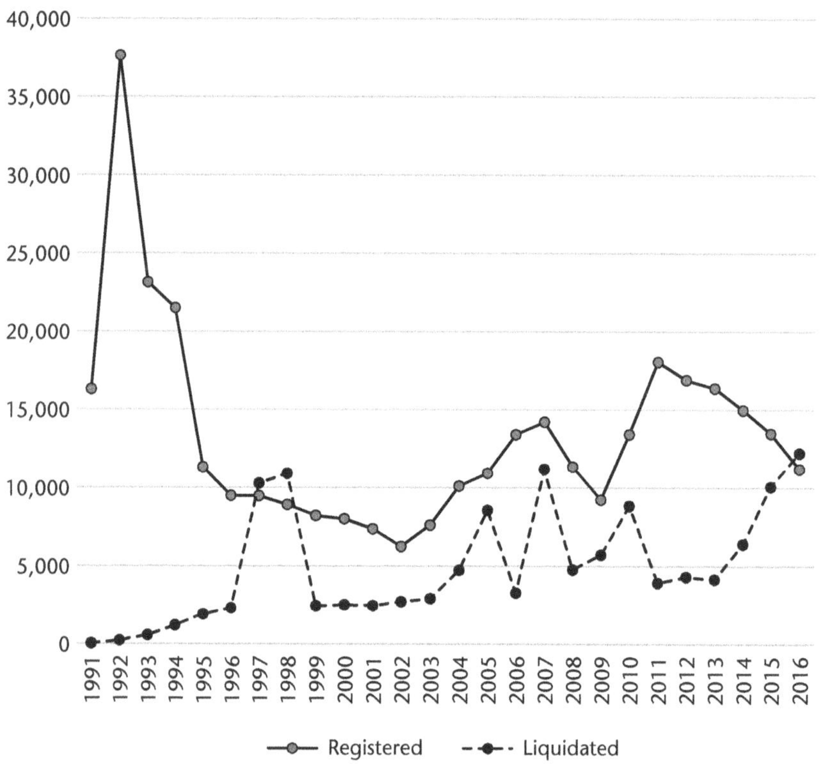

FIGURE 3.3 Registered and liquidated companies in Latvia, 1991–2017.

Source: Official statistics, CSB (2017).

TABLE 3.2 Number of economically active companies in Latvia, 2007–2014

2007	*2008*	*2009*	*2010*	*2011*	*2012*	*2013*	*2014*
54,844	56,108	54,481	56,789	65,522	54,381	50,844	58,397

Source: EM (2017).[1]

Note

1 Here and further in this chapter, EM (2017) represents data that were kindly provided by the Ministry of Economics of Latvia in May 2017. Thse data repersent official statistics of Latvia.

Latvian business and the resulting export increase constituted one of the drivers behind Latvia's recovery from the economic crisis of 2008. Namely, in 2010 Latvian exports increased by almost 30 per cent as compared to the previous year, with approximately 70 per cent going to EU countries (LIAA, 2011[2]). Both the export of goods and the export of services have continued to grow since 2010, reaching 10,281 EUR and 4,202 million EUR in 2016, respectively (see Table 3.3).

The most important commodity groups of Latvian exports are agricultural products and food (19.4 per cent in 2016), followed by machinery, appliances and electrical equipment, and wood and wood products (see Table 3.4).

The structure of Latvian exports is further presented in Table 3.5, whereas the main trade partner countries of Latvia are presented in Table 3.6.

Putnins' (2013) article summarises key information, including the challenges of companies exporting from Latvia. Drawing on a survey of approximately 500 medium-sized Latvian companies, Putnins (2013) concludes that Latvian companies are active in export activity, i.e. approximately 60 per cent of interviewed companies with an annual turnover between 500,000 and 50 million EUR that have been operating for at least five years are involved in direct export. The most common destinations according to Putnins' (2013) article are Lithuania and Estonia, but a substantial proportion of the sample also export to Scandinavia, Germany, Russia and other EU countries. Typically, a company exports to five different countries.

Putnins (2013) also concludes that growth in export turnover and in the number of countries to which exporters sell their goods and services has been fairly stagnant during the past five years. Namely, according to this study, a typical exporter has experienced zero growth in export turnover and only one additional export destination. Thus, considering that total turnover growth of the companies researched was positive, this suggests that Latvian exporters overall, and smaller companies in

TABLE 3.3 Export of goods and services, Latvia (million EUR)

	2010	*2011*	*2012*	*2013*	*2014*	*2015*	*2016*
Export of goods	6,657	8,300	9,646	9,810	10,215	10,322	10,281
Export of services	2,968	3,438	3,773	3,931	3,853	4,039	4,204

Source: EM (2017).

TABLE 3.4 Export of goods in Latvia, 2016; key community groups (%, FOB prices)

	Structure	*Changes*	*Contribution to changes*
Total	**100**	**−0.2**	**−0.2**
Agricultural products and food	19.4	4.1	0.8
Mineral products	5.0	−26.5	−1.8
Chemical industry products	11.1	9.4	1.0
Light industry products	3.6	−14.9	−0.6
Wood and wood products	17.3	4.9	0.8
Metal and metal products	8.1	−6.0	−0.5
Machinery, appliances and electrical equipment	17.6	−8.1	1.6
Vehicles	6.4	21.4	1.1
Other goods	11.4	5.6	0.6

Source: EM (2017).

TABLE 3.5 Structure of Latvian exports: countries (million EUR)

	2010	*2011*	*2012*	*2013*	*2014*	*2015*	*2016*
EU-15	2,332	2,779	3,110	3,122	3,267	3,326	3,630
Estonia	901	1,164	1,286	1,276	1,217	1,208	1,249
Lithuania	1,085	1,546	1,576	1,724	1,916	1,989	1,891
Other EU countries	473	698	893	999	1,049	1,011	879
CIS	1,007	1,257	1,534	1,621	1,533	1,248	1,171
Other countries	883	1,090	1,473	1,279	1,266	1,582	1,518

Source: EM (2017).

TABLE 3.6 Main trade partner countries of Latvia in 2016 (million EUR)

	Export	*Import*
Lithuania	1,891	2,160
Estonia	1,254	982
Russia	788	949
Germany	741	1,472
Sweden	621	442
UK	585	239
Poland	538	1,322
Denmark	478	270
The Netherlands	298	503
Norway	237	44
Finland	205	560

Source: EM (2017).

particular, have not been very successful in expanding their export activity. Putnins (2013) also reports that direct exporters pay higher average wages and seem to have higher labour productivity or utilise more skilled labour on average. Employees of export companies on average speak more languages and companies involved in direct exporting also seem to be more innovative, proactive and risk taking, and therefore have a greater entrepreneurial orientation. Furthermore, according to Putnins (2013), the most severe obstacles faced by Latvian exporters are strong price competition in foreign markets, legal barriers, customs requirements, breakage/spoilage and a lack of information about the exporting process.

Apart from understanding the export patterns of local companies, it is also interesting to explore the patterns of foreign direct investment as well as some of the potential reasons behind these numbers. In this light, Table 3.7 summarises the inflow of foreign direct investment in Latvia and the other two Baltic countries. As shown in the table, Latvia has achieved considerable inflow of foreign direct investment since 2011, yet the amount dropped significantly in 2016.

To investigate the reasons for this decrease, the key concerns of foreign investors are summarised by Sauka's study (2016), which, among other things, shows the major drawbacks faced by entrepreneurs in Latvia overall. Namely, key foreign direct investors in Latvia express major concerns with regard to demography and access to labour in Latvia. Emphasising the quality of the existing labour force, the investors highlight the lack of quantity of all types of labour – both white-collar and blue-collar. In this light, companies are calling for controlled, regulated immigration as well as smart re-emigration to solve the increasing demographic challenge. Since lack of employees directly influences business activity, we can expect that companies might take steps to import labour at any cost in the nearest future. Needless to say, policymakers in Latvia should be very cautious with regard to this trend.

According to Sauka (2016), investors are also calling for improvements in the level of education and vocational training in Latvia. Among other things, investors are concerned about the quality of mathematics, physics and chemistry teaching in high schools. Access to good engineers seems to be a problem for manufacturers, but the need for educated and, most importantly, innovative managers, is also obvious. Cases also demonstrate specific needs for ICT, retail and other industries, yet altogether companies would like to see value added, innovation-driven education and training of labour as priorities in Latvia. Furthermore, a broadly defined

TABLE 3.7 Inflow of foreign direct investment in Latvia, Lithuania and Estonia (billion EUR)

	2010	*2011*	*2012*	*2013*	*2014*	*2015*	*2016*
Lithuania	604	1,040	545	353	−18	785	−188
Latvia	286	1,045	863	680	590	600	114
Estonia	1,139	723	1,218	565	455	117	787

Source: EM (2017).

issue – legislation and support from the government, including business regulation, taxes, the tax system and legislation to protect investors – has been emphasised by foreign investors in Latvia as a challenge within the entrepreneurship climate in Latvia (Sauka, 2016). More specifically, investors express concern when it comes to the tax regime, especially competitiveness of labour taxes. Furthermore, several companies also highlight the need for improvements in the Latvian tax system 'as a whole'. Here, companies' major concern seems to be the inconsistency of tax policy, rather than the amount of taxes to be paid (except in the case of labour taxes).

Furthermore, as also highlighted by Putnins and Sauka (2014, 2015, 2017), the presence of unethical and/or illegal behaviour as well as the size of the shadow economy in Latvia's market is an important concern for foreign investors in Latvia (Sauka, 2016). Investors are also calling for improvements in the court system as well as the healthcare system, yet praise development patterns within the overall entrepreneurship climate in Latvia, especially since 2004, when Latvia entered the European Union. The highly developed IT support infrastructure, shared service centres, efficiency of labour, financial infrastructure and market regulation are among the factors that foreign investors find to be highly developed in Latvia. These factors are also likely to contribute to the growth of (export-oriented) companies in Latvia, including the company described in the following section.

Case study

Introduction to the study

Following global trends and taking advantage of locally available resources, such as the high speed of the internet and long traditions in engineering, Latvian companies are increasingly entering global markets with complex high-tech products and services. Yet despite this trend, which most probably will shape the development of the entrepreneurship climate as well as the internationalisation of businesses in Latvia and many other countries, the focus of this case study is on a company from the manufacturing industry in the food sector – representing what was 'traditional' in Latvia for many decades.

Laima is one of those companies, or more specifically, brand names whose history is as colourful as the history of Latvia itself. The company was established long before Latvia actually become an independent country, continued to exist during the first independence period and Soviet times, when manufacturing was developed, and has weathered all the transition years since the collapse of the Soviet Union. In a word, the company itself can be seen as a part of the history of the country and a part of the development of the entrepreneurship ecosystem within Latvia. Furthermore, given the international focus of Laima since it was established, the company also seems to be very suitable as case material for exploring international pathways – and various external and internal factors affecting internationalisation – of traditional manufacturing firms based in relatively small countries.

The origins of Laima chocolate date back to 1870, and thus it would be impossible to tell the whole internationalisation story of Laima in one chapter, of course. Just as the territory of Latvia was part of different countries, Laima also had different owners over these years. Major changes with regard to the ownership of the company also happened recently, in 2015, when the company was sold to Orkla Group, thus becoming part of a large international corporation. As is often the case, this has influenced the product range and strategy, including developments in international markets. Many factors, including financial and human resources, Orkla Group's other products in various markets, etc., have most likely shaped decisions in repositioning Laima. Whether this is positive or not for a well-established brand is not the scope of this case study – we leave this question open for further case studies covering the history of Laima's development since 2015. This case focuses on Laima's internationalisation patterns a few years before the acquisition – a period of time when Laima's internationalisation strategy was reformulated.

The case of Laima: the very beginning

NP Foods, Ltd. is a merger of a number of companies, including the chocolate producer Laima, the juice manufacturer Gutta, the cake and sweets manufacturers Staburadze, *Staburadze konditoreja* and *Saldumu tirdzniecība*, and the logistics company NP Logistics. The decision to consolidate these companies, which in fact belonged to the same owners, was made in 2008. As we sit comfortably in the Laima office amidst chocolate and fresh coffee aromas, the export sales director of NP Foods, Ieva Jonsone, who no longer works for the company but was responsible for Laima's internationalisation back in 2013, explains: 'This was a clever decision as it did not make sense for sales agents from each of those companies to approach the same distributors here in Latvia or abroad.' Administrative costs such as bookkeeping were also reduced substantially by the consolidation decision, thus making the companies more efficient.

In 2013, NP Foods exported to some 27 countries, including Germany, Great Britain, Scandinavia, the USA, Israel, Australia, Japan, Mongolia, China and Russia, and the total amount of the export share for all products reached 42 per cent. The number of employees employed by NP Foods has reached 1,100 and the company had a turnover of 64.32 million EUR in 2013, as compared to 58.77 million EUR in 2012. Also, the profits of NP Foods increased substantially in 2013 (i.e. 1.107 million EUR), if compared to 2012 (304,584 EUR). As Ieva Jonsone emphasises, however, NP Foods is more an administrative item than a brand as the company does nothing to promote itself as a brand: 'On the contrary, we are still promoting various brands that are included in NP Foods as a result of the merger.' Each of the brands within NP Foods has its own story and thus deserves a separate case study. For this reason, we will focus here on Laima, a brand whose history, needless to say, dates back far longer than 2008.

More precisely, the origins of Laima chocolate date back to 1870, when the German entrepreneur Teodor Riegert, who is considered to be the founder of the confectionery industry in Latvia, established a chocolate factory in Riga, Latvia. He founded Laima in 1921 and since then it has developed rapidly, constantly expanding its activities in the Baltic countries and beyond. To illustrate this, in 1931 Laima already employed as many as 500 people and was selling its production to countries such as France, England, Egypt, Lebanon and Palestine.

The history of Laima is as colourful as the history of Latvia itself. After the founder of Laima left the country, Laima became the property of Latvia in 1938. In 1941, however, when Latvia lost its independence, the factory, together with other factories in Latvia, became the property of the Soviet Union. Further on, after Latvia regained independence in the early 1990s, as a result of the consolidation of the major Latvian confectioneries, Laima became the key sweets manufacturer in the country. Yet the overall strategy of Laima when it comes to its target markets has remained similar to what the founder of the first chocolate factory envisioned.

We are, however, mostly interested in the story of the recent achievements of the company, which representatives of the company are kindly willing to share, starting our conversation on an important note: 'Today (i.e. in 2013), even though we are located in Latvia and are considered as a Latvian chocolate producer, our home market is the Baltic states. And this is evidence that we need and actually do view our target markets rather broadly.'

Chocolate or packaging business?

'2008, with the consolidation of a number of companies, is the time when export activities were re-started in Laima,' emphasises the export sales director of the company. Indeed, prior to 2008, at least for a couple of decades, the company was rather passive when it came to penetrating new export markets or gaining a bigger share in existing export markers: 'Laima was simply doing well and it was more like exporting was one of the self-evident options we could choose if there was some capacity left,' reveals Ieva Jonsone. Indeed, Laima operated in global markets such as Russia in the same manner as previous decades, sometimes without paying sufficient attention to improving the quantity and quality of those operations. In this light, as emphasised by the export sales director of Laima, 'the main problem was a lack of structured export policy, especially prior to the merger into NP Foods'.

Thinking about a more structured approach to exporting, the responsible persons at Laima considered various options. It was soon recognised that the product the company produces had much potential in itself: 'We realised we can sell what we already produce more effectively and widely.' Namely, when looking at potential markets and raising the question 'do we need to change the taste and appearance of Laima products substantially or can we enter these markets with the same product that we already have', the second option seemed to be more appealing. As Ieva Jonsone emphasises, 'for the producer it is very important for the production process to be changed as little as possible: changing the packaging design, the name of the chocolate or anything else is fine.' Namely, as a rather large company, Laima has a relatively large production capacity: 'In one go we produce six tonnes of a single chocolate item and it would be rather difficult and also inefficient to over-diversify our product assortment,' says Ieva.

Furthermore, the company also realised that the fact that Laima chocolate is produced directly from the cacao bean is something that should be emphasised even more. They also knew that it is not really the product itself that is being sold in their business, but rather a feeling, a story and a packaging material which should be different for each market even though the contents, i.e. the chocolate, remain the same: 'Our board member says we are in the packaging business and this is something we are paying more and more attention to when it comes to choosing our strategies in different markets,' says Ieva Jonsone, again emphasising that it is very hard to sell chocolate without any story behind the product that is represented on the packaging itself. 'No one is interested in hearing that you are a vertically integrated company or the like; it is the product and how it is presented that counts – for both distributors and customers,' she adds.

'When entering any international market it is crucial to have a good cooperation partner there,' emphasises the export sales director, adding that otherwise it is simply not possible to achieve anything – at least for companies such as Laima. Each market requires different approaches regarding how the cooperation partner is addressed and how further work is organised, and in considering this, a decision was made in 2008 to focus on three key markets. The first decision was to continue working in the Russian market, where Laima has the most working experience. Other markets were broadly defined as the United States and Asia.

Strategies for entering various target markets: Russia

'Russia is the market we have been working with for the longest time and there is not that much to say about recent developments,' says Ieva Jonsone. The export sales director indicates, however, that the recent growth of exports in the Russian market is determined by the fact that Laima is more actively cooperating with big supermarket chains in that country. 'By the way, there is literarily not a single day when I do not get a phone call from potential distributors in Russia that claim a willingness to sell Laima's products in the Russian market,' says Ieva Jonsone. The export sales director of Laima also reveals that long-time experience working in Russia has taught them the rules of the game – how work in that market needs to be done: 'If you know how to follow these rules, you can expect a 30 per cent rise in sales volumes in the Russian market; if not – blame yourself,' Ieva emphasises.

When it comes to regional coverage within the Russian market, historically Laima maintains strong positions in the St. Petersburg region, the northwest of Russia. Laima also operates in Moscow and the Moscow region and has been selling its products beyond the Urals, in Vladivostok, for a long time. 'When working in Russia it should be taken into consideration that this market is constantly changing,' says Ieva Jonsone. 'Not only have they changed the entire certification system, making life for exporters such as ourselves rather challenging at times; the whole system of the federal supermarket chain has also been modified recently.' The export sales director of Laima emphasises the necessity of being within the federal supermarket chains, indicating the large amounts in question – in terms of both net quantity sold and the scope of the assortment offered to the Russian market: 'In St. Petersburg the Laima assortment is simply huge if compared to other international markets. In Krasnoyarsk, however, the assortment is different and not that broad,' says Ieva.

'Speaking of assortment – producing chocolate in different countries is like producing borsch: even though all of us make the same borsch, for each of us the taste of the soup will be slightly different,' she continues. 'Even though the taste of Russian chocolate, depending on the producer, is of course slightly different than the taste of Latvian chocolate, the good news is that Russians accept the taste of Latvian chocolate.' Such acceptance is most probably associated with the long-term presence of Laima in the Russian market, which is also influenced by the partly common history of Russia and Latvia.

Acceptance of Latvian chocolate in Russia also lies in the origin of the original recipe. As Ieva explains:

> Since we produce the chocolate directly from the cacao bean, Latvian chocolate has a more pronounced taste and Russians seem to like it. Evidence for this can be seen in feedback Laima has recently received from Russia saying 'thanks a lot, your milk chocolate reminds me of real chocolate as we remember it from childhood!'

Ieva admits that 'of course you would not expect such a reaction from someone who has grown up with Scandinavian chocolate as Laima has a higher proportion of cacao in it and thus the taste is also different.' As we talk further, Ieva will emphasise that one reason why it is not that easy to work in the Russian market, and why not everyone is there, is the need for a very reliable partner. 'This partner should have a very good network, should be truly interested in your product and should also be able to tell you about the needs of the market,' she reveals, emphasising that the ability and willingness of the partner to tell you about the situation in the market is crucial: 'Russia is a huge market and it is thus simply not possible for us to travel and see everything that needs to be seen and known in order to be successful in this market.'

In this context, as explained by the export sales director of Laima, in Latvia many business-support institutions try to do a good job of enticing politicians or other 'highly ranked' people from various Russian companies to come to Latvia and visit local companies such as Laima. Yet, as she further emphasises:

> rather than politicians, however, it would be more important for business-people responsible for making decisions about supplies of Latvian manufacturers' products to various supermarkets in Russia to come; we could then present our products together with other big Latvian manufacturers of, for instance, fish products or alcohol and also offer a broader 'Made in Latvia' product range to be supplied to the same big supermarket chain.

What makes it even more difficult for any company, including Laima, is that, due to the size of such supermarkets in Russia, i.e. some chains have more than 100 supermarkets across Russia, various product categories, for instance, chocolate, cookies and the frozen torts that Laima supplies to the Russian market, each have their own supplier, 'thus we need to be very good at identifying whom to work with,' says Ieva Jonsone, emphasising that this is a key responsibility of the distributor in the Russian market, who builds relationships with all the suppliers.

'The distributor often invites me to come to various parts of Russia and give a presentation on Laima products to various suppliers to supermarket chains,' she continues, emphasising that Laima simply cannot export products to Russia directly due to the complexity of the process, including customs regulations and the like. So the way it goes is that the distributor buys production from Laima and sells it to the supermarkets and other customers in Russia. According to Russian legislation, this distributor is responsible for the entire assortment of Laima in the Russian market, including its quality. 'Such an approach is not unique in Russia,' says the export sales director of Laima, indicating that a similar approach is also taken in the US and Asian markets.

'There are a variety of ways in which distributors in export markets are found,' continues Ieva Jonsone. One way is directly, through participation in trade shows and exhibitions or direct visits to the market. Another way is by convincing suppliers of supermarkets that Laima products are important for a certain chain and thus pushing the distributor from the suppliers' side. 'In such cases, when we are lucky to convince the suppliers, they usually provide us with the contact details of their distributor, and, if we are also able to convince the distributor, cooperation can begin,' Ieva concludes, emphasising how important it sometimes is to establish a good relationship with suppliers to the big supermarket chains in Russia and other markets directly.

When Laima agrees with a distributor that Laima products will be sold in the Russian market, the next step is to agree on the terms of cooperation and, according to the export sales director of the company, the terms are usually similar:

> We agree on the portfolio of the product that will be sold in quantity 'x', usually expressed in monetary terms, per year. How this is achieved is the sole responsibility of the distributor, of course. Our interest is that products are on the shelves of shops and that the presence of Laima can be felt in certain shopping centres, and all we do is support the distributor with a variety of marketing materials.

Cooperation with the distributor, of course, also includes a pricing decision for each of the products, which is mostly determined by the potential shelf price:

> We sell products to our distributors so that they can sell them to target supermarket chains and other distribution channels for a price that is reasonably good, that is, adequately priced on the shelf for the middle and premium segment, where Laima is positioned in the Russian market.

Returning to the notion that Laima is more in the packaging business than the chocolate business, we might wonder what the specifics are of packaging design in the Russian market. 'Well,' says the export sales director of the company:

> on the way, we have learned a lot about packaging specifically for Russia. The key probably is that there are a number of things, including design-related issues, that for us Latvians seem not to be appealing at all, but ought to be considered if you want to work in the Russian market.

Rita Voronkova, the PR director of Laima, adds that 'you have to get the Russian mentality,' commenting that this is not such an easy task to accomplish. 'For instance, for the Latvian market we would never consider putting cathedrals, the Kremlin or colourful flowers on chocolate boxes, yet for chocolate boxes that go to the Russian market, this is what we do.' She emphasises the need to understand that 'what "beautiful" and "appealing" mean in one country might be completely different in another and Russia is not an exception in this regard'.

The tricky question in 'getting the mentality' is who should make the packaging design, i.e. should it be outsourced to someone in Russia or should someone in Latvia have to make it? According to Ieva Jonsone, the experience of Laima says that if the design is made in Russia, it will be 'too Russian, without a European touch'. Thus, the design is usually made in Latvia with very in-depth consultations with Russian partners. 'Moreover, our designers have worked with the Russian market so long that simply saying to them the design of a certain Laima product should be made for Russia is often enough,' concludes Ieva Jonsone.

Strategies for entering the United States

The reason Laima decided to enter the US market was because all the surveys and secondary information gathered on the market indicated that, even though in general competition in the chocolate and cookie market in the US is very fierce, the middle segment for these products is relatively free from competition. 'Our strategy was to sell a premium type of product for a better price.' Yet, perhaps even more than for other markets, participation in, or more specifically, networking at exhibitions is an important aspect when it comes to entering the US market. Ieva Jonsone, again emphasising the role of in-person conversations, and often simply luck, at such networking events, says:

> It has happened to us more than once that somebody from the US looking for manufacturers of, for instance, water, has approached us at an exhibition saying that even though they were looking for water, they liked our chocolate – and this is where cooperation often begins as these suppliers are interested in passing on information about Laima to distributors of chocolate products.

Furthermore, some decisions had to be made when it came to the assortment. Namely, Laima first entered the US market with chocolate, but experience from various degustations at exhibitions indicated that Americans also very much appreciate Laima's 'zefirs': 'thus, the decision to create a European marshmallow with dark chocolate brand, the same product that is sold under the brand name "Maigums" in Latvia, was made.' This marshmallow was different from what Americans perceived a marshmallow to be, yet 'they liked it, and also the product was packaged in a way Americans find appealing'.

> Overall our US market is divided in two groups: one is the ethnic market, or as Americans say, 'specialty shops' – Russians, Poles, Latvians and other people from CEE that live in the US. These people are located on two coasts – some in New York, others in Los Angeles, i.e. the East and West coasts. This market buys products they are used to, often influenced by memories, perhaps nostalgia for the past. The other group is the so-called 'local market' that consists of 'native-born' Americans. Here Laima has the intention that, on average, Americans entering the supermarket should have access to Laima products.

If specialty shops are fine with the existing products that Laima has, the situation with the local market in the US is quite different. Namely, as emphasised by the export sales director of Laima, the company has invested lots of resources in order to understand the needs of this market segment, with one intention – to acquire knowledge of how to get closer to what the 'average American' expects from chocolate.

> We have found our niche; this is the middle segment, which we can enter with two products. One product is a completely new product for the US market, yet well known in Latvia and other Baltic countries – the marshmallow with dark chocolate, which is sold under the brand name Moments by Laima.

The other product, however, has been newly designed for the US market and is not even available in Latvia. Ieva says:

> This is in contrast to what I said earlier – that we only adjust packaging without changing the product. In the case of the US market Laima has made an exception, mainly because Americans have long traditions of eating chocolate and thus have developed some 'taste habits'.

For this reason, Laima offers chocolate exclusively for the US market with three different dessert fillings: tiramisu, crème brûlée and key lime pie. These products are sold under the brand name Laima and the decision to enter the market with chocolate with fillings was simply following the market trend. In this light, as she further emphasises, it is indeed important to understand who the trendsetter is of a specific product group of your interest in each target market, and this is not always obvious. 'For instance, in the US market trends in chocolate consumption are mainly set by relatively young companies and in some price segments even by companies that are not of American origin,' she reveals.

'When it comes to the recognition of the brand in each market, we are frequently asked whether Laima has an English version of its webpage,' continues Ieva Jonsone.

> Of course we do, yet, especially when it comes to working in the US market, it is far from enough to simply translate the Latvian version into English and even far from enough to adjust the contents of the web page to the specific needs of the US market, including how the web page is designed.

What the export sales director means is that one mistake companies often make is having .lv in the address: 'Nothing that does not end with .com is considered in the US – even Mexican companies do not use the web extension used in Mexico, even though these two nations understand each other way better due to proximity,' she adds. As Ieva further emphasises, it is also crucial to include information in the web page so that consumers in the US market will notice it, 'and here again we rely on countless lessons we have learned on the way, spending countless hours working with the US market'.

Returning to the packaging business concept, as indicated by Ieva Jonsone, similarly to Russia, in the US packaging decisions are tricky and at the same time crucial:

> For instance, our American partners indicated that the packaging we have in Latvia includes too much description of the product. But this is what we have learned about the packaging – that we simply have to inform the customer what, for instance, the filling of the chocolate contains.

It turned out, however, that in the US market packaging ought to be as simple as possible, with only a very brief description: 'Everything should be expressed very straightforwardly – "dark chocolate", "milk chocolate" and the like is all you need for that market, whereas in the Baltic countries and other parts of the EU you would need to add much more description.'

Contrary to Russia, for which the packaging design is made in Latvia, the design for products sold to the US is made by a well-known designer in Mexico. 'This is because we simply do not understand Americans that well,' reveals Ieva Jonsone. 'For me, making Latvians think the American way is much more difficult than making them think the Russian way – simply because of the length of the presence in each market.' The export sales director further admits that 'when we look at the outcome – the US design – the conclusion is usually that this is nothing extraordinary, yet it is the way Americans perceive the message best.' Many other aspects for exploring, however, work quite the same way as in Russia – for instance, the importance of a close relationship between the distributor and the supplier of a specific supermarket chain as well as the role of Laima's export department in facilitating such cooperation. 'This is, for instance, the key reason why Laima products can be bought in some of the biggest US airports,' she continues.

As the export sales director of Laima explains:

> Not only is the packaging design different in the US market, so is the way Americans do business. While in Europe we discuss the taste and many other features of the chocolate, the very first thing that is discussed in the US is the business side of the deal. Americans first ask where the business is – what the price is, how much it will cost on the shelf – and only then look more into other features.

She emphasises that it is thus very important to be ready for such questions when talking to American distributors, and it indeed takes a lot of time to prepare for such meetings. When it comes to the pricing of the products, however, in the US, similarly to other markets, Laima usually benchmarks products with other products in a similar category as Laima. 'Having a great design, unique product or being slightly cheaper are the three key options one can choose in order to attract interest from final buyers of chocolate,' reveals Ieva Jonsone, indicating that in the US market Laima follows one of those strategies, depending on the target shopping chain.

Strategies for the Asian market

'We did not know more than anyone else about China or other Asian markets when we started; all we knew was that it is a big market with huge potential,' says Ieva Jonsone. Here networking also played a crucial role at the start of exporting activities. She remembers:

> Almost by accident I came into contact with a person who lives in Japan and has a company in China, and was interested in selling products from the Baltic countries to the Chinese market. This person had their own representative in the Chinese market and through our cooperation we gained both information and direct representation of Laima products in China.

The export sales director of Laima reveals:

> To work in the Chinese market you first need to be politically accepted in Beijing, which means going through 'different corridors' involving all the elements that come with such an approach to negotiations, including facing corruption. A lot of issues in such negotiations are influenced by the Chinese Chambers of Commerce, which in fact have the power to determine with whom local companies can work.

'Then, if everything is fine with Beijing, you should establish yourself in Shanghai,' she continues, emphasising that if the product is accepted in Shanghai, this means that it will be accepted in all of China – if not, then it won't be. 'It is important to emphasise that any relevant conversations are handled by your Chinese partner, and nobody really allows someone from, say, an EU country such as Latvia to join in – only if you are specifically invited to clarify some aspects,' she explains.

With such an approach, if everything is fine, you get your 'importer', i.e. if you are allowed to export to China, all your products are registered in the Chinese customs register, including packaging labels, etc. 'So even with your own importer, if you want to sell a different product to China, you first need to register its appearance in the Chinese customs register,' says Ieva Jonsone, revealing that it takes not only time but also a lot of money and in this regard it is important to have a person from China who can take care that expenditures are minimised, again due to the corruption issues that still exist in China. 'The importer then works with the distributor, who sells to suppliers of chains that in turn sell to the final user,' she explains.

Later on, one approach to determine whether, for instance, people in China like Laima products was going to an exhibition and simply giving away various Laima products to taste. 'We hired a local Chinese expert who translated the emotions of those Chinese that tried our chocolate and thus we gained unique information, more insights on which products are preferred and in which parts of the country,' reveals Ieva Jonsone. 'We also learned from our Chinese partners that, contrary to what is taught in business schools, it is not a good idea to translate labels on the chocolate boxes into Chinese,' continues the export sales director of Laima. Indeed, in China it is believed that products from the EU are of better quality, and thus all labels on boxes should remain in English, while translation into Chinese should be added with stickers.

'Yet another aspect that is very important in the Chinese market is correct writing in Chinese,' says Ieva Jonsone, adding that even in China not everyone can write in such a way that the majority of Chinese would understand what is written. For this reason, Laima has outsourced all the activities that are related to reading to their Chinese cooperation partners. 'For instance, if you write "Laima" in Chinese "normally" it would most often read as "mad horse", as the same words can be written differently by using hieroglyphs.' Ultimately, the word 'Laima' was written in a way that most Chinese would understand as 'I am in love' – close to the slogan of the company: 'Laima – choose love'.

In 2013, Laima was on their way to entering the Chinese market, as they were in a number of supermarkets with eight products, yet the intention was to do more, and as highlighted by Ieva Jonsone, further work in China requires lots of patience.

> If you do not have patience, do not even think of working in China. Many processes take a long time, much longer than initially expected due to the culture. Just to mention a few examples, in China no one will ever say 'no',

> even though they do not like the product at all. Also, the Chinese do not like it if you push them too much; this is simply considered to be rude and may end all business relationships. But the biggest mistake you can make in China, and this is indeed what many companies do, is to go to the market with the idea that you will teach or bring them something new. On the contrary, we all should realise that this is a nation with a very long history and strong roots and regardless of the country we represent, we should respect China and their traditions when working with them.

Yet, as further emphasised by the export sales director of Laima, the presence of the company in China and other markets – for instance, Russia – is not only dependent on what the company itself is doing:

> Many issues in these countries are either promoted or stopped at the political level and thus in my view politicians should be very careful when making decisions that can potentially influence business relationships between, say, Latvia and China. It is much easier to ruin a long-term business relationship than to create one.

Key conclusions: a take-away from the case of Laima

'My overall advice to all companies, especially to those that are only planning to enter export markets, is not to be afraid to do something outside of Latvia,' says Ieva Jonsone, adding back in 2013 that to do this it is important to acquire the necessary competence in each of the target markets. 'It is not only information about market trends, sales and distribution channels and the like that is important,' she continues, emphasising the crucial role of also understanding the mentality of each market.

> Only then will you know how to position your product in the most appropriate way, including creating an appropriate design so that you are able to meet the needs of your consumer in each target market, which is, in turn, crucial for the right value proposition of each and every company.

Indeed, according to the export sales director of Laima, the perception of what is attractive is very different in various parts of the world. As she further emphasises:

> Too often when trying to enter new markets, companies from various parts of the world start with the idea that they will show the market how good they are, without even thinking about the necessity to consider how this 'being good' will be interpreted from the viewpoint of the specific market.

Thus, a person who is responsible for exporting activities, especially when it comes to design, should be very flexible: 'Even though, from my own experience, I have to admit it is not that easy. Very often you need to overcome yourself, constantly changing your own perceptions.' To summarise, according to the sales export director of Laima, experience from working in various markets suggests that the aforementioned skills should be continually improved and this – i.e. (1) understanding markets where Laima is exporting its products, and (2) being able to adjust to specific market needs – remains one of the tasks for the future as well.

When asked which markets should be targeted in the future, the export sales director answers without much deliberation that the key target markets will remain the US, Asia and Russia. 'It is not that we do not work in Europe; of course there are markets in Central and Eastern Europe and also in the West where Laima chocolate can be found.' Yet, as the experience of Laima indicates, markets such as France, for instance, are simply too conservative:

> We had an intern from France at the company who conducted a survey on how the French choose chocolate and I have to admit that the results were not very promising for Laima. Indeed, it looked like the only way to sell Laima in France would be for a very low price and with home delivery, as consumers in this market would not change their already preferred chocolate brands so easily.

The lesson from this survey is that not all markets are meant for all products, or more accurately, that there are markets that require the investment of much more financial and other resources to gain some market share. Such investment may be too much even for big companies such as Laima, let alone for small and medium-sized firms.

'Globalisation is yet another aspect that should be considered when it comes to thinking about further expansion in export markets,' continues the export sales director of Laima. Namely, a big European chocolate brand recently bought a big American chocolate brand and, by doing this, substantially changed the market. Also, another big player in the US has recently announced that it has sufficient resources to buy another chocolate brand. 'In short, players in the markets change and market trends also change, often in unpredictable ways, and this requires constant monitoring of each of the target markets,' says Ieva Jonsone, emphasising that constant learning is crucial for any exporter, big or small, including Laima.

The price of the cacao bean also changes, i.e. it has been increasing and all the signs point towards further price increases. Ieva Jonsone reveals:

> Cacao beans are not an unlimited resource and demand for this product has increased substantially over the years, especially in China and Asia more generally – these are markets that have become consumers of chocolate relatively recently, and consumption continues to rise.

She adds that demand for chocolate overall has also grown in the US market. 'Thus, the struggle for market shares continues,' concludes the export sales director of

Laima – and we wish the company the best of luck, certain that we will hear more success stories about Laima's presence in various markets across the globe in the years to come – also as a part of the Orkla Group.

Notes

1 For further information on the development of the Latvian economy, see the IMF country report: www.imf.org/external/pubs/ft/scr/2015/cr15111.pdf.

2 Most recent trends in foreign trade statistics are summarised by the Latvian Investment and Development Agency (LIAA). See: www.liaa.gov.lv/en/trade/foreign-trade-statistics.

References

Avots, V., 2004, *Ulmaņlaiki: leģendas un fakti*, Riga: Jumava.

Bleiere, D., Butulis, I., Feldmanis, I., Stranga, A. and Zunda, A., 2005, *Latvijas vēstrure 20. gadsimts*, Riga: Jumava.

CSB: Central Statistical Bureau of Latvia, 2017, Central Statistical Bureau data, official statistics of Latvia. Available at: www.csb.lv. Accessed 1 July 2017.

Jansone, A., Robežniece, I. and Zelbārte, I., 2008, *90 Latvijas gadi: 1918–2008*, Riga: Latvijas Nacionālais vētures muzejs.

Krumina, M. and Paalzow, A., 2017, 'The business cycle and early-stage entrepreneurship in Latvia', in A. Sauka and A. Chepurenko, eds., *Entrepreneurship in transition economies. Diversity, trends and perspective*, Cham: Springer, pp. 135–152.

Putnins, T., 2013, 'Exporting by Latvian companies: Vitality, drivers of success, and challenges', *Baltic Journal of Economics*, 13 (3), pp. 5–35.

Putnins, T. and Sauka, A., 2014, *Shadow Economy Index for the Baltic countries, 2009–2013*, Riga: SSE Riga.

Putnins, T. and Sauka, A., 2015, 'Measuring the shadow economy using company managers', *Journal of Comparative Economics*, 43 (2), pp. 471–490.

Putnins, T. and Sauka, A., 2017, *Shadow Economy Index for the Baltic countries 2009–2016*, Riga: SSE Riga.

Sauka, A., 2016, *FICIL Sentiment Index 2015–2016. Development of the investment climate in Latvia: the viewpoints of foreign investors*, Riga: SSE Riga and FICIL Latvia.

Švābe, A., 1990, *Latvijas vēsture*. Riga: Avots.

4

THE INTERNATIONALISATION OF THE VIČIŪNAI GROUP

A case from Lithuania

Osvaldas Stripeikis and Irena Bakanauskienė

Introduction

The social, economic, cultural and political systems of post-communist countries have undergone considerable changes since the late 1980s. New ways have been opening up for the development of a market economy and democracy in these societies. After the declaration of independence from the Soviet Union, Lithuania has experienced radical political and economic changes. The main challenge was to shift from "planned" economy to liberal market economy. The development of entrepreneurship in Lithuania had significant benefits, both economically and socially. Within the last 20 years, various authors analysed entrepreneurship phenomenon in Lithuania (Markevičius, 2001; Strazdienė and Garalis, 2006; Lydeka, 1998; Žukauskas and Stripeikis, 2004; Gineitienė and Girdenis, 2004; Andriuščenka, 2003; Stripeikis, 2011).

The chapter analyses the context of the entrepreneurship process in Lithuania. Then it provides a case study of the Vičiūnai Group – one of the largest fish and seafood producers in Europe. The case study focuses on the evolution of the company as well as the success factors of development and internationalisation pathways.

Context of the entrepreneurship process in Lithuania

Based on the works of scholars (Dobravolskas and Černiauskas, 2011; Kuodis and Ramanauskas, 2009; Panovas and Černiauskas, 2012; Saboniene, 2015), we can identify five main periods of an emerging market economy in Lithuania: restructuring; market economy formation; boom period; recession and recovery periods.

Restructuring period (1990–1994)

During that period, economic reforms were focused on price liberalisation and small-scale privatisation. The beginning of this period in Lithuania was related to a transitional recession (43.86 per cent fall in real GDP and high annual inflation – 318 per cent in 1991 and 1163 per cent in 1992) (Kuodis, 2008). It was a painful process of learning to perform in a new unfamiliar environment of international markets, which was marked by liberalisation of prices and a radical improvement in consumer choice and quality. According to Dobravolskas and Černiauskas (2011, pp. 375–376):

> this had two effects on business: 1) increased competition-forced diversification of products and the increase in unit costs of production and additional costs of marketing of products; 2) the benefits from increased consumer choice seen as a net gain for consumers.

In 1992, the national currency (the litas) was introduced. This allowed for a stabilisation of inflation and the national monetary policy and to further encourage trade. The restrictive monetary policy was substituted by a currency board regime that was introduced in 1994.

Market economy formation (1995–2003)

This period was marked by intense opening up of the economy to international markets and a steady growth (average annual growth of approximately 5.4 per cent) of the economy until a recession in 1999. In 1995, real GDP grew by 3.3 per cent, in 1996 by 5.1 per cent and in 1997 by 8.3 per cent. According to Kuodis (2008), on the basis of price differences of the Lithuanian and Western European countries, entrepreneurs successfully exported cheap raw materials and goods, and exports grew successfully until the Russian financial crisis (in 1997, Lithuanian exports to the EU accounted for 32.5 per cent, and in 1998, 37.4 per cent). During that period (in 1995), Lithuania became a signatory of the General Agreement on Tariffs and Trade (GATT) and, after ratification of the World Trade Organization's (WTO) arrangements in 2001, it became a member of the WTO. Membership of the WTO has created stability and reliability in trade relations – factors that are highly significant for trade partners and investors. Membership of the WTO is of primary importance for export promotion and improvement of the business environment.

Until the Russian financial crisis, the majority of Lithuanian goods went to CIS countries and, first of all, to Russia (in 1998, export to CIS countries accounted for 35.7 per cent), and because of the crisis the Lithuanian economy experienced a shock – in 1999, real GDP compared with 1998 decreased by 4.1 per cent. The positive aspect of this stage was a change of direction of the Lithuanian export – re-orientation from unstable Eastern markets towards much more dynamic Western markets (in 1999, as compared with 1998, Lithuanian exports to EU countries increased by 6.8 per cent, and the main foreign trade partner became Germany). Since 2000, business has been recovering, and financial conditions have improved. One of the primary drivers of GDP growth was the export of goods, primarily in

Western markets (in 2000, export to EU countries, as compared with 1999, increased by 21.2 per cent).

Boom period (2004–2007)

Another phase of economic rise began in Lithuania, which was associated with the accession to NATO (29 March 2004) and the EU (1 May 2004). The economy strengthened, and EU financial support was received. In 2004, by joining the European Single Market, Lithuania began to strengthen its economic relations with the European Union. Fiscal stability of the country and a fixed currency rate strengthened by the currency board system convinced international markets to invest in the Lithuanian economy. The main features of this period were as follows: credit-based growth, inflation in real estate market, profits (commercial banks earned supernormal profits), public sector value-added and unregistered inflation during the bubble economy (Dobravolskas and Černiauskas, 2011; Saboniene, 2015).

EU membership had a significant impact on the further dynamics of Lithuanian foreign trade and, as a result, the average annual export growth rate reached 14 per cent in 2004 and jumped to 27 per cent in 2005 after trade barriers had been eliminated. As a result of economic integration to the European Union in 2005 and development of export promotion policies, the Lithuanian economy has significantly opened itself up to external trade.

Recession period (2008–2010)

The recession of 2008–2009 was caused by a number of factors: shadow economy, negative profits (profits of commercial banks suffered a huge loss of 4 billion litas) and reduced value-added in the public sector.

Recovery and development period (from 2011)

After the recession period, the Lithuanian currency, litas, was replaced by the euro in 2015, which is the basic assumption of the model for recovery. All main Lithuanian economy indicators for the periods analysed can be seen in Table 4.1.

Lithuanian business companies are challenged to act in the complex business environment, which is understood as a multidimensional construction with features like dynamism, unpredictability, globality, constant change and disequilibrium. One of the main challenges of the business organisation is the ability to balance all these aspects. The business environment requires organisations to implement such strategic orientations as autonomy, innovation, risk tolerance, research of possibilities and creativeness.

Table 4.2 shows that, by 2017, Lithuania's economy had recovered from recession and that the entrepreneurship climate is steadily growing. Regarding "ease of doing business", Lithuania is ranked 21 among 190 economies, according to the latest World Bank annual ratings. Lithuania's ranking has remained unchanged

TABLE 4.1 Main Lithuanian economic indicators (1996–2016)

	1996	*1997*	*1998*	*1999*	*2000*	*2001*	*2002*	*2003*	*2004*	*2005*	*2006*	*2007*	*2008*	*2009*	*2010*	*2011*	*2012*	*2013*	*2014*	*2015*	*2016*
GDP growth rate (annual %)	5.1	8.3	7.5	−1.1	3.8	6.5	6.8	10.5	6.6	7.7	7.4	11.1	2.6	14.8	1.6	6.0	3.8	3.5	3.5	1.8	2.3
Inflation rate (annual %)	23.1	8.7	5.4	1.4	1.1	1.5	0.3	−1.1	1.2	2.7	3.8	5.8	11.2	4.2	1.2	4.1	3.2	1.2	0.2	−0.7	0.7
Unemployment rate (annual %)	14.6	16.4	17.4	13.7	12.4	10.9	8.3	5.8	4.2	8.3	5.8	4.2	5.8	13.8	17.8	15.4	13.4	11.8	10.7	9.1	7.9

Source: Statistics Lithuania (2017), World Bank (2017).

TABLE 4.2 Lithuania's world rankings for "ease of doing business" and "competitiveness" (2008–2017)

	2008	*2009*	*2010*	*2011*	*2012*	*2013*	*2014*	*2015*	*2016*	*2017*
Ease of doing business (among 190 economies)	25	26	25	27	25	17	21	21	21	n/a
Competitiveness rank (among 138 economies)	38	44	53	47	44	45	48	41	36	35

Source: www.tradingeconomies.com.

at 21 since 2014. Lithuania is ranked 35 out of 138 countries for competitiveness, according to the 2016–2017 edition of the Global Competitiveness Report published by the World Economic Forum (World Bank, 2017).

Internationalisation of companies is regarded as an important measure of competitive performance at national and regional level. Results of investigation on internationalisation of Lithuanian enterprises (Korsakiene, 2015) disclose that firms aim to internationalise through export activities (62 per cent of internationalised firms) because exporting is the cheapest and quickest way to achieve internationalisation; own investment abroad is not so popular – 4 per cent of respondents mentioned this way to internationalise. The most important internal motives impacting internationalisation of Lithuanian SMEs are profit goals, personal relationships and networks. The least important motives are desire to reduce risk and unfavourable laws.

The following section presents the case of Lithuanian company Vičiūnai Group, as an illustration of entrepreneurship and internationalisation processes.

Evolution of the Vičiūnai Group

The presented case of the Vičiūnai Group is interesting in a way that it is in line with the whole Lithuanian entrepreneurship process. The date of the company's establishment corresponds with the beginning of the transition of the Lithuanian economy from a planned to market economy. Moreover, there are not many businesses that stay alive and, even more importantly, become successful in such a turbulent environment as that in Lithuania during the first decades of market liberalisation.

The Vičiūnai Group is a global producer and supplier of different food products, the biggest surimi processor on the planet and one of the largest fish and seafood producers in Europe. Along with its main business, the company is constantly expanding its different business portfolios – logistics, sales, agriculture, construction and restaurants. Currently, it exports production into 58 different countries across the world, and its 80 enterprises operate in 18 states.

The Vičiūnai Group is a privately held Lithuanian company established in 1991 – right after Lithuania restored its independence. At the time, it started with several local employees and currently it employs more than 8000 people in Lithuania, Europe and Asia. Its business development and marketing logic stem mainly from the fusion of traditions and innovation as well as through control of the whole business process. On top of being the largest surimi processor, the group's food product portfolio also includes frozen and ready-to-eat chilled products. In its 13 factories located in Lithuania, Estonia, Spain and Russia, the company produces surimi, salmon, herring, seafood and breaded fish, as well as dumplings, bread and pizzas. The annual production output exceeds 170,000 tons of food and has been growing steadily for the last five years.

The group's strategy is based on its production, logistics, warehousing and sales chain – it firmly adheres to the principle that total chain control is the best way to ensure quality. Its functioning is realised via 17 sales companies and 5 logistics companies across Europe. More than half of the sales come under the Viči brand, but the company also offers goods processing, logistics and distribution services to other major European supermarket chains and food producers.

The Vičiūnai Group is highly aware of the fact that success of its business is intertwined with the general well-being of the planet and people. Thus, social responsibility is deeply entrenched in its business model. The group is actively involved in a number of food safety, quality, sustainable fishery, green energy and social initiatives.

Along with a strong emphasis on the Lithuanian food traditions and the spirit of local entrepreneurship, the Vičiūnai Group puts considerable effort into finding better ways to produce its products and manage the ever-growing business. In 2016, investments in innovations accounted for 13 per cent of the total turnover.

The company is also one of the *Lean* pioneers in Lithuania. *Lean* management allows it to improve employee satisfaction and increase efficiency of operations and customer loyalty. All the factories are managed according to the *Lean* principles, and the efficiency of their operations is monitored by comparable systematic key performance indicators (KPIs).

Main stages of evolution of the Vičiūnai Group

As mentioned above, developments in the Vičiūnai Group have occurred in synchrony with all of the socioeconomic processes in Lithuania. The main milestones of the company's development can be seen in Table 4.3.

Retail phase (1991–1993)

The inception of the company took place 25 years ago – in 1991, the very first company of the current group, the transport enterprise Vičiūnai, was established. In the beginning, its business model was based purely on retail – Vičiūnai imported and sold various goods in Lithuania. It was probably the most popular *modus operandi* at the time, consistent with Lithuania's overall socioeconomic situation at the dawn of independence. There were no real attributes of internationalisation at this stage, except importing goods into the newly born market economy. The first phase was common to many Lithuanian companies at that time.

TABLE 4.3 Main milestones of the Vičiūnai Group

Date	*Main events of company development*
1991	*Vičiūnai UAB* is established in Kaunas (Lithuania). Main activities: transport services and trading canned food.
1994	Brand new fish products plant *Plunges Kooperatine Prekyba UAB* is opened in Plunge (Lithuania).
1995	Under its trademark *Viciunai* different fish products are presented to a wider scale of customers.
1997	*Plunges Kooperatine Prekyba UAB* acquires the first surimi products production line in Lithuania. An industrial bread bakery is purchased and the company *Plunges Duona UAB* is established.
1999	*Vičiūnai UAB*'s main activity is reorganised into two separate companies: *Vičiūnai ir Ko UAB* and *Vičiūnai UAB* (international logistics company).
2000	The beginning of internationalisation: • The trademark *Vičiūnai* is replaced by *Viči*. • The distribution company *Vichiunai Europe NV* is established in Bruges, Belgium. • The breaded fish production plant *Paljassaare Kalatööstus AS* based in Tallinn, Estonia is purchased and the distribution company *Vičiūnai Baltic OU* is established in Tallinn, Estonia.
2001	Export plans to the Russian Federation are implemented: distribution company *Baltko OOO* in Russia is opened.
2002	*Plunges Kooperatine Prekyba UAB* is reorganised: the fish processing department is separated and new company *Vičiūnai ir Partneriai UAB* is registered. The plant *Vičiūnai-RUS OOO* is established in Kaliningrad, Russia. The distribution company *Vicziunai-POL Sp.z. o.o.* is established in Poland. The distribution company *Vičiūnai – Ukraina LTD* is established in Ukraine.
2003	The distribution company *Vičiūnai-LAT SIA* is established in Latvia.
2004	Acquisition of *Makrill* in Estonia. The distribution company *Vičiūnai Czec Republic S.r.o.* is opened in the Czech Republic. The distribution company *Vičiūnai – Kazakhstan TOO* is established in Kazakhstan.

2005	*Makrill OU* is reorganised into *Vičiūnai Nordic OU*. The activity of footwear chain *Bona* is started.
2007	The plant *Vičiūnai Nordic OU* is reorganised: production lines are transferred to *Paljassaare Kalatööstus AS*. Due to a major fire, the oldest crabsticks production department of *Plunges Kooperatine Prekyba UAB* is destroyed. The logistics company *Frost Logistics OOO* is established.
2009	The footwear chain *Bona* is sold. The capacities of fish manufacture are expanded and the construction of new company *Baltic Food Partners* is started. The distribution company *Ekofort Sooo* is established in Belarus.
2010	Surimi production plant *Sistemos Britor S.L.U* is purchased in Santander, Spain. The trading companies' chain and geography are expanded: *VG Iberia* in Spain, *Vičiūnai Ser* in Serbia, *VG Handel* in Germany, *VG Italy* in Italy, *Vičiūnai-Bel* and *Vichiunai Logistic* in Belarus. Logistics is developed in Ukraine: new company *Ukr Logistika LTD* is established; the transport company *Vichiukrtrans LTD* is established.
2011	The new *Baltic Food Partners* UAB plant in Plunge is opened. The transport company *Vici-trans OOO* in Sovetsk is established. Online shop sales are started at www.e-vici.lt. *Eurobasket 2011* is mainly sponsored by *Vičiūnai*.
2012	Construction of new plant in Plunge is started. New company *VG Agro Holding* established and agricultural production and processing business development is started. Construction of new Baltic fish export processing plant in Kaunas Free Economic Zone is started.

Source: Vičiūnai Group (2017).

Production phase (1994–2000)

The period from 1994 could be characterised as the second development stage of the organisation. Together with his business partners, the principal shareholder of the company, Visvaldas Matijošaitis, saw a considerably higher potential in producing rather than only reselling the imported goods. The economic situation of the time was not very stable and was often described as "winner takes it all". The absolute majority of the big businesses established at the time ended up bankrupt, but the slim minority managed to lay the foundations for decades of sustainable growth in the future. Vičiūnai was one of the latter – surimi products manufactured on the first production line of Plungės Kooperatinė Prekyba have been the backbone of the whole group for 25 years now. At the moment, the Vičiūnai Group is the biggest surimi manufacturer in the world.

As is often the case with big international food producers, the evolutionary trajectory of the Vičiūnai Group has always been marked with the intertwined cycles of production growth vs. sales growth. Therefore, after having intensively developed production capabilities in Plungė, the group, in parallel, had to seek larger sales markets. And here comes the initial high wave of internationalisation and transnational business expansion marked by the establishment of the sales and distribution companies Vičiūnai Ir Ko in Lithuania, Vichiunai Europe in Belgium, Vičiūnai Baltic in Estonia, Vičiūnai-Lat in Latvia and Baltko in Russia during the period 1999–2001. The trend of aggressive international sales and development of distribution and logistics continued well into the 2000s. It is important to mention that the Russian financial crisis in 1998–1999 was not as crucial for the company as it was for other businesses in Lithuania. One of the reasons was a timely shift to Western markets.

Boost phase (2001–2011)

A boost in production capabilities is in line with the entire Lithuanian entrepreneurship context – a complete opening up of the economy to international markets and steady growth. As Lithuania became a member of associated structures (WTO, EU), it gained access to global markets. Consequently, the group's current strategic priority is to conquer existing and potential markets all around the globe even more aggressively. Efficient management and cooperation of the company's producers and local sales professionals has enabled it to dominate the surimi markets of the biggest European countries – Germany, UK, Russia, etc. Nevertheless, due to immensely increased production capabilities, the Vičiūnai Group is currently in pursuit of bolstering its position in Western Europe even further. This is to be achieved by applying a systematic mix of effective pricing, service level and product quality, thus strengthening the company's brand, Viči – probably the most internationally known Lithuanian brand name.

Consolidation phase (since 2012)

The next decade saw yet another boost in production capabilities – five new factories were established in different countries, starting from 2012, while the rest underwent vigorous modernisation. This stage was also the business consolidation phase. In 2012, VG Agroholding, a company managing and developing various agricultural businesses, was established and, in 2014, a holding of Vičiūnai Group saw daylight, turning the company into a fully-fledged international corporation.

Business development challenges or recipe for success

As is usually the case with international business, starting from the third evolution stage outlined above, the main challenge for the Vičiūnai Group all along has been to penetrate and then grow successfully in different markets, regions and even continents. Naturally, every time you enter a new market, you enter a different socio-economic reality marked with different regulations, levels of infrastructure, consumer preferences and mentalities, HR management peculiarities and, of course, competition. The group has constantly balanced its priorities and resources between different regions and markets, and expeditious growth, together with the constantly changing economic climate in different parts of the globe, has not made it any easier. Needless to say, there have been some failures in connection with this, but the bottom line is that at the moment the company is operating in around 60 markets and is constantly entering new ones. The annual income of the Vičiūnai Group is approximately 500 million euro and, in the long run, its financial results are also growing expeditiously.

The business scope of the group also varies immensely in different markets – from a few tons in some exotic markets in the Far East, North Africa or South America to domination in some categories in the markets of countries such as the UK, Spain, Russia or Germany.

The main component in successful business development and internationalisation is the aforementioned complete control of the whole business chain – production (even some raw materials), transportation, logistics, sales and distribution. It is achieved via state-of-the-art production sites in four states, five major regional logistic centres and 18 sales companies in Europe and Asia.

The strategic rationale behind managing 80 different enterprises scattered across various countries and regions is to appoint a Lithuanian professional who has been with the group for some time as the manager of a factory or sales company, and then to recruit or head-hunt the best local professionals, who are familiar with the peculiarities of the market, consumers and competition. "The company's golden rule, while expanding its business internationally, is to apply a well-balanced mix of its own production and business development know-how in conjunction with contextual and cultural knowledge of local sales professionals" (Ramunė Bičkauskienė, Corporate Administrative Director at Vičiūnai Group).

Having grown into a fully-fledged transnational corporation comprised of dozens of subsidiaries and enterprises in different locations, the Vičiūnai Group is also faced with some issues inherent to most international corporations. For instance, right from the beginning of its internationalisation in 2000, the management has sought to address the issue of effective communication and cooperation of employees of different nationalities, mentalities and origins. This has been achieved mainly by effective internal communication, charismatic leadership of the main shareholders and comparable systematic KPIs, on the basis of which the results are evaluated in all the markets.

The case of business development of the Vičiūnai Group is in many ways a living example of the economy of scale phenomenon. This is true not only in a traditional sense – thanks to unceasing expansion and modernisation, the company's annual production output has been growing steadily for the last five years (110,000 tons in 2011, and 160,000 tons in 2016); this also applies in terms of broader aspects of business development and internationalisation. In spite of the fact that Viči seafood and food production is available in nearly all European countries, there is no need to have subsidiaries in all of them. As stated by Mindaugas Snicorius (Head of Communication at Vičiūnai Group):

> once you establish an active affiliate hub, recruit suitable personnel and provide them with the necessary know-how, this hub can usually cater for the whole region. For example, our company in Belgium, Vichiunai Europe, is also developing business in other Benelux countries, VG Handel in Germany also caters for Austria and Switzerland.

This is also true when it comes to the management of human resources, negotiating with global supermarket chains or satisfying their extremely high audit criteria – once you invest the necessary financial, human and technical resources and enter several markets of the region, you obtain priceless know-how. Therefore, entering a new country, and negotiating with another retail chain or professional trade union becomes naturally easier.

Conclusions

The presented case of the Vičiūnai Group is compelling in a way that it reflects the entire Lithuanian entrepreneurship process. The main milestones of the company were analysed as well as the success factors of development. It could be said that the stages of the company's evolution mainly correspond with the development of the entire entrepreneurship process in Lithuania. In terms of internationalisation pathways, it is obvious that both kinds of factors are crucial: the general business environment of the country and the company's attitude and strategy towards internationalisation and entering new markets. The company was founded in 1991, which was the beginning of the first entrepreneurship development stage in Lithuania. In the beginning, the company's business model was based purely on retail (the first model of "doing business" at that time in Lithuania) and it imported and sold various goods in Lithuania. It is clear that at that point internationalisation, as we understand it now, was not on companies' agenda. The second entrepreneurship development phase in Lithuania, described as "market economy formation", took place from 1995 to 2003. In the context of Vičiūnai Group, this stage could be defined as shifting the main business models: higher potential in producing rather than only reselling the imported goods. Also, there were a few crucial factors – Lithuania becoming a signatory of the General Agreement on Tariffs and Trade (GATT), ratification of the World Trade Organization's (WTO) arrangements in 2001, the processes of entering the NATO and EU organisations – which enabled international markets to be entered (the first steps towards the Western European market: the trademark *Vičiūnai* was replaced by *Viči*, the distribution company *Vichiunai Europe NV* was established in Bruges, Belgium). The entire decade, starting from the 2000s, could be described as a boost in production capabilities. It is in line with the whole Lithuanian entrepreneurship context – a complete opening up of the economy to international markets and steady growth.

The main internal success factors of internationalisation in the company could be as follows:

1 Constantly balancing its priorities and resources between different regions and markets.
2 Complete control of the whole business chain – production (even some raw materials), transportation, logistics, sales and distribution.
3 Recruitment or head-hunting of the best local professionals who are familiar with the peculiarities of the market, consumers and competition. Applying a well-balanced mix of its production and business development know-how in conjunction with contextual and cultural knowledge of the local sales professionals.
4 Effective communication and cooperation of employees of various nationalities, with different mentalities and from diverse geographic locations, which is mainly achieved by effective internal communication and charismatic leadership.

The case of the Vičiūnai Group presents a success story and could serve as a model of corporate entrepreneurship and business development for other companies, of how to grow in different markets and operate in various entrepreneurial contexts.

References

Andriuščenka, J., 2003, "Strategic entrepreneurship: Conceptual attitudes in management paradigm", *Management of organizations: Systematic approach*, 26, pp. 7–25.

Dobravolskas, A. and Černiauskas, G., 2011, "Emerging of market economy in Lithuania (1990–2010)", *Intelektinė ekonomika*, 5 (3), pp. 371–387.

Gineitienė, Z. and Girdenis, J., 2004, "Mažų, vidutinių ir didelių įmonių vieta inovacinėje veikloje", *Organizacijų vadyba*, 30, pp. 81–92.

Korsakiene, R., 2015, "Internationalization of Lithuanian SMEs: Investigation of barriers and motives", *Economics and Business*, 26, pp. 54–60.

Kuodis, R., 2008, "Lietuvos ekonomikos transformacija 1990–2008 metais: Etapai ir pagrindinės ekonominės politikos klaidos", *Pinigų studijos*, 2, pp. 97–105.

Kuodis, R. and Ramanauskas, T., 2009, "From boom to bust: Lessons from Lithuania", in R. Martin, P. Mooslechner and D. Ritzberger-Grünwald, eds., *Recent Developments in the Baltic Countries – What Are the Lessons for Southeastern Europe?*, Vienna: Oesterreichische Nationalbank, pp. 102–115.

Lydeka, Z., 1998, "Aktyvieji ekonomikos subjektai ir jų tapsmas pereinamuoju laikotarpiu", *Organizacijų vadyba*, 64, pp. 137–155.

Markevičius, P., 2001, "Gamybos verslininkų verslumo išoriniai veiksniai", *Inžinerinė ekonomika*, 5 (22), pp. 38–43.

Panovas, I. and Černiauskas, G., 2012, "Lithuanian economy in 2011–2020: Forecast of main macroeconomic parameters as a tool to consider sustainable development of health financing", *Intelektinė ekonomika*, 6 (2), pp. 102–113.

Saboniene, A., 2015, "Lithuanian export competitiveness: Comparison with other Baltic states", *Engineering Economics*, 62 (2), pp. 49–57.

Statistics Lithuania, 2017, Indicators database. Available at www.stat.gov.lt/. Accessed 3 April 2017.

Strazdienė, G. and Garalis, A., 2006, "Verslumas: Ugdymo programos ir jų efektyvumo raiška", *Organizacijų vadyba*, 44, pp. 153–168.

Stripeikis, O., 2011, "Enterprising business formation in Lithuanian small and medium-sized firms", *Organizacijų vadyba*, 571, pp. 99–103.

Vičiūnai Group, 2017, Short history. Available at www.viciunaigroup.eu/about-us/short-history_en. Accessed 3 April 2017.

World Bank, 2017, Lithuania: Data. Available at http://data.worldbank.org/country/lithuania. Accessed 3 April 2017.

Žukauskas, P. and Stripeikis, O., 2004, "Smulkaus ir vidutinio verslo aplinka Lietuvos ir ES rinkose", *Organizacijų vadyba*, 31, pp. 209–228.

5

ENTREPRENEURSHIP DEVELOPMENT AND INTERNATIONALIZATION IN BELARUS

The case of transport company TTC KristallTrans

Alena Apiakun and Tõnis Mets

Introduction

The Republic of Belarus is situated in the eastern part of Europe with an area of 207,600 square kilometers. Its neighbors are the Baltic countries of Latvia and Lithuania in the north, Russia in the east, Ukraine in the south, and Poland in the west. The capital of Belarus is Minsk. Belarus is a former Soviet republic and proclaimed its sovereignty on July 27, 1990. After the fall of the Soviet Union, Belarus faced an economic crisis and had chosen its way of overcoming this crisis. Alexander Lukashenko, after being elected as the first President in 1994, launched the country on the path of "market socialism," which only partly and not with similar success followed economic reforms in China (Жуджунь and Ковалев, 2002). As part of the former Soviet Union, Belarus had a relatively well-developed industrial base; it retained this industrial base. The country also has had a broad agricultural base and a high education level. Compared to the former republics of the Soviet Union, Belarus had one of the highest standards of living. The dynamics of GDP is displayed in Figure 5.1.

Following its own development path, Belarus distinguishes from other post-socialist countries with a slower course of reforms (Smallbone and Welter, 2010; Filatotchev *et al.*, 1999). That has also emerged with the decrease in GDP in recent years (Figure 5.1). But some changes have appeared in government policy over the last few years. Therefore, this chapter aims to disclose recent developments in entrepreneurship in Belarus. With that purpose, the general economic situation of the country is first analyzed, followed by a short overview of entrepreneurship and business-related policy in Belarus. Entrepreneurial developments in the country are explained using examples from the transport and logistics sector and a firm called KristallTrans as a good model of the sector.

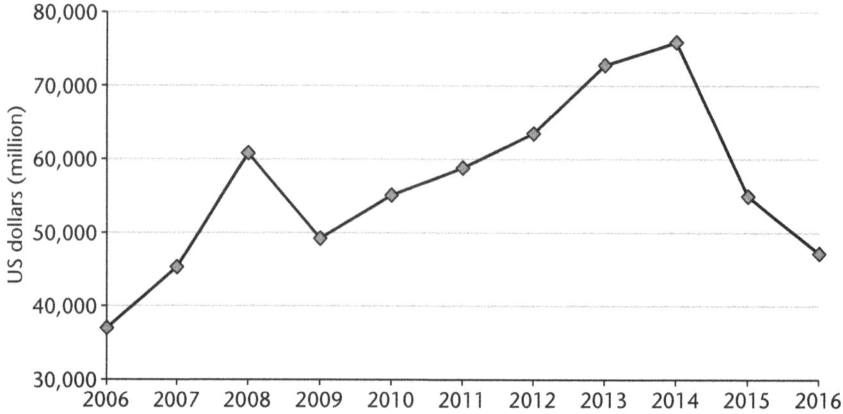

FIGURE 5.1 Dynamics of GDP of Belarus.

Source: Official statistics, NSC (2017).

Economic and entrepreneurial developments of Belarus

Overview of internationalization of the economy

The economy of Belarus has seen lower sustained growth in recent years. Belarus today still pursues a socially-oriented market economy model. The country remains in candidate status for accession to the WTO. It has needed several efforts to meet the requirements of membership, and now Belarus has been praised for its progress to date. The Belarusian economy is attractive for international trade because of the following factors:

- geographical location
- favorable investment climate
- highly skilled workforce
- industrially developed economy
- well-developed transport and communications infrastructure.

The competitiveness of the economy is characterized by its export capabilities. The main export groups of goods for the Republic of Belarus are:

- products of the petrochemical complex: oil products, chemical fibers, tires
- potash and nitrogen fertilizers
- metal products
- agricultural and lorry machinery
- meat and milk products
- sugar and other products of the agro-industrial complex.

The main volume of imports consists of raw materials: oil, gas, mineral raw materials, as well as components for machine building. General statistical data of foreign trade (Table 5.1) partly outrace the breakdown trend of GDP temporally.

TABLE 5.1 The main indicators of foreign trade of goods (million US dollars)

Indicator/year	*2011*	*2012*	*2013*	*2014*	*2015*	*2016*
The turnover of the Republic of Belarus foreign trade in goods	87,178	92,464	80,226	76,583	56,952	50,986
Export	41,419	46,060	37,203	36,081	26,660	23,416
Import	45,759	46,404	43,023	40,502	30,292	27,570
Balance	–4,340	–344	–5,820	–4,421	–3,632	–4,154

Source: NSC (2017).

Services made up 21.7 percent of the total volume of foreign trade in 2016. In recent years, its share has increased annually (19.3 percent in 2015) and has a positive balance. Despite the positive balance of services, the general trend of foreign trade relates to a reduction in the competitiveness of the Belarus economy and Belarusian businesses.

With the goal of improving the business climate, Belarus implemented several reforms in 2015–2016 in the areas tracked by the *Doing Business* report. The World Bank's (2017) report showed Belarus as one of the most enhanced economies, establishing a one-stop shop for all utility connection-related services, including the design and construction of the distribution line. In the 2017 *Doing Business* report, Belarus' global rankings were as follows (with 2016 rankings in brackets): starting a business – 31 (30); getting construction permits – 28 (25); getting electricity – 24 (74); registering property – 5 (7); getting credit – 101 (109); protecting minority investors – 42 (62); paying taxes – 99 (95); trading across borders – 30 (30); enforcing contracts – 27 (28); resolving insolvency – 69 (95).

According to the Index of Economic Freedom (2017), Belarus has a value of 58.6 (2016 was 48.8), wherein the global average economic index is 60.9 on a scale of 0–100. The positive dynamics of change show an improvement in the Belarus business climate over the last few years.

Another side of internationalization is joining Belarus to the Eurasian Economic Union (EEU, launched on January 1, 2015) together with Russia, Kazakhstan, and Armenia. There are different opinions (Точицкая and Кирхнер, 2014; Naūrodski and Valetka, 2015) regarding the potential form of this cooperation within a very complicated international situation. The Belarusian problem has partly been seen as a brain drain – a loss of human capital.

Belarus has achieved minor success in deregulation, but more liberal economic policies have not been a priority. Pervasive state involvement and control hamper the economy. Restructuring of the economic system has been very slow, and the small private sector is marginalized. Undercut by domestic structural weaknesses, the economy of Belarus has little resilience against external shocks.

Entrepreneurship and SME development in Belarus

In economically developed countries, the majority of innovations are generated by small and medium businesses – companies that are often seen as catalysts for new products and ideas (Akulava, 2012). In short, private initiative in these countries is regarded as the basis for the development of competition, where competition forces entrepreneurs to innovate constantly to achieve and sustain a competitive advantage. Arguably, also in Belarus, achievement of economic success largely depends on the development of the SME sector. Entrepreneurship as such has not, so far, become a "mass phenomenon." For instance, the share of employment in the individual and small private business sector in Belarus, including hired workers, is only 18 percent (NSC, 2016). The average number of employees, by ownership type, is shown in Figure 5.2.

One reason for a small share of private SMEs could be that Belarusians are simply afraid to risk founding their own businesses. They prefer to earn a relatively small salary, working for a state-owned enterprise, instead of starting their own companies. In many ways, the external environment does not support positive risk taking and the development of healthy private entrepreneurship initiatives in Belarus. Another reason may be that Belarusian entrepreneurs face challenges of low purchasing power demand, high tax rates and frequent changes in tax reporting, lack of transparency legislation regulating economic activity, and weakness of financial and non-financial support to SMEs. Therefore, it is no surprise that the entrepreneurial potential of Belarusians has not yet been disclosed.

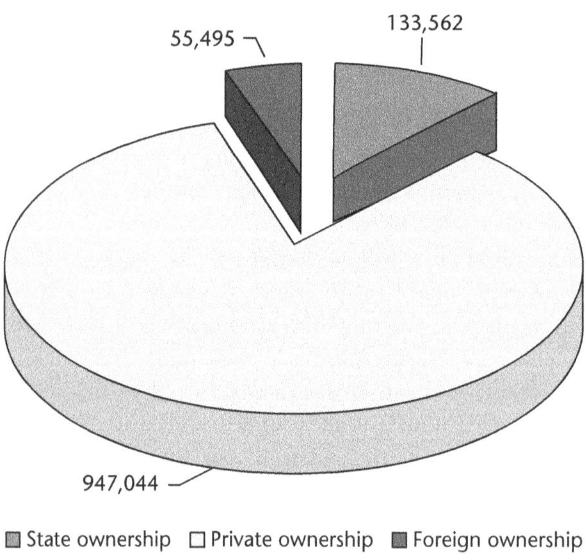

FIGURE 5.2 Average number of employees in the small business sector by ownership type, 2015.

Source: Authors based on NSC (2016).

Partly, entrepreneurial behavior can be found in "cross-border trading activity involving households and individuals" in the Belarus–Poland border areas (Smallbone *et al.*, 2012). This so-called "shuttle trading phenomenon" is not part of official statistics, but characterizes the potential of entrepreneurial behavior among Belarusian people.

The entrepreneurial environment in Belarus

The environment in which entrepreneurs are engaged in their activities is described as an ecosystem and we will analyze its impact on business life, its development, and its success in Belarus. There are, remarkably, four elements of the ecosystem represented in the country: education, financial support structure, the support structure in the field of business support, and state policy.

Education. In Belarus, there are 45 public and 10 private universities. Thirty Belarusian universities (accounting for around 54 percent) offer management programs – for example, *Economy and Management of the Enterprise* and *Business Administration, Economics and Management*. At the Belarusian State Economic University, as part of the Masters program, they offer the study module *Management of Business Development*. Business support centers operate at two universities: the *Business Support Center* and a *Young Entrepreneur* club for students of schools and colleges at the Belarusian National Technical University, as well as the Center for Business Education at the Belarusian Trade and Economics University of Consumer Cooperatives. In addition, the Belarusian University of Informatics and Radio Electronics opened and successfully operates a business incubator. At the secondary level, there are two elective courses, which are aimed at the assimilation of the economy and business fundamentals. Business schools organize various training programs, seminars, and entrepreneurship courses, as well as consulting and training agencies, several development programs at public institutions, business support centers, business incubators, and NGOs. There are about ten schools and agencies providing education and training in the field of business.

Financial support structure. The investors' circle includes family and friends, business angels, and venture capital funds. To obtain a bank loan for starting a business a deposit is required, which is not always available. In Belarus, there is only one official community of business angels and venture capital investors, *BAWIN*. In 2015, three crowdfunding platforms started in the Belarusian market, among them *Ulej*, the social platform *Talaka*, and a charity auction of meetings, *MaeSens*. The Belarusian microfinance market is in a stage of renovation. Approximately half of Belarusian banks are now offering loans to small and medium-sized businesses and startups exclusively for working capital, commercial mortgage, or purchasing of equipment. Information about options for credit can be found on banks' websites, as well as at the financial web-portals Myfin.by, InfoBank, Benefit.by, and others. The majority (11) of these banks are partners of the SME support programs of the European Bank for Reconstruction and Development (EBRD).

The state also promotes and implements a special program for the development of SMEs. Over the next few years, to support SMEs, US$325.53 million will be allocated from the state budget. The Belarusian government also provides financial support to SMEs through the executive committees of the Belarusian Fund for Financial Support of Entrepreneurs, the Belarusian Innovation Fund, and the State Committee on Science and Technology of the Republic of Belarus. To receive support from these structures, the company needs to work in certain priority areas: the production of goods and services, particularly export-oriented or import-substitution; production-oriented energy and resource efficiency; or new technologies and innovations.

Support structures in the field of business. There are two officially recognized types of business support for SMEs: entrepreneurship support centers and small business incubators. More than 80 percent of them are privately owned. According to statistics from the Ministry of Economy (Минэкономики, 2016), there are 88 small business support centers and 19 business incubators in Belarus. Their infrastructure provides/includes energy supply, relatively good roads, and access to the internet. However, state research centers have very few linkages to real business – that is, there is a lack of innovation.

Support in the external environment. Although the role of state policy appears in the factors already mentioned above, recent developments need more attention. The Vice Minister of Economic Affairs, Irina Kostevich, has said in an interview to the Belarusian Agency of Telegraphy (BELTA, 2016b):

> Belarus has adopted a National Strategy for Sustainable Socio-Economic Development for the period until 2020, in which it is determined that the share of small and medium-sized businesses should reach 50 percent of GDP. It is an ambitious figure, but we have to strive for it and to understand the country and the business will move towards this goal. As for the strategy of development of small and medium business in Belarus until 2030, the deadline of its development is 2017.

She added that before the end of the current five-year plan, till 2020, there should be about 48,000 operational SMEs in Belarus. The share of employment at SMEs should reach about 35 percent of total employment up to 2020; today, in 2016, this figure is 31 percent, so nearly 100,000 more people are required to work in small or medium-sized businesses to meet the 2020 target (BELTA, 2016b). The current situation of Belarusian private business and entrepreneurship provides extensive room for further development, as discussed in the next section.

State and business in Belarus

According to a study by Bogdanova (2013), among the obstacles that prevent normal development of businesses in the country are inflation and macroeconomic instability (54.7 percent), lack of and difficulty in attracting funding (30.9 percent), high tax rates and a complicated tax system (26.8 and 18.4 percent, respectively), legal insecurity (23.4 percent), and public administrative regulation, licensing, and certification (19.4 percent). To some extent, it can be claimed that the state and businesses in Belarus do not trust each other (Bogdanova, 2013).

In a favorable economic situation, entrepreneurs are more inclined to act as innovators and engage in calculated risks. In transition countries, where the institutional framework is not yet in place, and in particular during the economic downturn, starting your own business is often seen as the only way to escape poverty and unemployment (Welter and Smallbone, 2011). At the same time, studies show that the growth in efficiency of the real (economy) sector in Belarus is restrained by excessive employment in state-owned enterprises (Sokolova, 2016).

Following the results of the *Doing Business 2017* report, Belarus has created favorable conditions for starting a business – registering a company can be done quickly and easily. But shortly after registration, the problems begin. One of the main barriers to business development over the years is the instability of legislation, as well as access to finance, which is particularly relevant for new, innovative firms (Ivanova, 2005). This is because, for banks, it is much safer to loan to a large company for operating activities than to provide money for the implementation of new ideas in risky SMEs.

The share of the private sector is still low – about 21 percent of GDP (NSC, 2016; see also Table 5.2). The privatization of companies is proceeding slowly, and it is one of the reasons why an insufficient number of Belarusian companies are competitive in the international market.

The total number of employees of micro, small and medium-sized businesses decreased in 2015 (compared to 2010, a decrease of 109,000), to 1.136 million people, or to 27.3 percent of all employed in the economy. The share of small and medium-sized enterprises, including individual entrepreneurs, in the country's GDP last year also declined and amounted to 21.1 percent (2014 – 21.7 percent) (NSC, 2015, 2016).

TABLE 5.2 SME sector's contribution to the main macroeconomic indicators, %

Year	*2009*	*2010*	*2011*	*2012*	*2013*	*2014*	*2015*
GDP	18.8	19.8	21.2	23.5	21.9	21.7	21.1
Number of employed	28.1	28.0	27.5	27.6	28.4	28.0	27.3
Output	20.0	20.0	22.2	22.6	20.8	20.9	20.6
Industrial production	14.7	15.1	17.5	19.4	15.6	16.0	15.7
Investments	38.0	39.7	36.0	37.9	38.9	42.3	36.7
Export	37.9	42.9	46.1	41.3	37.3	41.5	48.1
Import	33.5	37.4	31.1	34.7	35.7	35.0	35.5
Retail trade turnover	41.9	40.9	37.6	34.5	36.1	33.3	31.7
Wholesale trade	80.3	81.5	90.6	76.1	81.6	79.1	83.2
Revenue	37.7	37.2	39.5	37.7	37.7	37.1	37.9

Source: Authors based on NSC (2016).

The total number of SMEs in Belarus, for the last year, dropped nearly to the level of 2012. Moreover, the number of medium-sized organizations, in general, has decreased below the figure of 2010. In the past year, the total number of SMEs has reduced in all regions of the country.

The volume of production[1] (works, services) by type of organization and type of economic activity in the Republic of Belarus for 2015 is presented in Table 5.3.

On average, the profitability of SMEs was 8.2 percent last year. The share of unprofitable small and medium-sized enterprises increased quite sharply in 2015; the net profit of SMEs halved in comparison with 2014. Moreover, an adverse situation formed in the hotel and restaurant business. The agriculture and mining industry was unprofitable, and there was sharply reduced profitability in the construction sector.

The majority of small and medium-sized enterprises in Belarus are privately owned. Table 5.4 shows the distribution of Belarusian SMEs by fields of activity in 2015.

The Ministry of Antimonopoly Regulation and Trade has developed a draft decree which significantly simplifies conditions for doing business in the sphere of trade, public catering, and consumer services, especially in small towns and rural areas. The decree (project) offers a moratorium on planned inspections by the end of 2020. It is proposed that business entities that operate in small and medium-sized cities and rural areas be given the right not to pay value added tax, income tax (legal persons), and that income tax on individuals (sole proprietors) be applied under the simplified system of taxation at the rate of 1 percent.

By the decision of President Alexander Lukashenko, Belarus has taken steps to stimulate business activity with the elimination of unnecessary requirements for business entities, as well as by improving control and surveillance activities. President Lukashenko, in his speech at the fifth Belarusian People's Assembly, said that 250,000 jobs would be created, and he considers private business to be one of the most promising areas in the next five years. "Going into business people can provide income for themselves and their families, as well as employ two or three people." The President believes that the liberating business initiative should be the driving force for the recovery of economic growth and job creation, and it is necessary to simplify and accelerate the involvement of inefficiently used state property into economic circulation to expand opportunities for renting state property objects (BELTA, 2016a).

Outlook of the entrepreneurial environment in Belarus

Compared with state-owned companies, private business is hugely profitable. According to experts, using the same technology, the efficiency of private production is 30–40 percent higher than in the state-owned sector. This also means that private ownership of industry increases productivity. There is the need to dispel the myth that once the private owner comes to the factory, workers remain without jobs. The Ministry of Justice will improve the legal framework of business, including among other measures the decriminalization of economic risks (BELTA, 2017).

TABLE 5.3 Annual volume of production by size of enterprise and field of economic activity, 2015 (million BYN)

Type of economic activity	*Large*	*Medium*	*Small*	*Micro*
Agriculture, hunting, and forestry	66,383,853	33,364,828	4,514,100	1,724,788
Fishery, fish farming	133,106	144,645	95,804	22,910
Mining industry	9,419,875	246,686	160,521	26,138
Manufacturing industry	468,969,768	42,248,629	51,163,658	13,235,441
Production and distribution of electricity, gas, and water	76,086,967	777,225	282,817	176,990
Building	57,824,075	12,671,343	16,187,234	5,935,734
Trade; repair of cars, household goods, and personal items	58,533,696	15,180,939	36,882,324	24,986,670
Hotels and restaurants	6,335,479	1,907,285	2,340,055	1,088,594
Transport and communication	77,392,069	5,804,229	12,263,493	10,692,279
Financial activities	4,231,178	706,604	2,077,543	1,424,920
Transactions with real estate, renting, and provision of services to consumers	27,893,785	11,367,782	19,358,371	13,351,514
Education	96,242	35,264	329,145	297,980
Health and social services	2,359,029	1,272,141	963,364	597,036
Provision of communal, social, and personal services	8,097,185	2,859,652	2,091,015	2,090,491

Source: Authors based on NSC (2016).

TABLE 5.4 Distribution of Belarusian private SMEs by fields of activity in 2015

Type of economic activity	*Number*	*%*
Manufacturing	15,249	14
Agriculture, forestry, and fishing	4,394	4
Building	9,803	9
Trade and repair	40,724	38
Hotels and restaurants	2,710	3
Transport and communications	12,843	12
Financial activities, real estate transactions	15,065	14
Services	4,726	4
Other	57	2
Total	107,441	100

Source: Authors based on NSC (2016).

The number of licensed activities will be reduced and administrative procedures simplified. The special guarantee fund will be created to support small businesses. New industrial enterprises will be exempt from paying VAT on the import of technological equipment. In towns with a population of at least 6,000, people will be provided with the necessary transport and engineering infrastructure.

The development of wholesale and, particularly, retail trade is accompanied by dynamic growth in demand for transportation and logistics services. Belarus has a geographically strategic position in the center of Europe, between the European Union and the EEU. There are good road and rail networks in the country. On the other hand, transport services have the leading share of export services of the Republic of Belarus – 28.5 percent (NSC, 2016). More than 1,000 companies and individual entrepreneurs work in the market of transport and logistics services, which, in addition to cargo transportation in international traffic, provide cargo escort services, customs, freight, and other documents. Active integration of Belarus into the system of international transport corridors will create additional opportunities for economic development, as discussed in the next section.

Trends in the development of transport and logistics services in the Republic of Belarus

The advantageous geopolitical position of the Republic of Belarus contributes to the development of freight traffic both internationally and inside the country. For the Republic of Belarus, located at the crossroads of trade routes between Europe and Russia, the Baltic and the Black Sea (via the territory of the Republic) are two of the ten major international transport corridors, with routes which have been identified as top priorities: №11 corridor (Berlin – Warsaw – Minsk – Moscow – Nizhny Novgorod) and №1H corridor (Helsinki – St. Petersburg – Pskov – Vitebsk – Gomel – Kiev – Chisinau – Bucharest – Dimitrovgrad Alexandroupolis) and its branch IXB (Kaliningrad/Klaipeda-Vilnius-Kaunas – Minsk – Kiev); it is becoming an increasingly urgent task for Belarus to keep up with general trends and not weaken its position in the market of international transport of goods (UNITER, 2016).

The transport and logistics complex of the Republic of Belarus is essential to support its diversified economy and the implementation of social policy. The transport complex of Belarus today (data 2015) consists of: more than 100,000 kilometers of roads, more than 14,000 organizations, all forms of property, and one million units of commercial vehicles. About 6 percent of total employment in the economy is in the transport system, with the proportion of GDP around 7 percent, the share of GDP of exports of services at 48 percent, more than 8 percent for investments in fixed assets, 25 percent of foreign investments made in the economy, and taxes and fees from transportation companies totaling 7.9 percent of revenues in the country (NCS, 2016).

Revenue per employee in the transport sector is the fourth largest economic activity of the Republic of Belarus after the petrochemical, energy, and wholesale trade, and more than 90 percent of the positive balance of foreign trade is formed by transport services. Moreover, statistics (Eurostatica, 2017) of the trucking market in the Republic of Belarus from 2015/2016 (Figure 5.3) show that, in 2016, 10.6 percent fewer goods were delivered by road to the Republic of Belarus from the EU than in 2015. Export trucking from Belarus to the EU in 2016 increased by 18.2 percent compared to 2015.

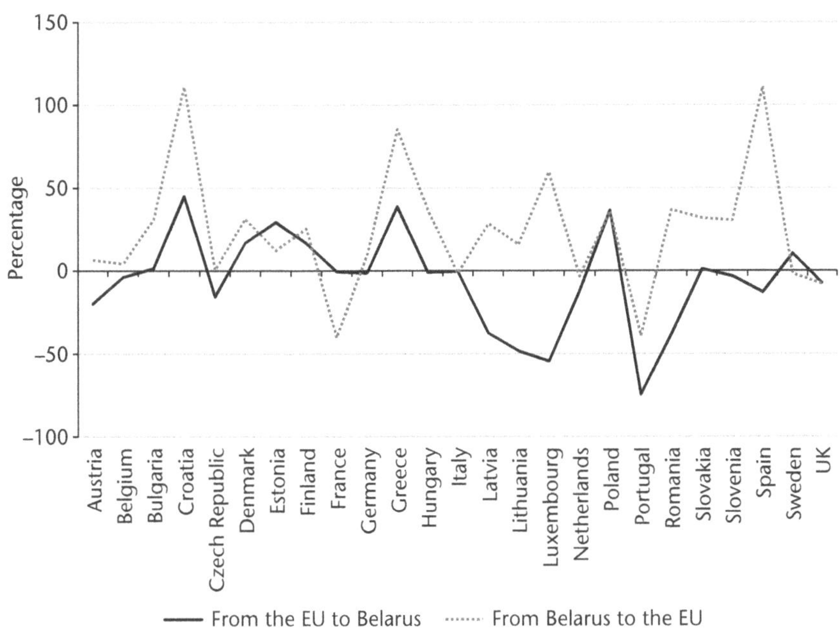

FIGURE 5.3 Changes in the trucking market in Belarus by country, 2015 compared to 2014.

Source: Authors based on data by Eurostatica (2017).

The bulk of cargo in international road traffic across the territory of the Republic of Belarus is transported by transit – about 16 million tons annually. The share of Belarusian road carriers accounts for 11 percent of the total number of transit traffic crossing the Republic of Belarus, with 89 percent being foreign carriers (Russia, 51 percent; Poland, 24 percent; and Lithuania, 11 percent). However, profitability of the industry fell almost twofold – from 5.4 to 2.8 percent. Similarly, volumes of transport also decreased, and this trend is continuing in 2017. High competition in the transport market, the reduction of tariffs, and the non-favorable economic situation in the country hinder the development of the freight sector. The volume of freight forwarding services dropped by 18 percent in 2015, while there was an increase of 20 percent in logistics services compared with the previous period. Volumes of road transport companies fell by 5 percent, and transit cargo handling volume of logistic centers increased by 42 percent; revenues from forwarding services declined by 24 percent in Belarus (NSC, 2016).

The problem of keeping pace with general trends and not weakening the Belarusian position on the international cargo transportation market is becoming increasingly urgent. According to Данильченко (2007), regarding the main reasons "hampering the development of foreign economic activity," business leaders have noted the strong competition from foreign companies – external factors – and internal factors:

- insufficient level of technical production base
- lack of interest in investment by foreign firms, partly because of an unstable legal environment
- lack of knowledge about the conjuncture of the world market
- poor product quality
- low qualifications of staff
- customs policy.

The main measures to meet the challenges and further develop the transport sector at the state and business level in the future are as follows (Ivut *et al.*, 2015):

1 Implementation of the state program of development of road transport in Belarus for 2015–2019, which is comprehensive and contains a list of activities and the mechanism for the implementation of measures for the development of road transport.
2 Formation of integrated information and technology space, with road freight transport based on current market monitoring, analysis, logistics and statistics, transport links and processes.
3 The implementation of an innovative development program; identification of areas in which to create new capacities and production; the introduction of new technologies in transport sphere.
4 Technological and structural upgrading of freight transport services by companies.

Thus, the role of the road transport sector in the Republic of Belarus is quite significant; its competitive advantage is that it is still a relatively inexpensive service, and it can be used to deliver cargo to almost any destination in a short time period.

The primary outcomes of the international cargo activity are created by enterprises of private ownership, 96 percent of which are small and medium-sized businesses. They own 79 percent of the fleet of trucks that carry out international cargo transportation. Now, trucking is quite a demanding and promising business. In this market, there are already numerous competitors for moving goods. To successfully withstand competition, an entrepreneur needs to find a niche and continually evolve, such as is shown in the following case study of Truck Trailer Company KristallTrans (TTC KristallTrans).

Case study: Truck Trailer Company KristallTrans

History of the company

The founder of the company, Alexander Starohatny, has worked in the transport industry since 1977. He started as a mechanical engineer, and later on he was promoted to the director's position during Soviet times. Even then, his desire was to work in the sphere of international transportation. After the "parade of sovereignties," in 1995, he created a production and commercial company, "KristallTrans." The main activity of the business was organizing international transportation. Starohatny knew that this area required a lot of specialist transport, a well-established material base, and a professional team. It all started with two MAZ trucks. Then they acquired their first MAN truck, previously used, from Germany. It was the first one of its type in the Grodno region. They repaired the lorry perfectly, effectively turning it into a new one. For the development of the company, they studied foreign experience, created a solid partnership, and established business contacts in Germany. Starohatny concluded the contract with the owner of the German company, which provided rental trailers, loaded cargo, and, on the Belarusian side, in turn, provided the trucks.

From this point, KristallTrans began its work in the field of international transport. They got the international carriage (European Conference of Ministers of Transport, ECMT, multilateral road haulage permits) certification and other international approvals. The company developed and the trucks improved. There was a need within the maintenance station because new vehicles included a lot of new electronic systems, support of which required specialized equipment, computers, and staff understanding. In Belarus, there was no place to repair foreign-made trucks; it was expensive to order from abroad. So Alexander Starohatny decided to learn to make truck repairs. Today, the company can carry out all kinds of repairs.

KristallTrans started to grow in cooperation with *Belkargo* and *Sovtransavto*, and later on, in collaboration with their German partner, very quickly and successfully continued to explore the international cargo market (Figure 5.4).

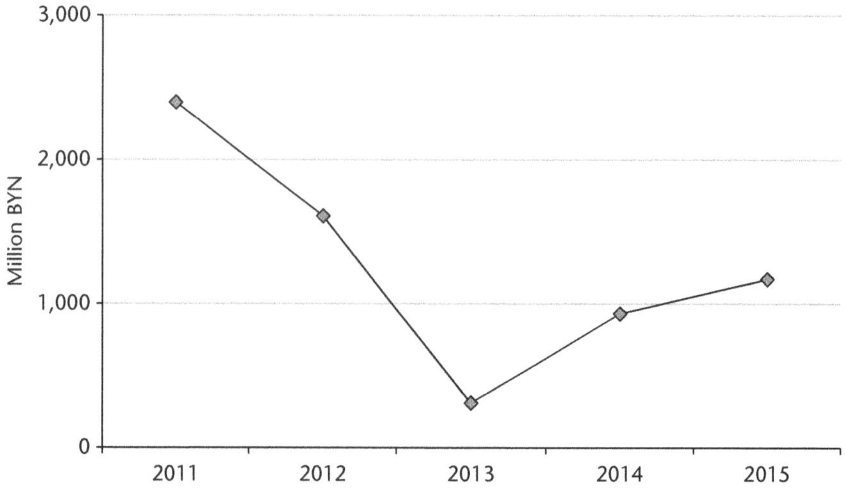

FIGURE 5.4 Company revenues.

Source: Authors based on company data, 2016.

The founding of KristallTrans was a response of the entrepreneur to the changes in society and changing market conditions. Under the leadership of Starohatny, the company mastered, implemented, and consolidated a business following standards in the field of international transport at all levels – from engineering and technology to logistics. More than 20 years of successful business in the area of regional and international trucking allowed for the accumulation of great experience and the establishment of good partnerships with companies engaged in trade, processing, and production of a wide variety of products and services.

KristallTrans today

Today, the primary activity of KristallTrans is the international transport of goods in Europe and Asia. Currently, the company is a member of BAMAP (Association of International Road Carriers) and stands in the freight market, not only as a transport company with its fleet of vehicles but also as a freight forwarder, offering a full range of freight forwarding services for cargo and customs clearance. The business fields of the company, according to its statutes, are the following:

- road freight transport
- cargo logistics services
- storage and warehousing
- maintenance and repair of motor vehicles
- retail sale of automotive parts and accessories
- lease of own real estate.

In its main field – transport of goods – among others, the company runs carriage of liquid cargoes, transports freight that requires special temperature conditions, and carries out the transportation of groupie cargoes – small transport shipments to different customers with one vehicle – from Europe to a warehouse in the destination country. This latter type of transportation is the most cost-effective solution for the delivery of small consignments of goods over long distances. Besides, container transport and freight forwarding are part of the business and logistics services provided by KristallTrans.

Traditionally, the majority of freight services of KristallTrans are international, even if the client is a Belarusian resident (Figure 5.5). As seen in 2013, there was a decline of economic indicators in Belarus also reflected in the service volumes of KristallTrans. This is likely a result of a fall in production and consumer demand in the country. The largest decline observed was in imports. Also, international sanctions, after Russian military intervention in Ukraine in 2014, decreased the flow of goods between European countries and Russia. Despite the current situation, due to competent management policies and highly qualified personnel, a gradual increase in freight traffic can be observed.

Despite the difficult economic situation, the company has retained its profitability (Figure 5.6) and even increased its fleet of trucks (Figure 5.7).

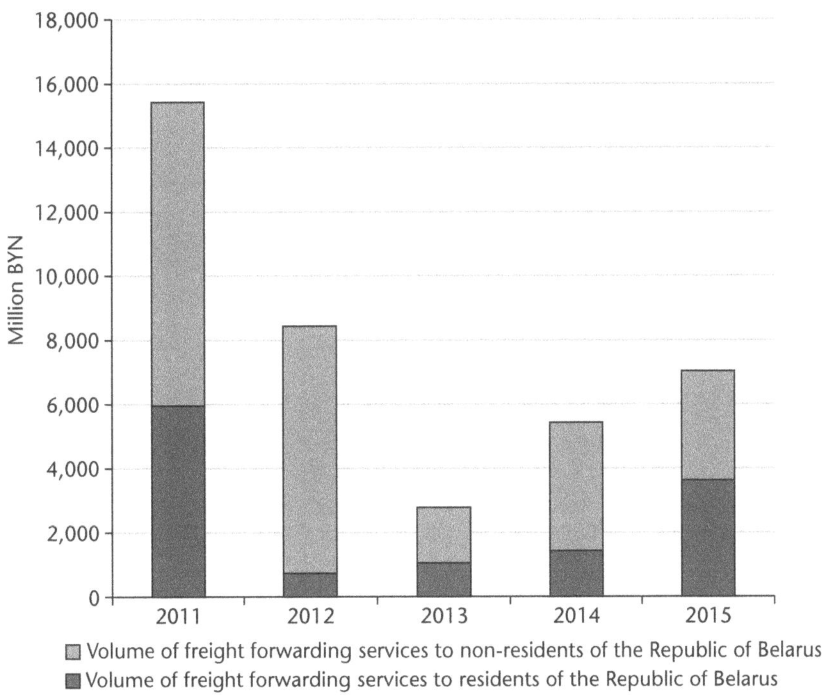

FIGURE 5.5 Volume of company freight.

Source: Authors based on company data (2011–2015).

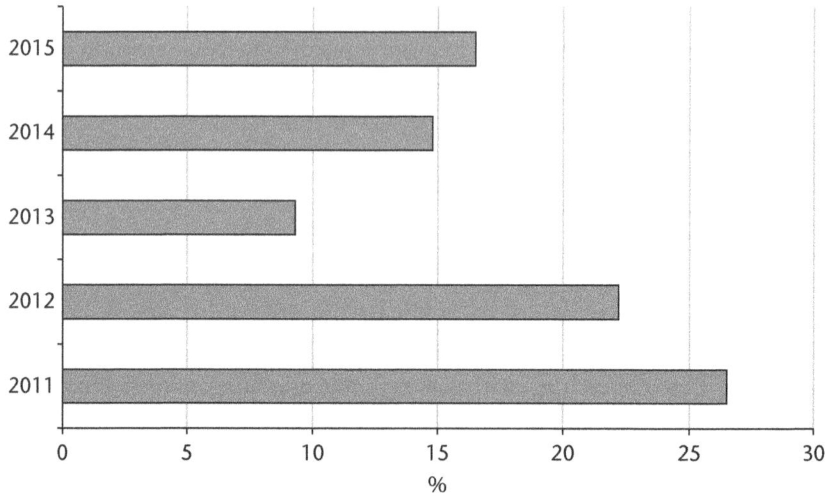

FIGURE 5.6 Profitability of service sales.

Source: Authors based on company data (2011–2015).

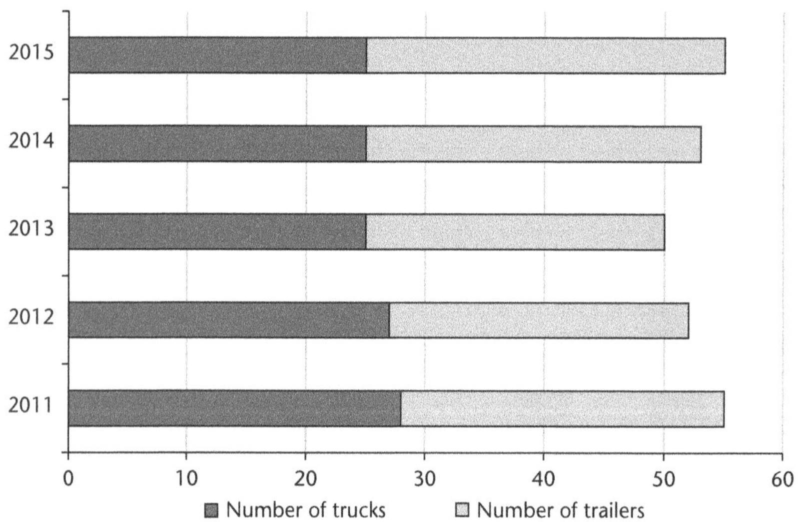

FIGURE 5.7 Fleet of trucks.

Source: Authors based on company data (2011–2015).

Optimization of the personnel structure and reduction in the numbers of staff (Figure 5.8) took place, first – in the administrative staff, through the introduction of modern information technologies in the management process.

As shown above, in Figure 5.8, KristallTrans adapted its business to dynamic changes in the business environment. These were entrepreneurial efforts, balancing tangible and human capital to achieve the company's own development potential.

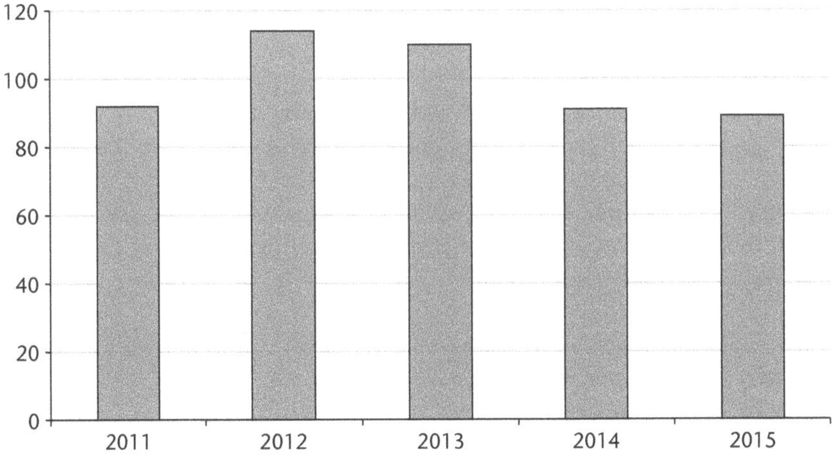

FIGURE 5.8 Number of employees.

Source: Authors based on company data (2010–2015).

Challenges and ways of overcoming them

The flow of documents. KristallTrans has to meet the same red-tape requirements as any other company in Belarus. On the company's website (KristallTrans, 2011), Irek Schnitzer, their manager of international business partners, makes critical points on dealing with bureaucratic rules in Belarus:

> You have one agency dictating to another some of the things that prevent the development of the prospective market. Company managers are sometimes required to do what there is absolutely no need for in specialization. Too many papers and each must have seals and stamps, multiple signatures.

To reduce paperwork, modern information technology can be used, such as electronic signatures, provided with the necessary confidential attributes. Now, Belarus is on its way, and the first steps have been made with the widespread use of electronic invoices.

The necessity of customs procedures simplification. Currently, many of the issues are solved for border crossing, taking into account the interests of carriers. For example, providing the border checkpoint with information about loads documents in electronic form in advance. This allows customs officers, beforehand, to decide on a fast pass or thorough check. Almost all border checkpoints have X-ray machines for monitoring compliance with the declared goods, which shortens the border crossing time significantly. The reduction in checking time for Belarusian carriers passing the border supported growing turnover and increased the number of crossings. Evidence of that can be found in the reports of the Border and Customs Committee. However, because of competition from foreign carriers, Belarusian carriers lose out. Transportation must always be optimized to accelerate the delivery of goods. Hours of queues at the border break plans of all interested parties in transportation. A good example of arranging border crossings can be seen in Germany. There they have built special terminals and storage platforms, solving problems and benefiting the carriers.

The fleet of KristallTrans contains about 50 trucks. They should give high output; recouping investment into new facilities can only be achieved by keeping trucks in continuous motion. Thus, the primary ways to improve transport logistics, in the Republic of Belarus, include different measures from the state as well as from companies. This collaboration includes:

1 Developing road service conditions in all transport corridors of the country.
2 Reducing downtime at the border.
3 Improving the capacity of vehicles.
4 Increasing the exploitation rate of transport.
5 Promoting the use of mileage.
6 Accelerating loading and unloading.

One of the ways to improve company–government collaboration could be by involving more private businesses in logistic services on the state border of Belarus. Such decisions support further developments in the transition to market economy context. That also means more opportunities for entrepreneurs.

Conclusions

The Belarusian economic model supposes the formation of a socially-oriented market economy with the same functioning of the various forms of ownership and state regulation of economic activities. Its main features are the coexistence of public and private sectors, privatization of enterprises with the saving of social guarantees for employees. The government pays great attention to the development of SMEs, as it sees that as one of the factors of maintenance of stable high employment and economic growth.

Socioeconomic development of the Belarusian state, in the future, is considered to be dependent on the development of entrepreneurship and market infrastructure, including effective state regulation. The country already has an infrastructure of entrepreneurship support: funds for financial support of entrepreneurs, business support centers, small business incubators, innovation centers, and a society of mutual crediting. Small businesses in Belarus already have a rather broad legal framework, but it is still insufficient. The problem is that adopted legal regulations and policy measures have not been fully implemented. In addition, although certain activities have been carried out in Belarus with the aim of creating favorable conditions for business, some obstacles remain. Key issues among them are the imperfect tax legislation, the negative attitude of the population toward entrepreneurship, active state intervention in economic processes, the lack of precise mechanisms of financing businesses, and high rents in the governmentally regulated market.

The government, having the aim of intensive business development, has a wide circle of tasks to address:

- to improve the entrepreneurial climate and create a favorable market environment to accelerate the development of small businesses
- to eliminate the reasons causing the outflow of human capital (the basis for entrepreneurial and scientific-technical potential) and financial capital to foreign countries
- to ease the tax burden
- to build a sustainable financial basis of development for small and medium-sized businesses
- to improve the system of state support for the development of entrepreneurship and state regulation of the activity of business entities.

For the economic structural changes and reduction of the number of state-owned enterprises, the SME sector is seen as an important source of new businesses and employment. The necessary conditions for the efficient development of the economy are the liberation of the initiative and freedom of enterprise. The economic nature of entrepreneurship is characterized by its attributes: initiative, business risk, and responsibility, combining factors of product and process innovation. And private property, an individual initiative of the entrepreneur, and his or her own risk guarantee the freedom of entrepreneurship. The success of these declared aims depends on the capability of Belarusian leaders to accelerate transition processes remaining behind developments in other CEE countries.

Thus, the dynamics of the development of international business activity depend on the internal potential of the firm, the business and investment climate of the external environment, and the stimulating operations of the government. The role of the state, in growing the competitiveness of the Belarusian economy, could be seen in the creation of conditions that encourage starting with the simplest forms of exports and ending with direct investments. A good example of the outlook for this approach, and what can be achieved in the entrepreneurial way, is seen in the transport company TTC KristallTrans.

The transport sector is one of the primary sources of GDP growth for Belarus, and its entrepreneurial development is one of the necessary conditions for the further growth of the welfare of the people. The attraction of investment in the development of transport infrastructure gives a real multiplier effect of GDP growth in the country. The increase in the volume of transit cargo flows through the regions' transport systems stimulates entrepreneurial activity, creates additional jobs, and provides increased investment in the construction and modernization of transport infrastructure facilities, as well as tax revenues to local budgets.

The Republic of Belarus is a kind of bridge between Western and Eastern European and Asian economies. Being at the crossroads of transportation routes, Belarus has become a significant center mediating the international movement of goods. But to avoid losing its position in this market, Belarus needs to further develop the environment for private business. This is the premise for the efficient operation and internationalization of transportation and logistics companies, which is one of the most important features of a successful economy. Before transport enterprises can be successful, there is the task of enhancing the efficiency and internationalization of their economic activities.

Entrepreneurship, as the fourth subjective factor of production of goods and services, depends on the personal qualities of the manager (initiative, dedication, resourcefulness, etc.). Real entrepreneurs make strategic decisions for crossing borders and finding opportunities between domestic and foreign business, political, and legal environments. Starohatny sees a common future for his company – TTC KristallTrans – and homeland – Belarus – a country of transit; where trade relations between Europe, Russia, and Asian countries are meeting each other, there is hope for further entrepreneurial developments.

Note

1 According to old Soviet traditions, official statistics measure volume of production not sales or turnover of companies.

References

Akulava, M., 2012, "Portrait of a Belarusian Entrepreneur," *BEROC Policy Paper Series*, PP, No. 6.

BELTA, 2016a, Выступление Президента на Пятом Всебелорусском Народном Собрании (Speech by President Lukashenko, June 23, 2016), Наш край. Available at www.nashkraj.by/2016/06/vystuplenie-prezidenta-na-pyatom-vsebelorusskom-narodnom-sobranii/. Accessed August 8, 2017.

BELTA, 2016b, Стратегию развития МСП в Беларуси до 2030 года разработают в течение года. Available at www.belta.by/economics/view/strategiju-razvitija-msp-v-belarusi-do-2030-goda-razrabotajut-v-techenie-goda-190666-2016. Accessed August 8, 2017.

BELTA, 2017, В Беларуси вводят дополнительные меры по совершенствованию деловой среды (Interview with the Minister of Economic Affairs Zinovsky, February 20, 2017). Available at http://bel.biz/news/ekonomika/sovershenstvovanie-delovoj-sredy?utm_source=relap&utm_campaign=relap&utm_medium=relap. Accessed August 8, 2017.

Bogdanova, L.V., 2013, "Prospects of innovative development of the Republic of Belarus," *IV International Scientific-Practical Conference*, Brest, April 25–26, pp. 325–326.

Данильченко, А.В., 2007. "Интернационализация деловой активности: проблемы и перспективы развития белорусской экономики," in А. В. Данильченко and Л. Петровская, eds., Финансы. Учет. Аудит, 3, pp. 19–25. Available at http://elib.bsu.by/handle/123456789/121761. Accessed November 5, 2015.

Eurostatica (Аналитического бюро *Eurostatica*), 2017, Статистика рынка грузовых перевозок. Available at www.eurostatica.com. Accessed August 10, 2017.

Filatotchev, I., Wright, M., Buck, T., and Zhukov, V., 1999, "Corporate entrepreneurs and privatized firms in Russia, Ukraine, and Belarus," *Journal of Business Venturing*, 14, pp. 475–492.

Index of Economic Freedom, 2017, Country rankings. Available at www.heritage.org/index/ranking. Accessed August 11, 2017.

Ivanova, Y.V., 2005, "Belarus: Entrepreneurial activities in an unfriendly environment," *Journal of East-West Business*, 10 (4), pp. 29–54.

Ivut, R., Zubritsky, A., and Zinevich, A. 2015, "Transit capacity development in the Republic of Belarus in the context of its transport-logistical system formation," *Новости науки и технологий*, 1 (32), pp. 19–33.

KristallTrans, 2011, У них – бизнес, у нас – бумаги. Available at https://kristalltrans.by/a27657-nih-biznes-nas.html. Accessed August 13, 2017.

Минэкономики, 2016, *Об инфраструктуре поддержки малого и среднего предпринимательства*. Available at www.economy.gov.by/ru/activities-of-infrastructure-to-support-small-businesses-ru/. Accessed August 10, 2017.

Naūrodski, S. and Valetka, U., 2015, "Will Belarus fully benefit from the Eurasian Economic Union?" *CASE Network E-briefs*, 01, June, pp. 1–16.

NSC (National Statistical Committee of the Republic of Belarus), 2015, 2016. Industrial output. Available at www.belstat.gov.by/. Accessed July 15, 2017.

NSC, 2017, Small and medium business. Available at www.nalog.gov.by/ru/svedeniyapred-prinimatelstvo. Accessed July 15, 2017.

Smallbone, D. and Welter, F., 2010, "Entrepreneurship and government policy in former Soviet republics: Belarus and Estonia compared," *Environment and Planning C: Politics and Space*, 28 (2), pp. 195–210.

Smallbone, D., Welter, F., and Xheneti, M., 2012, "Entrepreneurship in Europe's border regions," in D. Smallbone, F. Welter, and M. Xheneti, eds., *Cross Border Entrepreneurship and Economic Development in Europe's Border Regions*. Cheltenham: Edward Elgar, pp. 1–20.

Sokolova, G.N., 2016, "Belarusian labor market under conditions of structural changes in economy: Effectiveness of mechanisms for adjustment," *Sociological Almanac*, 7, pp. 111–119.

Точицкая, И. and Кирхнер, Р., 2014, *Участие Беларуси в Евразийском экономическом союзе*. Минск, Исследовательский центр ИПМ.

UNITER, 2016, Transportation and logistics infrastructure. Available at www.uniter.by/upload/iblock/250/2508019da0857995c8a8a043ba4cc137.pdf. Accessed June 7, 2017.

Welter, F. and Smallbone, D., 2011, "Institutional perspectives on entrepreneurial behavior in challenging environments," *Small Business Management*, 49 (1), pp. 107–125.

World Bank, 2017, *Doing Business: Measuring Business Regulations*. Belarus. Available at www.doingbusiness.org/data/exploreeconomies/belarus. Accessed August 8, 2017.

Жуджунь, Д. and Ковалев М. М., 2002, *Китайские экономические реформы: опыт, возможности применения в Беларуси: Монография. Минск*, БГУ.

PART III
Born to become global

6

ENTREPRENEURIAL DEVELOPMENTS TOWARD A KNOWLEDGE-BASED ECONOMY IN ESTONIA

The case of Fits Me – venture-capital-backed startup going global

Tõnis Mets

Introduction

Estonia had not yet regained independence when Porter published his *The Competitive Advantage of Nations* (1990). The following year, at the end of August 1991, Estonia reached recognition of state sovereignty by Iceland, Lithuania, Latvia, Russia, France, and Sweden. On September 6, the Soviet government recognized Estonia's independence. The Soviet Union collapsed in December 1991; it took three more years to get the Soviet (later Russian) Army (the aftermath of Soviet occupation) out of Estonian territory. Already, since 1987, Estonians started to develop a concept of economic independence, IME (*isemajandav Eesti*; Gilles *et al.*, 2002). But, just after 1991, a transition from command to market economy started from great disorder caused by a disconnection from the Eastern system and re-orientation to the West. From that moment, Estonia found itself among poor countries with a low developmental level where "economic growth is determined by the mobilization of primary factors of production" (Porter *et al.*, 2002, p. 179). This is called the *factor-driven* stage of development by Porter *et al.* (2002), partly described as having an inexpensive semi-skilled labor force (Porter, 1990). That stage, for the Baltic countries and Estonia, was different compared to many African and Asian developing countries with a low level of education for the population.

Since 1991, the Estonian government has implemented radical reforms of economic infrastructure, including national convertible currency (kroon), and the privatization of land, production plants, and state-owned living space. These and many other steps encouraged property ownership and entrepreneurial activity for people. A flat tax system and absence of income tax on reinvested profit supported an inflow of foreign direct investment (FDI). All those policy measures were implemented by the Estonian government stimulating the speed of growth in the "catching-up" period realized with the accession to the European Union (EU) and

NATO in 2004. This could also be called the period of bold political entrepreneurship in an activity chronology of the Estonian government (Mets, 2017a). In a relatively short time, Estonia moved from the lowest development level to the next – *investment-driven* – according to Porter *et al.* (2002). When exactly this happened is not easy to identify, due to the incomplete statistical data for the first half of the 1990s. Further growth was resource-based mainly (Figure 6.1). But this extensive growth could not be sustained. The problem became evident in the global crisis of 2007–2008, with the drop of GDP to –14.1 percent in 2009. This meant the need for a new paradigm in a wider societal meaning (Lauristin and Vihalemm, 2009) as well as in the economic strategy of the country – direction to higher productivity (Varblane *et al.*, 2008).

The global crisis had a stronger impact on the Estonian economy compared to other EU countries, generally due to its smallness and dependence on export markets. The drop of consumption, by a few percent in the target countries, caused a decrease in exports of more than 20 percent from Estonia. Also, internal consumption dropped. Industry reacted to the financial crises by cutting staff. After the crisis, growth was reached with fewer employees, i.e., by growing productivity in 2010 (Hansson, 2015). But, in the next year, productivity growth lessened (ibid.).

The government responded by growing entrepreneurial competencies among the Estonian population and supporting new high value-creating business development. Entrepreneurship education became a compulsory part of education (Mets *et al.*, 2017). New startup programs have given their first outcomes. Estonia is well-known for new technology ventures becoming global (Joeveer, 2014; Mumbai, 2013). But the behavior of these *new economy* technology ventures is much different

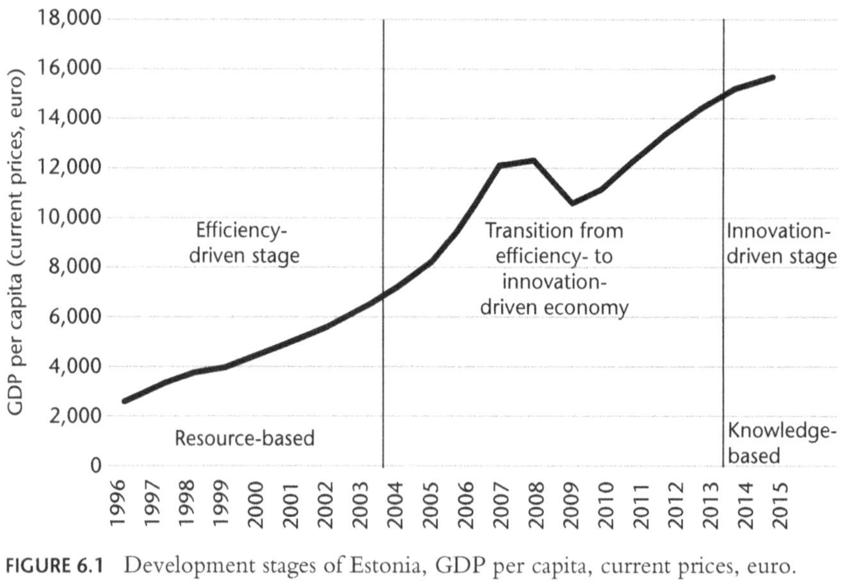

FIGURE 6.1 Development stages of Estonia, GDP per capita, current prices, euro.

Source: Based on WEF (2014); SE (2017).

from traditional ones. Frequently, they must start a global business from inception. Often, globalizing startups, which could be the engines of economic development in Estonia, move their headquarters to global centers in the UK and USA. There are several sound voices asserting that these government programs are not contributing to the living standard of ordinary people in Estonia (Eisermann, 2014). In addition, there is a supposed need to support more traditional (oil shale retorting, furniture, shoe production, etc.) industries which, in the opinion of industrialists, create more jobs and welfare (BNS, 2015; *Äripäev*, 2016).

The last reports of the World Economic Forum (WEF) include Estonia among *innovation-driven* economies (WEF, 2014), the highest development level by Porter *et al.* (2002). This new situation calls for an analysis of whether the ecosystem created for the *efficiency-driven* economy is still supporting innovation and growth – a central part of the recent strategy – smart specialization. In the context of smart specialization in Estonia, it has been found that ICT could be among the drivers of further economic development and growth of welfare. This understanding is based on several achievements, partly as the result of the IT-Tiger and e-Government programs initiated by the Estonian government in the 1990s. On the state level, that means public e-services such as an electronic tax filing system, the Electronic Health Registry, e-Prescription system, internet voting system, and e-business registry systems. In terms of new business creation, one could mention success stories of globalized ventures, including Skype, Playtech, GrabCAD, and TransferWise. Although the value of these ventures has been assessed from $100 million to $8.5 billion, they all are described with the same attributes: (1) they have moved from Estonia to global centers, (2) they have lost their independence, and (3) they do not belong to Estonians anymore (partly, exceptions are still TransferWise and Playtech). All these facts raise a question about the effects of (seed) funding startup programs and R&D by the public sector and the contributions of venture-capital-backed startup ventures on the welfare of Estonians.

This chapter aims to analyze the pros and cons of the startup ecosystem and programs in Estonia drawing on the case of venture-capital-backed Massi Miliano OÜ (2006), known internationally for the name and trademark Fits Me (2010). Fits Me, as a venture, is a "kid" (outcome) as well as a "parent" (one of the contributors enabling recognition of the innovation-driven stage) of transition in economic development from efficiency to the *innovation-driven* stage in Estonia. The company has designed a virtual fitting room for e-shoppers to try on clothes before making a purchase in e-shops, with a flexible bio-robot-mannequin adjusted to mimic the buyer's body and visualizing how a piece of clothing fits her/him. In 2012, Fits Me moved its headquarters to London and, in 2015, it was sold to a Japanese e-commerce giant, Rakuten (Lunden and Lomas, 2015).

This story calls on the researcher to learn more about the role of entrepreneurs and the ecosystem around new venture creation in the economic development context, how Estonia has moved from the *efficiency-driven* to *innovation-driven* economy. At the same time, we can mention that many countries, being on the *factor-driven* economic development level, as noted above, remained there (WEF,

2014). Next, the question is raised about the sustainability of the Estonian entrepreneurial ecosystem: is it working for its own people's welfare in Estonia or feeding multinational companies worldwide? What can we learn from the experience of Fits Me, and what could Estonia do better on the new *innovation-driven* economic development level? The author tries to answer these questions in the following sections.

The framework of entrepreneurship development in Estonia

Short history of economic development and entrepreneurship

As mentioned above, in trying to periodize Porter's economic development stages in the trajectory of Estonia, one can meet some difficulties. These deviations are related to the dating of stages as well as transition periods and identification of assumptions of the development trajectory. Partly, they are also related to institutional as well as resource aspects. Overall, it seems that Porter's concept originates from the presumption of the traditional capitalist trajectory of society, where state regulations are based on private property ownership. Yet, Estonia came from an entirely different state system as regaining independence from Soviet occupation and a command economy in 1991 had partly symbolic meaning. The transition process, which began with the so-called "singing revolution" in Estonia, had started four years earlier. The Estonian government initiated the concept of transition from a communist state and collective ownership regulations toward the private property of land, inventory, and living space (Gilles *et al.*, 2002).

In 1991, when the transition process started, Estonians, still being poor, were well educated[1] but not yet skilled in market economy rules. There were high-level research institutes operating in Estonia, among them four in different fields of physics belonging to the Academy of Sciences, formerly more or less funded by the Soviet military and space programs. For example, in 1989, when the author of this chapter visited Ireland – a country with a much higher living standard and a population two-and-a-half times bigger than Estonia – no institute of such specialization could be found there. Departments of physics were just a part of university structure in Ireland. Although these institutes of physics and other fields had very little in common with the Estonian economy, a high level of science competencies existed there. Therefore, the categorization of labor as unskilled, according to Porter's division in that stage, is not entirely true for Estonia – innovation skills partly already existed then. Estonians used these competencies successfully to find researchers previously. (e.g., Högselius, 2005).

Between 1991 and 1994, there was a period of radical reforms in society, constituting new political and social order, sometimes called "rough entrepreneurial capitalism." The new policy meant releasing of prices, disclaiming roubles, disconnection from the former Soviet economic system, and establishing its convertible currency, the Estonian Kroon. But, also, the government started to solicit FDI and privatize state enterprises. A telecommunication concession was transferred to the private company AS Eesti Telekom in 1992. Governmental programs of Sweden (NUTEK) and Finland, but also from the European Union (EU) with PHARE, supported an influx of entrepreneurial competencies through training programs, consultancy, and direct help for founding entrepreneurship development centers. Politically, it was still a critical period until the occupying Russian Army troops left, in August 1994. After that, Estonia took a course to integrate with the EU and NATO. These targets were reached in 2004.

The 1990s was also a period described by growth, due to natural enterprise. The number of active companies doubled in the ten years from 1995 to 2004, mainly due to micro-firms with fewer than ten employees (Table 6.1, data of the Commercial Registry). Because of the dual system of registration of businesses – the Commercial Registry and the Tax Department until 2010 – many private entrepreneurs, having few sales and therefore no VAT registration, are not included in these numbers from the Commercial Registry.

Liberal economic policy attracted FDI, which supported the fast restructuring of industry – Estonia, as a small open economy, became a good example of a CEE transition country from the early stages of the 1990s. An inflow of FDI lasted until the crisis of 2007 (Varblane, 2017). The effect of FDI was partly from the growth of export, which made up 56 percent of GDP in 2000 and 75 percent in 2011 (Kerner, 2012). With that indicator, Estonia was one of the most export-oriented (and internationalized) economies in the EU after Belgium, Slovakia, Hungary, and the Netherlands (ibid.). But Vahter (2004) has also shown that FDI-based exporting companies are oriented on lower average value added in Estonia. He did not find the same, for example, with FDI in Slovenia (ibid.). This is a warning signal about FDI for Estonia. Partly, changing the balance of FDI since 2011 (see Table 6.1) provides the next warning signal. That shows that zero taxation of reinvested profit of FDI does not support the goals Estonia had 20 years ago. The Estonian government has not decided how to continue with FDI.

The share of services, in the GDP of Estonia, since 1995, has been 62 percent or more; the trend is growing (Kerner, 2013). In the Russian crisis of 1999 and global (post-)crisis years of 2008–2010, the importance of services grew up to 69–70 percent of GDP and 33 percent of export; in more stable periods, it has been 66 percent of GDP and 25 percent of export (ibid.). That means, if foreign demand for Estonian goods declines, services are influenced less by that. Seventy-seven percent of the positive balance in service export is created by three sectors: logistics/transport – 47.8 percent; ICT services (mainly software) – 16.6 percent; and building – 12.6 percent. The dynamics of exports from these industries are depicted in Figure 6.2.

Political reasons could be seen to be behind the decline of logistics (transportation and storage of goods) – namely, the sanctions on trade between the EU and Russia after Russian military intervention in Ukraine in 2014. But, the exports of this sector, as well as of the food industry, have suffered under Russia's unpredictable policy before. Therefore, the best perspective, in the near future, could be considered to be ICT and building services. Both of them are based on Estonian

TABLE 6.1 General data of the entrepreneurial startup ecosystem of Estonia

Development stage	*Efficiency-driven*		*Transition from efficiency- to innovation-driven*						*Innovation-driven*		
Year	*1995*	*1999*	*2004*	*2008*	*2010*	*2011*	*2012*	*2013*	*2014*	*2015*	*2016*
GDP per capita, euro	1,935	3,910	7,125	12,353	11,054	12,556	13,613	14,427	15,186	15,405	15,883
Population, million	1.437	1.376	1.363	1.337	1.331	1.327	1.323	1.318	1.315	1.315	1.316
Employed, 1,000	633.4	579.3	601.9	656.0	568.0	603.2	614.9	621.3	624.8	640.9	644.6
No. of active companies:	30,527	46,305	60,882	77,948	100,216	103,833	108,884	112,760	113,765	117,398	120,450
by no. of employees: > 250	223	182	167	201	149	165	173	182	191	195	196
50–249	1,348	1,262	1,258	1,376	1,088	1,114	1,115	1,126	1,162	1,200	1,184
10–49	5,980	6,296	6,304	7,137	5,551	5,533	5,705	5,793	5,874	6,281	6,293
< 10	22,976	38,565	53,153	69,234	93,428	97,021	101,891	105,659	106,538	109,722	112,777
software, % of startups				2.03	1.57	8.27	3.56	8.26	13.73	9.33	
TEA index			5				14.3	13.1	9.4	13.1	16.2
Perceived opportunities, %							49	50.1	74.48	51.4	52.3
Public R&D costs, % GDP		0.52	0.52	0.72	0.79	0.85	0.90	0.90	0.81	0.80	
Total R&D costs, % GDP		0.68	0.85	1.26	1.58	2.31	2.11	1.71	1.44	1.48	
Startup investment, million euro				7.3	18.5	8.2	22.3	30.9	68.4	97.8	103.4
FDI* balance, million euro	140.2	258	362.6	450.6	921.6	–390.7	474.6	17.8	377.8	–1,115.4	–40.8

Source: Author's compilation and synthesis based on GEM (2016); WEF (2014); SE (2017); martin@garage48.org (2017) and EP (2017).

Note

FDI* – balance of foreign direct investment without re-invested profit.

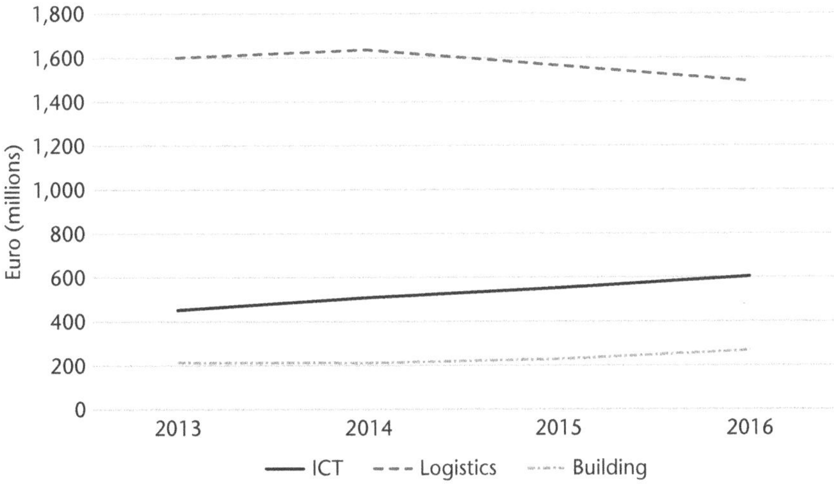

FIGURE 6.2 Dynamics of the three main sectors of Estonian service export 2013–2016.

Source: Author based on SE (2017).

human (and natural) resources. Building services are supporting, but also are entirely dependent on, the export of Estonian wooden module-houses and construction components. Altogether, this sector made €521 million in 2015 and €577 million in 2016 (Eesti Metsa- ja Puidutööstuse Liit, 2017). If building is a reborn sector, based on traditional industries, then ICT services is a new industry, with its economic value having appeared during the last 10–15 years, as analyzed in the next sections.

Propositions for the knowledge-based economy and entrepreneurship

Central propositions, for the new knowledge base of the innovation-driven economy in the framework of the entrepreneurial ecosystem, are discussed by several authors (Stam, 2015; Cohen, 2006; Isenberg, 2010; Foster *et al.*, 2013; Venkataraman, 2004). According to the World Economic Forum (WEF), there are two groups of pillars supporting the creation of new ventures (WEF, 2014): systematic conditions (networks, leadership, financing, talent, knowledge, support services) and framework or macro-level conditions (formal institutions, culture, physical infrastructure, available markets). Although these circumstances, for the Estonian entrepreneurial ecosystem, have been described previously by the author (Mets, 2016, 2017b), more particular knowledge base aspects of entrepreneurship are analyzed below.

Besides the stabilization of the economy, the restructuring of business infrastructure and old industries, and the birth of new companies, the 1990s were remarkable for the events which made Estonia famous as an ICT and e-governance country. Estonian President Lennart Meri announced the "Tiger Leap" program – the national ICT strategy – in 1996. A year later, 97 percent of schools were connected to the internet, starting computer literacy training. This was also the period when several technology startups were founded that, later on, became good examples of business globalization; among them Regio (1988/1990) – a GIS software and mobile positioning firm, Solis Biodyne (1995), Asper Biotech (1999), Quattromed (1999) – biotechnology, and others. Although these new companies got their initial ideas from universities, their role in the economy remained modest. In general, the same could be concluded about university–industry collaboration (Mets, 2006).

The strategy "Knowledge-based Estonia" (2002), which aimed to improve the situation, was targeted at research more than innovation and the real economic outcome of R&D. The goal of R&D funding, 0.9 percent of GDP for 2003, was reached in 2005 and a target of 1.5 percent, for 2006, was reached in 2010. The given numbers for 2011–2013 (Table 6.1) could be considered excellent compared with other innovation-driven countries (OECD, 2015); however, behind these figures is an investment into the factory by a single company in that period, and this indicator can no longer be sustainable at that high value. At the same time, the share of public funding in total R&D expenses never reached the values established by the strategy. The target of the next strategy, "Knowledge-based Estonia 2007–2013," for the public R&D expenditures of 1.4 percent of GDP, in 2014, have remained far from reality during the last two to three years; public funding of science has even decreased (Table 6.1). Considering that nominally the state budget of research did not increase between 2008 and 2014, growth came from European structural funds, which reached 54 percent of the public funding of R&D in 2014 (Varblane, 2014).

The current strategy, until 2020, is pointing to smart specialization in the fields of ICT (including horizontally through other sectors), health technologies and services, and a more efficient use of resources (MoE&R, 2014). There are no signs that the government has prepared for the situation where it is expecting a decrease in European R&D funding. Also, the number of employees engaged in industrial R&D remains less than five per 1,000 people employed in the industry; with that figure, Estonia lags four times behind recognized innovation-driven Nordic countries (OECD, 2015). Also, although Estonian science is highly recognized (Allik, 2015), the number of patent applications is still modest (Mets *et al.*, 2016). This means that, on the whole, the achievements of Estonian science are not developed for technology applications by Estonian companies.

The first data about Estonians' entrepreneurial attitude, comparable with international data, measured similarly to GEM (Global Entrepreneurship Monitor), were provided with a questionnaire by the Estonian Institute of Economic Research (EIER) in 2004 (Table 6.1). The value of that – 5 percent, measured by EIER (Lepane and Kuum, 2004) – was not very encouraging for further development as it was at approximately the same level as for highly developed countries like Finland or Germany. Estonia joined the GEM consortium in 2012, and its TEA (Total Entrepreneurial Activity) index, measured then at 14 percent, was one of the best in Europe. The opportunity entrepreneurship component of TEA was, and has remained, very high, even in 2014, when the main index dropped slightly to 9.4

(Table 6.1). Since 2010, the number of new startups presenting their annual reports has grown quickly, with a particularly high number of software startups among them in the last few years. Partly that might support the indication of opportunity perception measured by GEM studies.

At the beginning of the twenty-first century, the Estonian government also launched programs for entrepreneurship development, including SME support, entrepreneurship training for adults, startup seed funding, and later on, the implementation of entrepreneurship training at all levels of the educational system. The Estonian government has also been active in the implementation of European structural funds for those purposes. Very little has been studied on the impact of governmental decisions on startup activities. A good illustration of the effect of the startup Estonia program can be seen in the startups' investments. This is partly due to the Estonian Development Fund's (EDF) investment into startups which started from €5.7 million (100 percent Estonian origin funding) in 2006. Now that has reached a level of €103.4 million, in 2016, with about 90 percent coming from abroad (see also Table 6.1). Frequently, foreign investment into startups remains overseas because Estonian startups move their headquarters to global centers. Therefore, these investments may partly not be included in the FDI data (Table 6.1). This will be discussed below as we consider whether government startup policy is sufficiently justified.

Rise of new wave entrepreneurs

The challenge of smart specialization calls for innovative entrepreneurs who are able to create new technological solutions. The decision for ICT, as the primary technology field of national strategy, does not only come from the EU smart specialization goals or Estonian "Tiger Leap" program. Estonia already has traditionally good IT science from the founding of the Institute of Cybernetics, as one of the institutes of the Academy of Sciences in 1960. Now the leading research institutions are Tallinn University of Technology and the University of Tartu.

Similarly, the R&D basis for biotechnology and material technologies is created in these two leading Estonian universities. Although there are several success stories of entrepreneurial new ventures in these fields (see, e.g., Mets, 2012, 2016, 2017a, 2017b), they are in the clear minority of the Estonian startup scenery. But common to the majority of better-known technology companies is their early internationalization or even globalization orientation. The reason for that is not just the openness of the Estonian economy. There are "push" and "pull" factors for that, coming from their knowledge base, which need significant resources for product development. They need to cover R&D expenses, which is not realistic for the tiny market of Estonia (push-factor); global markets are more attractive for those purposes (pull-factor). These types of startups, oriented to global markets from inception, are called "born globals" (Luostarinen and Gabrielsson, 2004).

Not all technology startups, particularly in the IT field, are based on university R&D. But practically all are based on university professional training and knowledge (see, e.g., Mets, 2012). IT firms provide services in data processing and storage, publishing, and sales of software, design, and hosting of websites, but the biggest share of them are producing software for different purposes, making 83 percent of sales in IT services (2014). The number of people employed in software companies is growing fast (Figure 6.3). But a significant share of software developers work in other sectors, which are not categorized as programming businesses. For example, banks in Estonia have large ICT departments; nearly 7,000 Estonian firms have their own ICT unit or specialist (Mets 2017b).

In the period 2005–2015, the number of software companies reporting activities grew from 740 to 2,733 (SE, 2017). Figure 6.3 depicts this group of businesses as very dynamic, with 72.9 percent of new ventures started in the last ten years. This could be called a real IT startup boom in Estonia (Dumas, 2014). The trigger for the IT startup boom is partly attributed to the success stories at the beginning of the twenty-first century, such as IT company MicroLink and portal Delfi, sold in 2004 and 2005. Most remarkable is the sale of Skype (for $2.6 billion, to eBay in 2005), revolutionizing the telecommunication sector. Four Estonian technology developers-cofounders of Skype became investors for new businesses. All these have an international orientation from inception. The Global Entrepreneurship and Development Institute (GEDI) ranks Estonians' internationalization aspiration as fourth in the EU, although other attitude and ability related success factors/pillars are positioned between tenth and nineteenth. Particularly low is the ranking of risk capital, at twenty-seventh (GEDI, 2014).

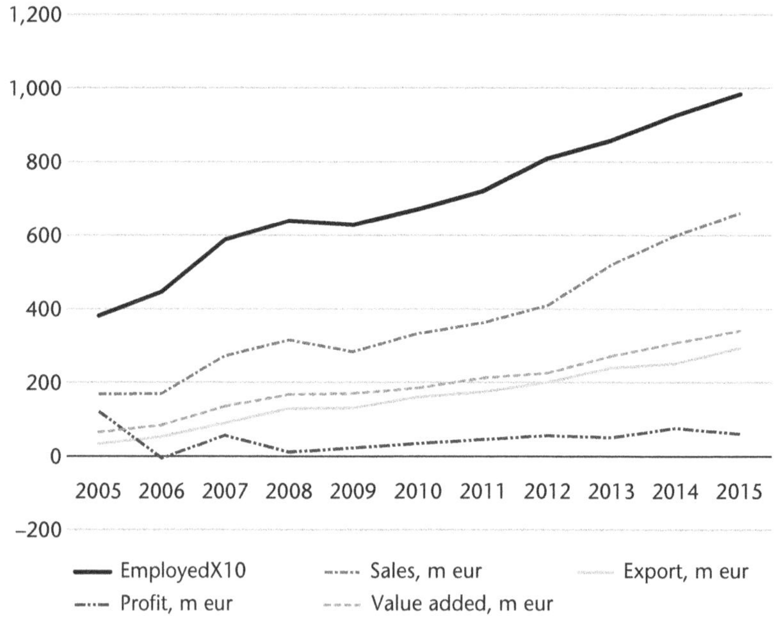

FIGURE 6.3 Number of people employed, sales, export, profit, and value added of software companies.

Source: Author based on SE (2017).

Methodology

The current study, based on empirical data, analyzes a particular Estonian technology startup in the context of the knowledge-based innovation-driven economy. The country has just passed the transition stage from the efficiency-driven phase. A case study is a way to study the development of the startup business in the society transition process context longitudinally. At the same time, the case of a startup should characterize entrepreneurship in Estonia during that period. There are several aspects to consider. What is crucial is to learn the factors describing Estonia as a new innovation-driven economy; that means existence, production, and application of ideas, R&D, technology, and funds of Estonian origin. Besides, it is necessary to answer doubts about the rationality of national startup programs and international orientation.

The main criteria for the selection of a case study company were as follows:

- The startup should be of Estonian origin, including the idea and knowledge base.
- It is a success story; it should already be an active international business.
- It should integrate different technologies, not software only.
- The main development track of the startup and entrepreneurs' activities can be examined.

It was not too difficult to find a case company in Estonia due to its small size. Estonian startup community Garage48 has its own portal (http://hub.garage48.org/estonian-startups) providing very useful information about state-of-the-art startups. A further selection of success stories among the 30 biggest investments also meant studying market reach, profitability, IP (intellectual property; patents), and sourcing knowledge. Among five startups, having protected IP based on university R&D, three were more or less already published by the author before and the final decision was partly subjective in order to find answers to doubts mentioned about Fits Me (2010) and its subsidiary Massi Miliano (2006).

Methodologically, a process approach is used (McMullen and Dimov, 2013). This enables the trajectory (journey) of a startup to be followed in real time with all its tumbles and feedback loops. The empirical study includes (1) mapping (critical) events and resources of the entrepreneurial journey, collecting information from interviews (including published interviews in the press/media), (2) learning about business reports and public media reflections on Fits Me, and (3) patent and article search on the persons and Fits Me/Massi Miliano and the business field to put the process into context. During the study, more than 50 documents and ten interviews were analyzed, including those published in the media and in students' studies. The data of the company were collected from the annual reports in the Commercial Registry, from the company's webpage, and from public media (see the Appendix). These multiple sources were considered to interpret and code the information. The validity of the results was examined in the personal interview. In the following text, key players figure under their name. All the essential facts and sayings cited below originate from the public documents. The sources of information (indicated in the Appendix) for the case description are not referenced unless they are direct citations.

Data analysis includes operations for systematization, pattern recognition, and process data interpretation, as presented in Table 6.2.

A framework for the mapping of variables is divided into three parts: (1) the entrepreneurial process facts (ideas, intentions, activities, actions, processes, stages), (2) additional data for framing the entrepreneurial journey (actors, resources, environment, the beginning and end of the journey, other essential facts), and (3) the entrepreneurial journey pattern based on collected data.

Practical implementation of the methodology requires some further explanation on how the journey information could be presented, in the next section. The entrepreneurial journey is not a linear process; it includes bigger and smaller tumbles and feedback loops, i.e., some sub-processes and activities may be repeated several times before reaching the final combination of product mix. That also means there are parallel processes at different stages. The complexity of the business concept grows during the journey. Therefore, the course of the trajectory may happen via various routes. In Table 6.3, structuration of the entrepreneurial process follows only the central trajectory and some additional facts of the parallel processes are given. The graphical presentation provides an opportunity to disclose some ups and downs and parallel paths.

The case of Fits Me

Starting under the name Massi Miliano, the virtual fitting room for e-shoppers is publicly known by its trademark and international name Fits Me, or Fits.me (2010). It is one of the success stories of the Estonian startup community, although not everything succeeded, maybe, as many people expected. It is also a good example of the application of university R&D in robotics science reaching the global business application. The case of Fits Me, as the technology developer, innovator, value creator, or target of investors, has been studied by several

TABLE 6.2 Case study analysis

Technique for case study analysis	*Explanation*
Chronologies	Events and facts organized by date
Coding	Sorting data according to the entrepreneurial journey
Clustering	Categorizing sorted data according to the stage of the e-l process
Pattern recognition	Comparison of process events/facts with observed final patterns
Process interpretation	Sense-making and interpreting findings of the processes

Source: Own elaboration.

researchers (e.g., Abels and Kruusmaa, 2013; Kallaste, 2013; Dumas, 2014; Rungi *et al.*, 2016). On the company's web page, one can find success stories of brands such as Henri Lloyd and Thomas Pink. All these sources disclose technology and marketing challenges that entrepreneurs experience. Less studied is the content and logic of the entrepreneurial process and the journey of the startup and consequences of its globalization.

The British Council (http://creativeconomy.britishcouncil.org/people/heikki-haldre/) characterized the founder of Fits Me, Mr Heikki Haldre, in 2014, as an "entrepreneur having created and exited five companies," and his ambitions and background are as follows:

> In internet years, Heikki is an e-commerce veteran. His company, which is dealing with e-commerce logistics, gave an in-depth look at the problems of today's apparel e-commerce – how difficult apparel is to sell online, and the problem with garment returns, all of which are mostly due to the wrong size. While another of Heikki's companies, sold since, was a chain of fashion shops reaching several countries, he was also the manager of the largest political campaign which made Estonia part of the European Union. His lust for innovation and commitment to outward thinking have been the key to creating new things. He believes that the best way to predict the future is to invent it.

The need for innovation grew partly from the entrepreneur's experience of difficulties in obtaining well-fitting clothing from shops. The process of learning, in the idea development stage, started with the aim of creating scanning technology for the human body for tailoring purposes. He wished to produce tailor-fitted suits as cheap as fabricated ready-made clothing in shops (Table 6.3).

Massi Miliano was founded in June 2006, by Heikki Haldre, with the idea of creating robotic mannequins for virtual tailoring fitting rooms (from the level of Propositions, P_{2006}; see Figure 6.4). The firm started as a technology developer with the support of the state agency Enterprise Estonia (EE) and partly convertible loans from private and institutional investors. Paul Pällin, being experienced in mediating R&D funding for universities, had good contacts with scientists. Researchers at the University of Tartu and Tallinn University of Technology were involved in the development process from the very beginning; the first patent applications were dated from the year 2007. With the first patent application, the role of mannequins was widened to online shopping. So the initial idea of human body scanning was transferred to the idea of the tailor- mannequin, and further to the idea of the mannequin for clothing e-shops providing visual information to customers on how the clothing fits them. The use of mannequins was expected to decrease returns of garments, which could reach 20–35 percent of sales. Online clothing retailers' sales were assessed as $26 billion, a huge opportunity for the entrepreneur. During the first two years, this research collaboration was the main development effort; the number of employees in the firm was kept minimal until 2008. In 2009, the number of staff increased to nine.

TABLE 6.3 Features and events of the entrepreneurial journey of Fits Me

Feature of the model		*Description of observed features*	*Remark*
Entrepreneurial process pattern	(Re-shaping) Propositions Pre-incubation	Experienced in e-commerce and fashion shops, Heikki Haldre had the initial idea to create scanning technology for the human body for tailoring purposes	Start-point based on former competencies
	Intention	Interest in creating innovative technology for garment fitting services for e-shopping; founding of Massi Miliano OÜ	Idea, 2006; early funding: loans
	Idea development	Feasibility study of technology, R&D, prototype of robot-mannequin, first tests, first patent application in 2007	2006–2008
	New venture idea (NVI)	Idea of virtual fitting room	2008
	Concept development	The concept of virtual fitting room SaaS, development of robot-mannequin, customer tests in the UK and USA, 2009–2010, Fits Me Holding, 2009: virtual fitting room solutions on a software-as-a-service (SaaS) basis	2009, EE: €0.7m, involvement of new owners
	Opportunity confidence (OC)	Starting sales of services in UK, USA, Germany, Italy, Estonia	2010–2011
	Business development	Continuous development with customer tests. Fit Advisor service, 2013.	HQ in London, 2012
	Venture launch	Sales 2013: €~2.8m, profit €0.27m declared, 57 employees	Massi Miliano
	Post-launch	Merger with US startup Clothes Horse, December 2014. Acquired by Rakuten, July 2015; positioning as data acquisition and analytics company, 2017: Fashion IQ – insights tool	

Complimentary data	Beginning of the journey	Idea of human body scanning for tailoring idea, robot-mannequin, 2006	Real start 2006?
	Idea	Idea saw dynamic changes in 2006–2008, integration of new concepts, 2013 and 2017	
	Ecosystem	State support, 2006; seed and venture capital: Estonia and USA	Developed
	Resources	R&D in robotics; software competencies; engineering knowledge; capital available	Needs mainly covered in Estonia
	Innovation	Virtual fitting room SaaS platform	
	Financial viability	Sales ~€2.8 m and profit reported for Massi Miliano, 2013; Data missing for Fits Me	Potential value for Rakuten
	End of the journey	Sales of firm 2015? A new concept of analytics company?	Re-start?

Source: Author's compilation based on sources in Appendix.

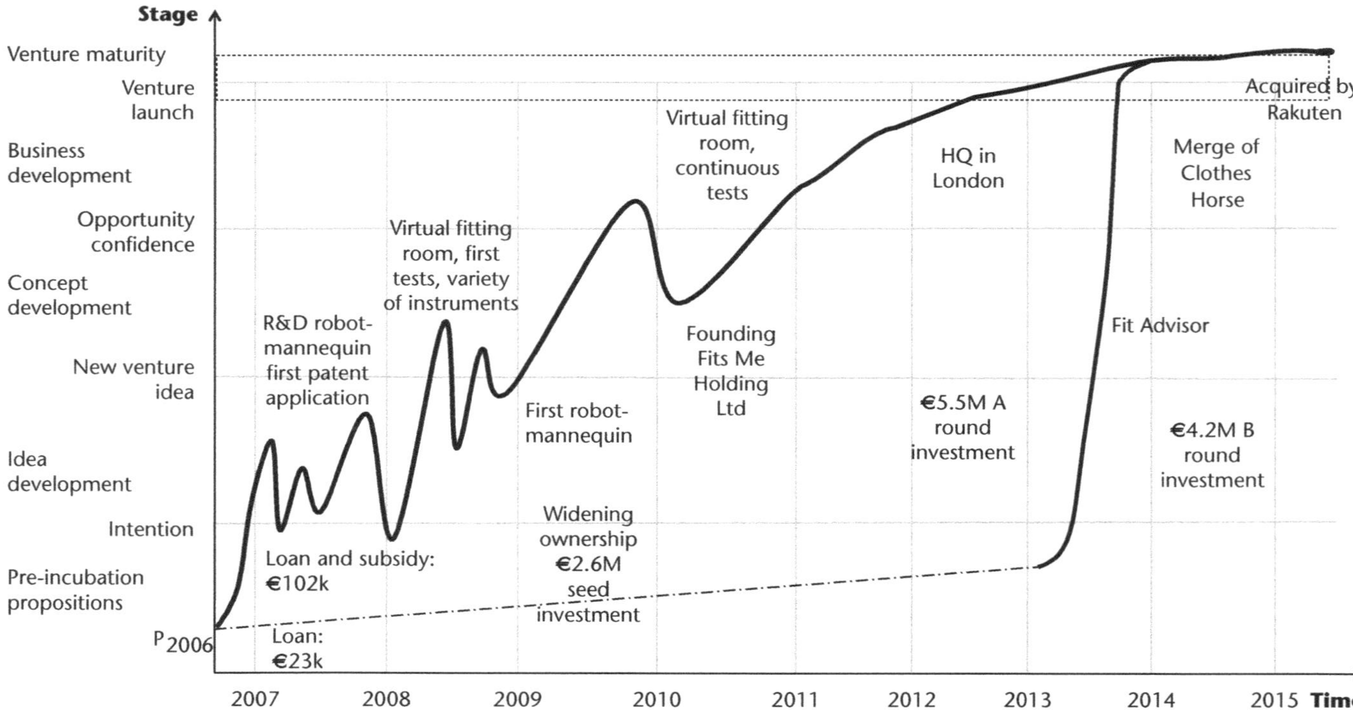

FIGURE 6.4 The entrepreneurial journey of Fits Me.

Source: Own elaboration.

Initial technology ideas included 3–4 alternative solutions, starting from combining Lego-details to rapid prototyping, using 3D printing for modeling the human body. The idea of using bio-robotics was inspired by the work of Maarja Kruusmaa for the creation of robot-fish. To simulate the human body with robots, developers obtained the database of German company Human Solutions, covering approximately 80 percent of shapes and dimensions of the human body, excluding extremities. The development of the robot-mannequins all took place in the Tartu studio. From an early stage, tailors and fashion designers were involved, providing the specific know-how and feedback. One of the most difficult tasks was achieving flexibility for the robot-mannequins while keeping costs down. From piece-by-piece actuator-controlled panel construction of the body, they improved their design by using a skin-like stretching material for covering over the robot-mannequin.

Massi Miliano, with support from the Eurostars program of the EU in 2009, involved Webmedia AS, the EDF, and other investors as new owners of the company. The first bio-robot-mannequin was ready in 2009. Massi Miliano won the business plan (pitching) competition against 47 IT startups in Silicon Valley's Plug and Play Techcenter in October 2009.

Fits Me Holdings Ltd was founded in 2009 by Heikki Haldre and Paul Pällin. Massi Miliano, a subsidiary of that, remained as the development unit in Estonia. The new startup secured seed financing to the tune of €1.3 million in 2010. The round was led by the Estonian Development Fund (SmartCap) bringing total funding, together with initial investments, to €2.6 million.

Fits Me moved its headquarters to London in 2012. Fits Me closed a €5.5 million investment Series A round in April 2013. That also covered €1.5 million tranches in January 2012. Backers included existing investor SmartCap, plus new participation from Conor Venture Partners, Fostergate Holdings Ltd, and The Entrepreneurs Fund. Massi Miliano reported global client brands (Superdry, Hugo Boss, Mexx, Ecko) and recorded profits from 2013.

The Fitting Room service means, for the client businesses, that photos of clothes on (bio-) mannequins in all versions of online shopping are presented on their webpage. A customer has the opportunity to test the fit of a particular item on his/her body according to his/her measurements. Preparing different items for sale is quite a laborious process for photograph sessions. Also, it was found that not all online shops are ready for that. Therefore, to simplify garment selection for online shopping, a new solution based on developed competencies, Fit Advisor, was launched in 2013. Fit Advisor provides fitting information and recommendations without photography. In 2014, James B. Gambrell joined the company as an investor and managing director. Some investors had expected new top management in the company two years earlier.

Although Massi Miliano announced a profit in 2013, Fits Me needed more investment, and round B, in October 2014, involved an additional €4.2 million. Former investments and the value of the company were discounted. A representative of SmartCap explained the additional funding with the need to protect initial investments. *Äripäev* (*Business Daily*) wrote about difficulties for Fits Me as sales turnover of Massi Miliano came mainly from the holding company. Doubts were also raised by some initial investors. Soon the company acquired (merged with) a competitor, US-origin startup Clothes Horse, in December 2014, ensuring the North American market.

Fits Me, having total investments of €15.42 million, was acquired by Rakuten, a Japanese internet business corporation, in July 2015. The new owner declared that Fits Me will operate as a standalone business within the corporation. The technology development department, with 50 employees and a joint laboratory with the University of Tartu, remained in Estonia (Hansalu, 2015). Also, co-founders Heikki Haldre and Paul Pällin stayed with the firm. Although the value of the deal is not known, in some interviews it was said that investors were happy. Nevertheless, doubts about the deal and the rationality of state-owned SmartCap investments of €1.4 million and Enterprise Estonia (EE) €0.9 million remained. This is a topic for later discussion.

The annual report of Massi Miliano, signed by board member Haldre in 2015, showed a profit of €0.74 million and a decreasing number of full-time employees – 44. Later on, Heikki Haldre became a board advisor and Paul Pällin became chief scientific officer. In March 2017, Stuart Simms, new CEO of Fits Me, announced that:

> we made a transition from positioning ourselves as a virtual fitting room company to a data acquisition and analytics company that uses data acquired at scale to help inform brands and retailers about the products and services they should be offering to consumers.

This repeats the idea Haldre had expressed in an interview on November 6, 2012 (Bortolan, 2012).

Discussion

The story of Fits Me includes multifaceted and controversial sides of a technology startup. From its inception, Fits Me was a business founded to be sold. There was a tiny space for it in the Estonian garment market, and few resources to feed its growth. The only solution was the very early international orientation of the business. Fits Me followed role models created by several Estonian startups previously, including Skype and Regio (Mets, 2012). The entrepreneurial ecosystem in 2006 had become more mature since the 1990s, when Regio started. Analysis of the case of Fits Me should be part of the wider view on the role of startups in a small emerging country.

The answers to the questions about the role of Fits Me in the Estonian entrepreneurial ecosystem and economy also characterize several other startups that moved out of their homeland. Is this firm a success story, as mentioned by activists, or is it a failure, as skeptics believe? The reason for the skepticism comes from the fact that former investments and the value of the company were discounted before the last investment, round B. Even a statement from the representative of the EDF, that investors were happy after the acquisition of the firm by Rakuten, can have a different meaning. First, it could be saving the investment as he mentioned – that might mean also minimizing losses. Second, discounting recent investments after the appointment of a new CEO and before round B of investment in 2014 indicates the feasibility problem. We can only speculate about the price of acquisition and profitability of the deal. Considering that only 15 percent of the total investment, €15 million, came from Estonia, this was not too high a price for 50 highly paid jobs and competencies development in the local ecosystem. Besides, it should be considered that jobs in high technology companies indirectly induce up to five times more jobs in other (traditional production and service) sectors (Moretti, 2012). That suggests that, in the socio-economic context, Fits Me remains a success story.

Analysis of the entrepreneurial ecosystem demonstrates how this type of foreign investment, which has supported the extensive growth of the Estonian economy in the past, is no longer mainly targeted to grow the knowledge-based economy. Besides, the investors have found ways to move earned capital out of Estonia without any taxes. This makes questionable the continuation of the policy implemented in transition to the efficiency-driven economy. In the last six years, new investments into Estonian startups have been even more remarkable than traditional FDI (see Table 6.1), but the character of seed investors is very different. The investment money frequently comes to Estonian startups after they move their headquarters to global centers. The case of Fits Me is proof of that. A further task for the policy is to differentiate different foreign capital depending on the target of the knowledge economy.

Although the idea comes from the entrepreneur, the case of Fits Me demonstrates the creation of IP in collaboration with university researchers. That happened by involving public and private seed and venture capital to fund R&D, reaching initial market success, and finally, sales of the venture to Rakuten, a Tokyo-based electronic commerce and internet company in 2015. Similar cases of Estonian startups show that inflow of startup seed capital is facilitated by new ideas coming from outside the public R&D system. Partly, these ideas feed university research. There are no predictions on how long a generation of spontaneous, original ideas could feed an Estonian startup booming (process), and when the initial contribution of academia would be needed. But one thing is clear – by not following a national smart specialization strategy, the government compromises the future of innovative knowledge-based Estonia.

Besides being based on university R&D, peculiar to Fits Me is the creation and protection of its own IP growing value of the business. Patenting of technical solutions and widening the view on the venture idea were a part of IP strategy. In this process, the idea has seen dynamic changes. Although started from the entrepreneur's visionary intention, the development of the concept followed the logic of causation and effectuation intermittently (about these two approaches, see, e.g., Sarasvathy, 2008). So, in the entrepreneurial process, the initial body scanner idea was replaced by bio-robotics, integrated further to the virtual fitting room. The latter was complemented by the Fit Advisor. And finally, in the Rakuten Corporation, Fits Me became the advisor for brand owners and retailers. This is a long journey of learning and competence development, but this is also the story of reshaping a business idea and its technological embodiment.

The story of Fits Me demonstrates that the business development process in the knowledge economy is a more complex phenomenon than it has been before in the endogenous development of entrepreneurial competencies. That points to the need to prepare entrepreneurs-technologists to manage uncertainty and complexity. This is a challenge for the knowledge-based Estonia.

Note

1 In 1997, 30 percent of the population of 25–64-year-olds had tertiary education (OECD, 2017). This is mainly a legacy of the Soviet period as reforms in the education system had just started.

Appendix

Sources used for the compilation of the case study

Äripäev, www.aripaev.ee.
Commercial Registry, https://ariregister.rik.ee/index?lang=eng.
Crunchbase Pro, www.crunchbase.com/app/info/pro.
EDF – Estonian Development Fund, www.arengufond.ee.
ERR – Estonian Public Broadcasting, http://news.err.ee.
Estonian Research Information System, www.etis.ee.
Estonian World, http://estonianworld.com.
Fits Me: https://fits.me/.
Interview with Paul Pällin (May 3, 2017).
Linkedin, www.linkedin.com (public biographies).
Postimees, www.postimees.ee.
TechCrunch, http://techcrunch.com.

References

Abels, A. and Kruusmaa, M., 2013, "Construction of a female shape-changing robotic mannequin," *Journal of Automation and Control Engineering*, 1 (2), pp. 132–134.

Allik, J., 2015, "Progress in Estonian science viewed through bibliometric indicators (2004–2014)," *Proceedings of the Estonian Academy of Sciences*, 64 (2), pp. 125–126.

Äripäev, 2016, "Enn Veskimägi: Idufirmadelt pole midagi õppida," *Äriuudised, Majandus24.ee*. Available at http://majandus24.postimees.ee/3855689/ennveskimagiidufirmadeltpolemidagioppida. Accessed June 17, 2017.

BNS, 2015, "Anvar Samosti sõnul on Eesti idufirmad näitemäng," *Äriuudised, Majandus24.ee*. Available at http://majandus24.postimees.ee/2889205/anvarsamostisonuloneestiidufirmadnaitemang. Accessed August 16, 2016.

Bortolan, U., 2012, "Industry voices: Fits.Me virtual fitting room," *Internet Retailing*, November 6. Available at http://internetretailing.net/issue/internetretailing-november-2012/spotlight-feature-fits-me-virtual-fitting-room/. Accessed September 21, 2016.

Cohen, B., 2006, "Sustainable valley entrepreneurial ecosystems," *Business Strategy and the Environment*, 15, pp. 1–14.

Dumas, M., 2014, "The rise of the Estonian start-up sphere," *IT Professional*, 16 (4), pp. 8–11.

Eesti Metsa- ja Puidutööstuse Liit, 2017, "Puidupõhiste toodete väliskaubandus 2016." Available at http://empl.ee/wp-content/uploads/2014/11/1-kuu-eksport-2016.pdf. Accessed May 16, 2017.

Eisermann, R., 2014, "Estonia: The start-up country," *Design Management Review*, 25 (2), pp. 18–24.

EP, 2017, Databases of the Estonian Bank. Available at www.eestipank.ee/en. Accessed May 31, 2017.

Foster, G., Shimizu, C., Ciesinski, S., Davila, A., Hassan, S., Jia, N., and Morris, R., 2013, *Entrepreneurial Ecosystems around the Globe and Company Growth Dynamics. Report Summary for the Annual Meeting of the New Champions 2013*. Geneva: World Economic Forum.

GEDI, 2014, *Towards a More Entrepreneurial Estonia. Call for Action*. Washington, DC: The Global Entrepreneurship and Development Institute.

GEM, 2016, *Reports of the Global Entrepreneurship Monitor*. Available at www.gemconsortium.org. Accessed May 16, 2017.

Gilles, J., Leimann, J., and Peterson, R., 2002, "Making a successful transition from a command to a market economy: Lessons from Estonia," *Corporate Governance*, 10 (3), pp. 175–186.

Hansalu, K. 2015. "Fits.me jääb Eestisse ja peab laienemisplaani," *Äriuudised, Majandus24.ee*. Available at http://majandus24.postimees.ee/3258927/fitsmejaabeestissejapeablaienemis plaani. Accessed June 17, 2017.

Hansson, A., 2015, "Miks on täna majanduskasvu raskem saavutada kui 10 aastat tagasi?" Presentation of the Governor of the Estonian Bank, November 11. Available at www.eestipank.ee/press/ardo-hansson-tootajate-tootlikkuse-kasv-toppama-jaanud-12112015. Accessed June 16, 2017.

Högselius, P., 2005, *The Dynamics of Innovation in Eastern Europe. Lessons from Estonia*, Cheltenham, UK and Northampton, MA: Edward Elgar.

Isenberg, D.J., 2010, "How to start an entrepreneurial revolution," *Harvard Business Review*, June, pp. 41–49.

Joeveer, M., 2014, "Estonia's rise as a high-tech leader boils down to one notion: Think globally from the start," *Forbes*. Available at www.forbes.com/sites/mamiejoeveer/2014/12/31/estoniasriseasahightechleaderboilsdowntoonenotionthinkgloballyfromthestart/print/. Accessed June 16, 2017.

Kallaste, K., 2013, *Value Creation of Innovative Service on Example of Fits.Me*, Bachelor thesis, Tartu: University of Tartu (in Estonian).

Kerner, R., 2012, "Estonia's trade in the world of globalisation," *Quarterly Bulletin of Statistics Estonia*, 2 (12), pp. 20–26.

Kerner, R., 2013, "Exports of goods and services and the domestic value added embodied in exports," *Quarterly Bulletin of Statistics Estonia*, 3 (13), pp. 57–61.

Knowledge-based Estonia, 2002, *Estonian Research and Development Strategy 2002–2006*, Tallinn: Research and Development Council.

Lauristin, M. and Vihalemm, P., 2009, "The political agenda during different periods of Estonian transformation: External and internal factors," *Journal of Baltic Studies*, 40 (1), pp. 1–28.

Lepane, L. and Kuum, L., 2004, *Enterprise of Estonian Population*, Tallinn: Estonian Institute of Economic Research (in Estonian).

Lunden, I. and Lomas, N., 2015, "Rakuten buys virtual fitting room startup Fits.Me in a fashion commerce play." Available at https://techcrunch.com/2015/07/12/rakuten-buys-virtual-fitting-room-startup-fits-me-in-a-fashion-commerce-play/. Accessed May 16, 2017.

Luostarinen, R. and Gabrielsson, M., 2004, "Finnish perspectives of international entrepreneurship," in L.-P. Dana, ed., *Handbook of Research on International Entrepreneurship*, Cheltenham: Edward Elgar, pp. 383–403.

martin@garage48.org., 2017, "Funding of Estonian startups." Available at https://docs.google.com/spreadsheets/d/1csgtaNSl949AumfOBhwhD_S-o7wc1UIhKZdWUS4Vy-Q/edit?pref=2&pli=1#gid=5. Accessed June 16, 2017.

McMullen, J.S. and Dimov, D., 2013, "Time and the entrepreneurial journey: The problems and promise of studying entrepreneurship as a process," *Journal of Management Studies*, 50 (8), pp. 1481–1512.

Mets, T., 2006, "Creating a knowledge transfer environment: The case of Estonian biotechnology," *Management Research News*, 19 (12), pp. 754–768.

Mets, T., 2012, "Creative business model innovation for globalizing SMEs," in T. Burger-Helmchen, ed., *Entrepreneurship – Creativity and Innovative Business Models*, Rijeka, Croatia: InTech, pp. 169–190.

Mets, T., 2016, "Is Estonia becoming a better home for 'born globals'?" in D. Smallbone, M. Virtanen, and A. Sauka, eds., *Entrepreneurship, Innovation and Regional Development*, Cheltenham: Edward Elgar, pp. 101–124.

Mets, T., 2017a, "Entrepreneurship in Estonia: Combination of political and entrepreneurial agenda," in A. Sauka and A. Chepurenko, eds., *Diverging Paths: Entrepreneurship in CEE and CIS*, New York: Springer International, pp. 115–133.

Mets, T., 2017b, "Is ICT the solution of the problem for Estonia?" in H. Kaur, E. Lechman, and A. Marszk, eds., *Catalyzing Development through ICT Adoption: The Developing World Experience*, New York: Springer International, pp. 273–288.

Mets, T., Kelli, A., Mets, A., and Tiimann, T., 2016, "From patent counting towards the system of IP strategic indicators," *Engineering Economics*, 27 (3), pp. 316–324.

Mets, T., Kozlinska, I., and Raudsaar, M., 2017, "Patterns in entrepreneurial competences as the perceived learning outcomes of entrepreneurship education: The case of Estonian HEIs," *Industry and Higher Education*, 31 (1), pp. 23–33.

MoE&R, 2014, *Estonian Research and Development and Innovation Strategy 2014–2020 "Knowledge-based Estonia"*, Tartu: Ministry of Education and Research.

Moretti, E., 2012, *The New Geography of Jobs*, New York: Mariner Books.

Mumbai, A.A.K., 2013, "The Economist explains: How did Estonia become a leader in technology?" *The Economist*, July 31. Available at www.economist.com/blogs/economist-explains/2013/07/economist-explains-21. Accessed May 31, 2017.

OECD, 2015, *OECD Science, Technology and Industry Scoreboard 2015: Innovation for Growth and Society*, Paris: OECD Publishing.

OECD, 2017, Adult education level (indicator). Available at http://dx.doi.org/10.1787/36bce3fe-en. Accessed May 15, 2017.

Porter, M.E., 1990, *The Competitive Advantage of Nations*. New York: Macmillan.

Porter, M.E., Sachs, J.D., and McArthur, J.W., 2002, "Executive summary: Competitiveness and stages of economic development," in M.E. Porter, J.D. Sachs, P.K. Cornelius, J.W. McArthur, and K. Schwab, eds., *The Global Competitiveness Report 2001–2002*, New York: Oxford University Press, pp. 16–25.

Rungi, M., Saks, E., and Tuisk, K., 2016, "Financial and strategic impact of VCs on start-up development: Silicon Valley decacorns vs. Northern European experience," In *Industrial*

Engineering and Engineering Management (IEEM), 2016 IEEE International Conference on Industrial Engineering and Engineering Management (IEEM), pp. 452–456.

Sarasvathy, S.D., 2008, *Effectuation: Elements of Entrepreneurial Expertise*, Cheltenham: Edward Elgar Publishing.

SE, 2017, Databases of Statistics Estonia. Available at www.stat.ee/en. Accessed May 31, 2017.

Stam, E., 2015, "Entrepreneurial ecosystems and regional policy: A sympathetic critique," *European Planning Studies*, 23 (9), pp. 1759–1769.

Vahter, P., 2004, "The effect of foreign direct investment on labor productivity: Evidence from Estonia and Slovenia," *University of Tartu Faculty of Economics and Business Administration Working Paper No. 32.*

Varblane, U., 2014, *Health of the Estonian Science?* Presentation, November 5, Tallinn (in Estonian).

Varblane, U., 2017, *Growth Factors of Estonian Economy*. Lecture slides (in Estonian).

Varblane, U., Eamets, R., Haldma, T., Kaldaru, H., Masso, J., Mets, T., Paas, T., Reiljan, J., Sepp, J., Türk, K., Ukrainski, K., Vadi, M., and Vissak, T., 2008, *The Estonian Economy Current Status of Competitiveness and Future Outlooks. Short Version of the Report*, Tallinn: Estonian Development Fund.

Venkataraman, S., 2004, "Regional transformation through technical entrepreneurship," *Journal of Business Venturing*, 19, pp. 153–167.

WEF, 2014, *The Global Competitiveness Report 2014–2015*, Geneva: World Economic Forum.

7

BORN POLAND, GONE GLOBAL

The case of successful Polish ICT company Aiton Caldwell[1]

Ewa Lechman

Introduction

For the last two decades, the global landscape has been profoundly reshaped by the rapid diffusion of new technologies (ICT), which significantly contributed to the functioning of the global economy, enhancing shifts in productivity, and impacting society and the economy (Bersnahan and Trajtenberg, 1995). Also, rapid ICT development has provided a solid background for the improvement of the entrepreneurial climate across countries, driving dynamic development of various forms of entrepreneurial activity, including the internationalization process.

Since the 1980s, Central and Eastern European economies have been profoundly transforming, both in terms of creating a friendly environment for entrepreneurial activities, but also in terms of dynamically growing access to and using new information and communication technologies (ITU, 2015). Undeniably, these two overlapping processes have generated extensive changes in internationalization patterns in all transition economies (Rao, 2001; Taylor and Jack, 2012; Onetti *et al.*, 2012; Zapletalova, 2015). According to Kshetri (2014), one very important and decisive trend in enhancing entrepreneurship development in post-communists countries was moving from a state-controlled economy to a free-market-based economy. Along with the latter, all of these economies have actively undertaken public policies to promote entrepreneurship, as one of the major channels of boosting economic growth and development.

Poland, as a transition economy, since the 1990s, has been recognized as one of the most dynamically developing countries in Central-Eastern Europe. Between 1991 and 2015, the Polish economy was continuously growing, achieving about 1.2 percent annual *per capita* growth.[2] Table 7.1 presents the most up-to-date data on economic growth both in Poland and in other Central-Eastern European countries.

TABLE 7.1 Selected macroeconomic indicators, Poland and selected Central-Eastern European countries, 1991–2015, averaged values

	Poland	*Czech Republic*	*Estonia*	*Hungary*	*Latvia*	*Lithuania*
GDP annual per capita growth	1.2	1.7	4.6	3.1	1.6	2.8
Foreign direct investment, net inflows (% of GDP)	3.1	7.6	8.1	2.6	2.8	7.3
ICT service exports (% of service exports, BoP)	15.9	24.1	16.6	24.9	16.7	16.9
ICT goods exports (% of total goods exports)	5.5	1.0	12.8	13.9	7.3	5.8
Trade (% of GDP)	66.5	109.2	142.6	122.7	97.6	115.5

Source: Author's calculations based on data derived from WDI 2016 databases.

Although the economic growth pattern was marked by several rapid ups and downs, the long-term trend demonstrates significant shifts in terms of economic development. Also, during this period, the average annual growth of gross fixed capita formation was at around 7.7 percent per annum.[3] Regardless of the fact that between 1992 and 2015 the Polish economy was exposed to several negative external shocks, like, for instance, financial crises in 2008, it demonstrates relative stability and is considered as one of the most dynamically developing countries with significantly growing per capita income.

Nowadays, according to the Attractiveness Survey 2013 (Ernst & Young, 2012), Poland ranks in first place among Central-Eastern Countries in terms of its macroeconomic competitiveness (according to the number of investment projects realized), and third in terms of the number of jobs created due to foreign direct investment flows (Ernst & Young, 2012). Due to the growing number of FDI, Poland has also become a highly competitive country with, notably, a growing manufacturing industry becoming more and more sophisticated and technologically advanced. The Polish manufacturing sector continues to shift towards innovative, technology- and knowledge intensive products, which provides perfect ground for growing international competitiveness; and successfully in 2016, Poland was ranked fifteenth (out of 40 countries listed) in the Global Manufacturing Competitiveness Index (Deloitte, 2016).

Growth of new companies is preconditioned by entrepreneurial skills to carry business functions effectively. Henceforth, in Poland, since the mid-1990s, national government has undertaken multiple efforts towards improvement of entrepreneurial skills and attitudes (the Polish Ministry of Education has introduced an 'entrepreneurship *curriculum*' at all educational levels). Creating a firm-friendly, and especially SME-friendly, environment has been effective enough, so that now in Poland SMEs' contribution to the national economy, both in terms of value added creation and employment, is steadily growing.

Furthermore, according to Global Entrepreneurship Monitor 2014 data and analysis, Poland is perceived as a country where the entrepreneurial sector is growing intensively, while the growth of small and medium sized enterprises is especially visible. Another seminal observation made in GEM 2014 is that in 2014 in Poland there was also an important change regarding the relationship between opportunity- and necessity-driven entrepreneurship, as in this year the first was reported as higher compared to the latter. The necessity-driven entrepreneurial activity, demonstrated mainly as the push-type factors, was determined by still relatively slow changing educational structure and low quality of work, which – in effect, due to high unemployment rates (especially long-term unemployment) – forces people to set up their own business. While among the pull-type factors we may indicate high pressure for 'going abroad' and starting export activities, growing international competition and rent-seeking behavior, as economic policy incentives for setting up new businesses.

This positive change may be interpreted as increasing 'quality' of entrepreneurship in Poland, which tends to be more and more innovation-driven and more oriented toward global markets. Other factors which have effectively contributed to entrepreneurship development in Poland were profound institutional reforms promoting new firms creation, significant shifts in terms of R&D, and providing solid foundations for financial and capital markets emergence (for instance, banking system or stock exchange) allowing for various sources of rising financial capital for investments. All these changes resulted in Poland, according to the World Bank's Ease of Doing Business Index 2013 (World Bank, 2013), being the global top improver in the entrepreneurial climate between June 2011 and May 2012, and in this regard Poland may be claimed as an entrepreneurially successful country.

Significant shifts and structural transformations encountered in the Polish economy are also demonstrated through growing export values, which, by definition, intensifies firms' internationalization activities. Transition economies have been undergoing significant shifts and structural changes in many areas of economic activities. Rapid trade liberalization and deregulation of markets, along with the growing pressure on introducing the Central East-European countries into global markets, enhanced most of these countries to boost both volume and value of export (Lechman, 2014), which became an important channel of firm internationalization. Figures 7.1 and 7.2 visually present the process of rapid changes in Polish export activities between 1992 and 2015. Figure 7.1 shows changes in the total value of export of goods during the period 1992–2015.

According to the OECD Bilateral Trade in Goods by Industry and End-use (BTDIxE), ISIC Rev.4 2016, from 1992 to 2015, the total value of export grew annually at about 11 percent, while the most abrupt increases are noted from 2002 onward, when the sudden 'take-off' in export value is observed. Along with significant shifts in value of total export, in Poland between 1992 and 2015, there are easily observable growing shares of ICT services and goods and high-tech goods exports in total value of Polish export (see Figure 7.2). In 1994, the share of ICT services in total Polish export accounted for about 15.5 percent, while in 2015 it grew to 33 percent. Regarding ICT goods and high-tech goods export share, they changed from 4.1 percent in 2000 to almost 8 percent in 2014, and from 3.5 percent

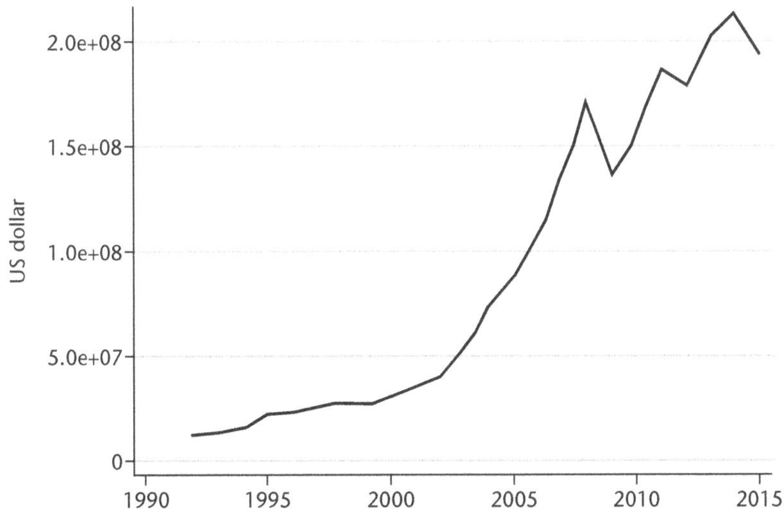

FIGURE 7.1 Export pattern in Poland, 1992–2015.

Source: Author's elaboration. Based on total trade in goods (values in thousands of USD) data derived from OECD Bilateral Trade in Goods by Industry and End-use (BTDIxE). ISIC Rev.4. 2016.

in 1992 to 8.7 percent in 2014 accordingly. Clearly, information and communication services export has been amongst the most dynamically expanding international trade component of Polish international trade, which – undeniably – paves the road for firms' internationalization and their greater engagement in global markets. It also shows that the ICT sector plays a major role in boosting domestic companies' internationalization, as it is highly globalized, and hence enhancing the globalization of other sectors. Undeniably, the growing role of the ICT sector is one of the most important features of modern economies, where producers of ICT goods and providers of ICT services are fast expanding worldwide; moreover, they seem to be pivotal for the intensification of the internationalization process.

The remainder of the chapter is organized as follows. The next section constitutes the contextual background and describes the main characteristics of the ICT sector in Poland. The subsequent section presents the case of Aiton Caldwell, a Polish company that succeeded in going global and internationalizing. The final section concludes.

The ICT sector in Poland

Central-Eastern European countries, as transition economies, are characterized by significant shifts toward investing in new technologies, and as claimed in the previous section, the latter is demonstrated through, *inter alia*, growing importance of the ICT sector, both in terms of number of enterprises as well as regarding the rapidly growing share of ICT services and ICT goods in the total value of Polish

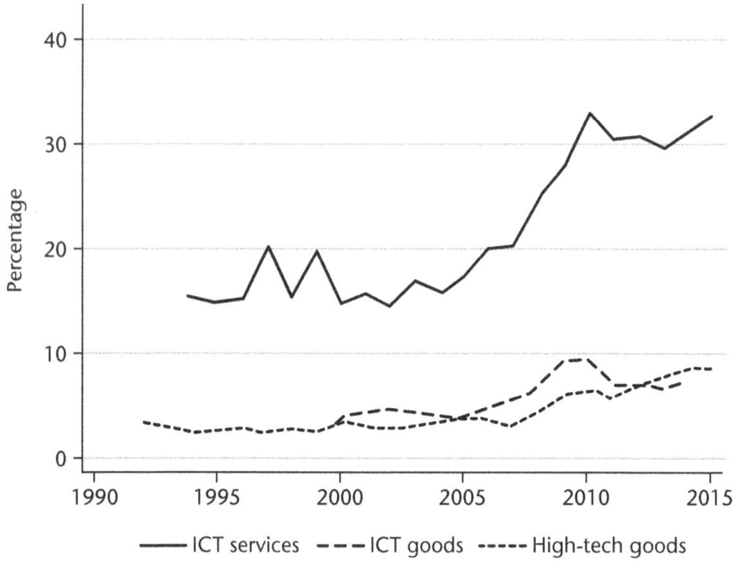

FIGURE 7.2 Export patterns of ICT services, ICT goods and high-tech goods (as % of total export value), Poland, 1992–2015.

Source: Author's elaboration. Based on data on ICT service export,[1] ICT goods export[2] and high-tech goods export[3] derived from World Development Indicators 2016.

Notes

1 ICT services export refers to information and communication technology service exports, including computer and communications services (telecommunications and postal and courier services) and information services (computer data and news-related service transactions). Original data source – International Monetary Fund, Balance of Payments Statistics Yearbook and data files.

2 ICT goods export refers to information and communication technology goods exports, including telecommunications, audio and video, computer and related equipment; electronic components; and other information and communication technology goods. Software is excluded. Original data source – United Nations Conference on Trade and Development's UNCTADstat database.

3 High-tech goods export refers to exports of products with high R&D intensity, such as in aerospace, computers, pharmaceuticals, scientific instruments and electrical machinery. Original data source – United Nations, Comtrade database.

exports. Since 2009, the development of the ICT sector in Poland may be recognized as being very dynamic and overwhelming. According to Eurostat data in Poland in 2010, the total number of ICT enterprises was 55,304, while in 2013 it grew to 70,084, which accounts for more than 26 percent growth in just a four-year period, and undeniably this rapid growth of number of ICT companies demonstrates the growing importance of this sector in the national economy.

According to the National Statistical Office (Rozkruta, 2013), in the period 2009–2012, the total number of ICT enterprises (with more than ten employees) grew by more than 25 percent (with ICT service companies by about 31 percent), and in 2012 it was 1,647. In 2014 (Rozkruta, 2015), the total number of ICT companies (with more than ten employees) grew to 2,146, which is more than a

6 percent increase if compared to the previous year; of which about 90 percent offered ICT services. Referring to revenues from sales, in 2014 companies from the ICT sector note almost 9 percent growth compared to 2011, and it accounted for 132 billion PLN; while the biggest share of revenues was generated by ICT telecommunication companies. Still during the period 2011–2013, the revenues obtained from both ICT manufacturing and ICT services enterprises systematically increased, but definitely the biggest share of these revenues was reported in ICT services – in 2014, it was at about 63.5 percent of total revenues generated by the ICT sector in Poland (Rozkruta, 2013).

Also, it is essential to underline that in Poland ICT service companies are these firms where a huge majority of R&D expenditures are incurred – according to National Statistical Office data, in each consecutive year it is about 90 percent of total R&D expenditures. The latter implies that the ICT sector is highly innovative, where new (or improved) products and services are introduced to the market most frequently according to the OEC report 'Telecommunications market in Poland 2015. Development forecasts for 2015–2020' (OEC, 2015); in forthcoming years, since 2016, the ICT market should continue to expand at about 4–5 percent annually, while the ICT service market, after a period of extremely dynamic growth, shall stabilize and increase (regarding its value) at about 1.8 percent annually. This further expansion of the ICT sector is to be mainly catalyzed by mobile telephone operators, whose total revenues comprise not only sales of services, but also hardware accompanying sales of services as well as sales of other electronic devices.

Compared to other Central-Eastern European countries, Poland's ICT market overall performs extraordinarily well. In 2016, in Deloitte's ranking '500 largest companies in Central Europe,' 42 firms are ICT companies, out of which 14 are enterprises operating in Poland.[4] Considering Deloitte's overall ranking, the Top 2016 covers 180 companies from Poland; while the majority of Polish ICT companies appear in the first half of the ranking. In 'Deloitte Technology Fast 50 Central Europe 2014' report, we read that 8 out of 20 companies in Central-Eastern Europe are from Poland, and 33 percent of the 50 fastest growing new technology companies originate from Poland; moreover, among the ten fastest growing small companies mentioned in 'Deloitte Technology Fast 50 Central Europe 2014' (the so-called rising stars), there are four enterprises from Poland.

All of this suggests that the Polish ICT sector is vitally developing, and its contribution to the national economy is increasing. The brief analysis of macroeconomic data for Poland (National Statistical Office, 2016; Eurostat, 2016) allows us to conclude that the ICT sector has good prospects for growth, and the overall contribution of this sector to the country's GDP may potentially increase to 10–13 percent before 2020, of which the decisive factors may be strong and growing internal demand for ICT products and services, rapidly growing number of ICT companies – both those offering ICT solutions for the domestic market and those which export – free diffusion of newly emerging ICT solutions, and highly skilled and educated ICT staff.

Arguably the process of ICT widespread adoption provides the perfect background for the 'born global' companies' emergence, profoundly transforming the business environment and bringing new challenges for companies to face to survive in global and heterogeneous markets. The unique role of ICT in leveraging 'born global' companies into global exposure provides them with a tool for effective and fast communication channels to operate with physically unreachable customers worldwide at almost zero cost (Cavusgil and Knight, 2009).

The concept of 'born global,' initially proposed by Rennie (1993), then developed by many scholars (e.g., Knight, 1996; Madsen and Servais, 1997; Moen, 2002; Sharma and Blomstermo, 2003; Jantunen *et al.*, 2008), has gained growing interest and attention worldwide for the last two decades. The term 'born global' generally refers to a company that wishes to operate on the global market from the very beginning of their economic activity. For instance, Moen *et al.* (2008) suggest that the true 'born global' company is a startup that does not operate first on the domestic market, but instead tends to conquer global markets from the very beginning. In Oviatt and McDougall (1994, 1997) or McDougall *et al.* (1994) we find arguments that 'born global' companies demonstrate tendencies to internationalize very early in their life cycle, and they claim that such companies may be also labeled as 'global startups' or 'instant internationals' (Fillis, 2001). Hence, it may be argued that 'born global' firms do not follow the traditional, incremental internationalization pattern, as suggested in several studies in the area (e.g., Andersen, 1993; Gankema *et al.*, 2000; Lu and Beamish, 2001; Ruzzier *et al.*, 2006; Johanson and Vahlne, 2009), but rather leapfrog several steps along the internationalization path and are globally exposed from the first day of their inception. The 'born global' firms are simply 'born' to operate both on national and on external markets, hence 'traditional' stages models of internationalization demonstrate little relevance in this case.

Obviously enough, the emergence of 'born global' companies is to a large extent preconditioned by broad adoption of new technologies, which effectively constitute a prerequisite, on one hand, but on the other – they simply enable and foster running a business as a globally exposed firm. Moreover, as underlined in multiple studies, 'born globals' are predominantly small 'technology-based' firms (see Acs and Audretsch, 1990; Colombo *et al.*, 2004; Colombo and Grilli, 2010), offering to the public high-tech solutions instead of producing commodities. Additionally, 'born global' companies show relatively little risk aversion; by definition, they aggressively compete on global markets and demonstrate high propensity to introduce leading edge innovations (Knight and Cavusgil, 2004).

The case of Aiton Caldwell[5]

As claimed in the previous section, the Polish economy has made great progress in the last two decades in terms of economic, institutional or educational performers. Also in terms of technology (digital) readiness, Poland has made great progress in the last decade (years 2000–2015). Fast diffusion on new information and telecommunication technologies among society members, and their adoption on educational and institutional levels, have created a solid base for demand creation for ICT services and products. New technologies are in common use in a multitude of spheres of life, by a great majority of individuals. Polish society adopts and uses ICT innovation for different purposes, especially education, running business, new markets search, marketing, logistics and many others. In the last few years, Poland has also 'given birth' to multiple ICT companies, which today successfully operate worldwide. Aiton Caldwell is recognized as such a highly innovative company, mainly operating on the cloud computing market. It is treated as one of the most successful Polish companies operating on the ICT market. The cloud computing market is one of the most dynamically developing markets in Poland. In 2013, Aiton Caldwell controlled more than 40 percent of the VoIP Polish market. In December 2011, the company debuted at the *NewConnect* market, and since then it has been listed on the stock exchange.

According to the BSA Global Cloud Computing Scorecard, in 2013, Poland was ranked eleventh, out of 24 countries, which has essential influence on the development of cloud computing technologies. Importantly, these 24 countries account for about 80 percent of total resources in the field of information and communication technologies. In the 2016 BSA Global Cloud Computing Scorecard ranking, Poland was classified as Top 10 in terms of improving its policy toward creating a friendly environment for cloud computing development.

Aiton Caldwell supplies world markets with high-tech platforms operating within the assumed model of computing; it successfully operates on Romanian and United States markets, where it offers to the public a broad array of products and services. Its major target group is still small and medium-sized enterprises, but also individual clients. For small and medium-sized enterprises and individual clients they mainly offer SaaS – Software as a Service (since 2006); while for foreign clients (mainly companies), PaaS – Platform as a Service. Aiton Caldwell may also be claimed as one of the most excellent examples of Polish companies which have successfully managed to internationalize. Arguably, Aiton Caldwell may be labeled as a 'born global,' as it did not follow the incremental internationalization pattern, but rather was intended to operate on global markets from its inception; and from that perspective this company is perceived as 'winning the game.'

From its very inception, Aiton Caldwell put special emphasis on investing in development of human capital; they also underline that people and their knowledge and skills are the most valuable capital from the company's long-term development strategy. By convention, the 'company's working team' consists of highly qualified specialists from different fields, *inter alia*, telecommunication engineering, marketing and sales of client support. The company also looks to cooperate with other companies, as well as research institutes, academics and organizations that provide support for entrepreneurs, i.e., Pomerania Employers, Pomerania Business Club, Pomerania Regional Business Chamber, National Electronics and Telecommunication Business Chamber.

Aiton Caldwell originates from Datera SA – the ICT company that was set up in 2003 in Gdańsk, by two graduates from Gdańsk University of Technology. For the next few years, the company's owners gained a growing share of the Polish ICT company; and in 2008 they decided to 'create' a new company – Aiton Caldwell (formerly named FreecoNet). The newly born company became an independent entity, and started to offer highly innovative ICT-based solutions, predominantly cloud computing services, to companies from the small and medium-sized sector, as well as for individual clients.

On the domestic market, for small and medium-sized enterprises and individuals they offer the product named SaaS – Software as a Service (since 2006); while for foreign partners, they offer PaaS – Platform as a Service. The SaaS as the cloud service is aimed to provide business and individual clients with high-quality telecommunication services, which may be accessed through the Internet network. The SaaS has several unique functionalities, which are easily and relatively cheaply acquirable without the necessity of having certain equipment or software installed on a personal computer. The major advantage of SaaS offered by Aiton Caldwell is that this type of service is fully hosted by the provider; and so the client does not need to bother about its functioning and work environment (the provider, Aiton Caldwell, takes care of all the issues associated with service, management, updating or any other specific technical support issues).

Another important advantage of the SaaS service is that the client pays exclusively for the actual use of the service; and thus no pre-payments are charged. Aiton Caldwell sells the SaaS service model through three various business lines: FreecoNet (VoIP telephony with wide range of added services for individual users and small-sized businesses allowing for reducing call costs), Vanberg Systems (Vanberg Systems Comprehensive is a hosted service for SMEs; the system is recognized as a telecommunication operator, telephone exchange system and supplier of office devices) and Smarto (integrated hosted service supporting management of SMEs; offers newly emerging companies wishing to facilitate and support their communication channels; allowing for effective cost reduction and optimization of business processes).[6] The other service offered by Aiton Caldwell is PaaS (Platform as a Service) – offering access to the cloud telecommunication platform, and this is mainly reserved for the firm's foreign partners. The cloud telecommunication platform provides ready-to-use solutions, which are fully customized and adjusted to clients' unique requirements and necessities. This type of the business model is aimed to provide a field of communication among business partners; however, this form of service requires from each partner his own hard infrastructure.

During the initial phase of internationalization, Aiton Caldwell was, however, operating mainly on the domestic market. The company was rapidly gaining the leading position on the Polish ICT market, which may be reflected not only by growing market shares and profits, but also by multiple awards and honors that the company was granted in 2007 and 2008. These were: Pomeranian Innovation Leader 2007, Innovation of the Year 2007, Cent for Future 2007, VoIP Leader 2008 and Kamerton Innovation 2008. This contributed significantly to the company's position on the Polish market, and they started thinking about extending their offer – both in terms of products and services sold, but also in terms of gaining new markets. The next three years of dynamic market expansion resulted in further awards and nominations. These were: Product of the Year 2010 – Readers' Choice of Networld – II place, Company with Future 2010 – nomination in the competition organized by Pomeranian Chamber of Craft SME, Regional Innovativeness and Development Leader 2010, Marketing Director of the Year 2010, Top Manager 2010 – nomination, The Most Promising Company of 2010 – nomination, Economic Griffin 2011 – nominee, A Responsible Company in Business 2011, Silver Innovations Medal 2011 – for the SMARTO brand, and Regional Leader of Innovativeness and Development 2011 – category of 'Innovative Company.' Next in 2012, Aiton Caldwell won a 'double prize' under the 'Company with the Future (Firma z Przyszłością)' competition, where they were awarded the first (main) prize, and – also in 2012 – the company was awarded 'Regional Leader in Innovations and Development', reflecting their efforts to boost national innovativeness, and thus contributing effectively to social and economic national development.

However, since the very beginning Aiton Caldwell's priority was gaining foreign partners and clients; and thus they permanently seek internationalization opportunities as they open new pathways for business development and product improvements. In 2012, the company signed two strategic partner agreements which allowed them to go abroad and effectively enter Romanian and United States ICT markets. In Romania, Aiton Caldwell has signed a business agreement with Media SAT, the telecommunication company, which gave birth to Alonia Business – the Aiton Caldwell branch targeting mainly small and medium-sized enterprises. Alonia Business offers high-quality and innovative solutions; operating as a platform for services it covers a wide range of services, like: Alonia Messenger – easing interpersonal communication; PC to PC free talks with anybody regardless of the place of residence; Video Telephones; and Alonia Services on VoIP, allowing for significant communication cost reduction. Also in 2012, Aiton Caldwell signed a business agreement with an American partner, which resulted in the emergence of SYNNEX CLOUDSolv SOHO VoIP – the Aiton Caldwell branch operating on the US market and offering the SaaS technology for business clients. SYNNEX CLOUDSolv SOHO VoIP is the solution offered to small and medium-sized enterprises; and by convention it works as a 'smart business phone service' using the VoIP solutions.

How Aiton Caldwell went global

The process of internationalization may bring companies big benefits, which may be identified as, for instance, access to foreign markets, creating new demand for the company's products, increasing the consumer base, financial profits generation, access to new technologies and innovation, risk sharing with external partner(s), new brands/products/services creation, growth in competitive power, offset in seasonal market fluctuation – to list just a few. Theoretically, companies want to internationalize for four major reasons: 'resource seeking,' 'market seeking,' 'efficiency seeking' and 'strategic asset seeking' (Dunning, 1998). Companies that enter foreign markets can act in different ways, which – in effect – leads to acquiring certain goals. The simplest way to go abroad is to start exporting products and services. It is relatively easy; however, it requires certain financial resources towards, for example, marketing actions. An alternative way to internationalize is to develop a joint venture, in order to sell the products and services through a company operating in a similar business, or to just sell a license to the company abroad and collect royalties. A similar way to internationalize is to create a contract with a foreign company to do the business for a certain percentage of sales. This is rather simple, but it does require deep research to find an appropriate partner. The last possible way to start operating abroad is to open an overseas office or subsidiary company.

Aiton Caldwell, once grounded in its position on the Polish ICT market, started to consider going abroad to gain some external markets. First, three different European economies were taken into consideration; those were: Hungary, Romania and Ukraine. After running thorough research on each market, which consisted of estimating each country's potential demand for products offered by Aiton Caldwell, country-wise legal regulations and government policies for foreign investors, they finally decided to choose Romania. The preparation phase to take the first step along the internationalization pattern consisted of ensuring accuracy for the target market, in order to minimize the risk of failure. Aiton Caldwell extensively studied the Romanian telecommunication market, which included identification of the potential demand, choosing the most adequate marketing actions and a profound study of the legal environment and regulations when entering the national ICT market. Bearing in mind Aiton Caldwell's major objectives, the seminal part of the analysis included a detailed study of the Romanian telecommunication/ICT companies which were potential competitors on the Romanian domestic market. After gathering all the necessary information, they classified, from the biggest to the smallest, all ICT companies regarding their market strength and position with respect to achieved revenues. In the next step, Aiton Caldwell 'cut off' four of the biggest Romanian ICT companies (referring to their decelerated revenues in the previous year). Next, they 'cut off' all ICT companies whose total annual revenue was below 1.5 million euro; hence the second 'cut' resulted in elimination of the smallest Romanian ICT companies.

Finally, they reached the target segment of medium-sized (medium-class) telecom companies, among which Aiton Caldwell started to seek its business partner. Initially, Aiton Caldwell wanted to adopt the joint venture scheme of internationalization, but finally they agreed on the revenue share model. The idea of the 'revenue share model' of companies' cooperation consists of sharing profits – but also losses – between companies in an agreed alliance. Finally, Aiton Caldwell decided to cooperate with one Romanian ICT company – Media SAT; and to finalize and prepare the final alliance agreement, both companies went for a four-month workshop, where the final version of the inter-company agreement was established. Specifically, they agreed on the following issues: business offer of products and services; target clients; services which were to be provided by Aiton Caldwell to Media SAT and reversely; detailed cooperation conditions and business plan; user's panel look(s); adjustment to Romanian legal conditions; price model (acceptable for an 'average Romanian'); provided services for clients; and monitoring.

Based on these, it is highly justified to state that Aiton Caldwell is an international company, enjoying a strong global position. They have gained such success within a few years of dynamic development and investment, mostly in human capital. It is an example of great success!

Today, in 2016, Aiton Caldwell is successfully cooperating with two external business partners. One of them is located in the United States of America and the second one in Romania. So far the cooperation, although not easy, has resulted in the creation of two new products which are sold exclusively abroad. Now, Aiton Caldwell is seeking business partners to enter Ukrainian, Hungarian, Czech and Irish markets.

On June 2, 2014, Aiton Caldwell successfully finalized the merger with Datera SA. Since then, the company has been offering to the public two trademarks – FNC (formerly FreecoNet), which mainly provides IT services for microforms, and Datera. As a strategic goal, both companies plan to achieve about 50–60 million PLN annually, which would allow them to leave the New Connect market, and move to the major Warsaw Stock Exchange.

Conclusions

The main aim of this chapter was to provide descriptive evidence on the state of development of the Polish ICT market and in this context to present, as a case study, the internationalization path of Aiton Caldwell. First, we briefly discussed the state of development of the Polish national economy, putting special emphasis on the entrepreneurial environment on the domestic market. We may conclude that for the last few decades the Polish economy has significantly moved toward a highly developed and stable economic system, gradually gaining a higher position in competitiveness rankings, showing relatively little vulnerability to external negative shocks, which is mainly due to sound monetary and fiscal policy, a well-established and governed banking sector, and – above all – long-term economic growth and development-oriented state policies. We may also conclude that, with respect to growing volumes on export, the Polish economy performs well, which suggests that Polish companies are undergoing an intensive internationalization process. Moreover, we have shown that the Polish ICT market is growing rapidly, and Polish ICT companies are gaining a leading position among other companies in CEE countries. Finally, the presented case of Aiton Caldwell, as an example of an ICT company that has managed to internationalize rapidly, perfectly reflects the expansion of the Polish ICT sector.

This work has demonstrated several crucial aspects of entrepreneurship development in Poland. First, we have learnt that, for the last three decades, Polish 'entrepreneurial sectors' have been gradually opening up to world markets, giving nationally based companies new opportunities in doing business, but also exposing them to global competition. The case discussed here of one of the most dynamically developing Polish ICT companies, Aiton Caldwell, has shown that the 'born-global-type' companies are of growing importance both for Polish national markets, but mostly from the point of view of their 'going abroad' strategies. The latter is – to a large extent – preconditioned and facilitated by effective market liberalization allowing for new businesses to open and to start trading on foreign markets.

Moreover, the rapid development of new information and communication technologies has, first, enhanced intensive ICT trade flows, and second, allowed for the setting up of new business offering various types of goods and services. Fast diffusion of new information and communication technologies has provided a solid background for starting totally new companies, offering to the public high-quality and competitive goods and services. ICT fostered the emergence of a totally new type of business – born global companies – which expansively gain new markets. Aiton Caldwell is an excellent example of such an 'ICT-enhanced' company, which in a short time period has managed to internationalize and hence open new opportunity windows for Polish entrepreneurship.

Notes

1 This research has been supported by project no. 2015/19/B/HS4/03220, admitted by the National Science Centre, Poland.
2 Author's calculation based on data derived from World Development Indicators 2016.
3 Author's calculation based on data derived from World Development Indicators 2016.
4 Orange Polska (forty-second place in ranking), Cyfrowy Polsat, Assecco, AB, Polkomotel, T-Mobile Polska, Samsung Electronics Polska, P4, Action, LG Electronics Mława, LG Electronics Wrocław, ABC Data, Flextronics International Poland, Komputronic.
5 Most of the information and materials on Aiton Caldwell were gathered during the realization of INNOCASE project no. 2012-1-PL1-LEO05-27456, which has been funded with support from the European Commission under the Lifelong Learning Programme (based on an interview with Jan Wyrwiński – Chairman of the Board at Aiton Caldwell), and after summarized in the final report of the project realization. The remaining information was exclusively gathered from freely available Internet sources.
6 Source: www.aitoncaldwell.pl/en/products/group (accessed September 2013).

References

Acs, Z.J. and Audretsch, D.B., 1990, *Innovation and Small Firms*, Cambridge: MIT Press.

Andersen, O., 1993, 'On the internationalization process of firms: A critical analysis,' *Journal of International Business Studies*, 24 (2), pp. 209–231.

Bresnahan, T.F. and Trajtenberg, M., 1995, 'General purpose technologies: Engines of growth?,' *Journal of Econometrics*, 65 (1), pp. 83–108.

Cavusgil, S.T. and Knight, G., 2009, *Born Global Firms: A New International Enterprise*, New York: Business Expert Press.

Colombo, M.G. and Grilli, L., 2010, 'On growth drivers of high-tech start-ups: Exploring the role of founders' human capital and venture capital,' *Journal of Business Venturing*, 25 (6), pp. 610–626.

Colombo, M.G., Delmastro, M. and Grilli, L., 2004, 'Entrepreneurs' human capital and the start-up size of new technology-based firms,' *International Journal of Industrial Organization*, 22 (8), pp. 1183–1211.

Deloitte, 2014, *Deloitte Technology Fast 50 Central Europe 2014*. Deloitte Central Europe.

Deloitte, 2016, Global Manufacturing Competitiveness Index. Available at www2.deloitte.com/content/dam/Deloitte/global/Documents/Manufacturing/gx-global-mfg-competitiveness-index-2016.pdf. Accessed December 18, 2017.

Dunning, J.H., 1998, 'The eclectic paradigm of international production – a restatement and some possible extensions,' *Journal of International Business Studies*, 19 (1), pp. 1–31.

Ernst & Young, 2012, European Attractiveness Survey. Available at www.ey.com/Publication/vwLUAssets/European-Attractiveness-Survey-2013/$FILE/European-Attractiveness-Survey-2013.pdf. Accessed December 18, 2017.

Eurostat, 2016, General and Regional Statistics. Available at http://ec.europa.eu/eurostat/data/browse-statistics-by-theme. Accessed December 18, 2017.

Fillis, I., 2001, 'Small firm internationalisation: An investigative survey and future research directions,' *Management Decision*, 39 (9), pp. 767–783.

Gankema, H.G., Snuif, H.R. and Zwart, P.S., 2000, 'The internationalization process of small and medium-sized enterprises: An evaluation of stage theory,' *Journal of Small Business Management*, 38 (4), pp. 15–27.

ITU, 2015, ITU ICT Eye – ICT Statistics, International Telecommunication Union 2015. Available at www.itu.int/en/ITU-D/Statistics/Pages/stat/default.aspx. Accessed December 3, 2015.

Jantunen, A., Nummela, N., Puumalainen, K. and Saarenketo, S., 2008, 'Strategic orientations of born globals: Do they really matter?,' *Journal of World Business*, 43 (2), pp. 158–170.

Johanson, J. and Vahlne, J.E., 2009, 'The Uppsala internationalization process model revisited: From liability of foreignness to liability of outsidership,' *Journal of International Business Studies*, 40 (9), pp. 1411–1431.

Knight, G., 1996, *Born Global. Wiley International Encyclopedia of Marketing*, Hoboken, NJ: John Wiley & Sons.

Knight, G.A. and Cavusgil, S.T., 2004, 'Innovation, organizational capabilities, and the born-global firm,' *Journal of International Business Studies*, 35 (2), pp. 124–141.

Kshetri, N., 2014, *Global Entrepreneurship: Environment and Strategy*, London: Routledge.

Lechman, E., 2014, 'Changing patterns in the export of goods versus international competitiveness. A comparative analysis for Central-East European countries in the period 2000–2011,' *Comparative Economic Research*, 17 (2), pp. 61–77.

Lu, J.W. and Beamish, P.W., 2001, 'The internationalization and performance of SMEs,' *Strategic Management Journal*, 22 (6–7), pp. 565–586.

Madsen, T.K. and Servais, P., 1997, 'The internationalization of born globals: An evolutionary process?,' *International Business Review*, 6 (6), pp. 561–583.

McDougall, P.P., Shane, S. and Oviatt, B.M., 1994, 'Explaining the formation of international new ventures: The limits of theories from international business research,' *Journal of Business Venturing*, 9 (6), pp. 469–487.

Moen, Ø., 2002, 'The born globals: A new generation of small European exporters,' *International Marketing Review*, 19 (2), pp. 156–175.

Moen, Ø., Sørheim, R. and Erikson, T., 2008, 'Born global firms and informal investors: Examining investor characteristics,' *Journal of Small Business Management*, 46 (4), pp. 536–549.

National Statistical Office, 2016, Basic data. Available at http://stat.gov.pl/en/basic-data/. Accessed December 18, 2017.

OEC (Office of Electronic Communication), 2016, 'Report on the telecommunications market in Poland in 2015,' Warsaw: Office of Electronic Communication. Available at https://en.uke.gov.pl/files/?id_plik=23825. Accessed August 27, 2016.

Onetti, A., Zucchella, A., Jones, M.V. and McDougall-Covin, P.P., 2012, 'Internationalization, innovation and entrepreneurship: Business models for new technology-based firms,' *Journal of Management and Governance*, 16 (3), pp. 337–368.

Oviatt, B.M. and McDougall, P.P., 1994, 'Toward a theory of international new ventures,' *Journal of International Business Studies*, 25 (1), pp. 45–64.

Oviatt, B.M. and McDougall, P.P., 1997, 'Challenges for internationalization process theory: The case of international new ventures,' *Management International Review*, 37 (2), pp. 85–99.

Rao, P.M., 2001, 'The ICT revolution, internationalization of technological activity, and the emerging economies: Implications for global marketing,' *International Business Review*, 10 (5), pp. 571–596.

Rennie, M.W., 1993, 'Born global,' *The McKinsey Quarterly*, 4, pp. 45–52.

Rozkruta, D. ed., 2013, *Information Society in Poland. Results of Statistical Survey in Years 2009–2013*, Warsaw: Główny Urząd Statystyczny.

Rozkruta, D. ed., 2015, *Information Society in Poland. Results of Statistical Survey in Years 2010–2015*, Warsaw: Główny Urząd Statystyczny.

Ruzzier, M., Hisrich, R.D. and Antoncic, B., 2006, 'SME internationalization research: Past, present, and future,' *Journal of Small Business and Enterprise Development*, 13 (4), pp. 476–497.

Sharma, D.D. and Blomstermo, A., 2003, 'The internationalization process of born globals: A network view,' *International Business Review*, 12 (6), pp. 739–753.

Taylor, M. and Jack, R., 2012, 'Understanding the pace, scale and pattern of firm internationalization: An extension of the born global concept,' *International Small Business Journal*, 31 (6), pp. 701–721.

World Bank, 2013, *Doing Business 2013: Smarter Regulations for Small and Medium-Size Enterprises*, Washington, DC: World Bank.

Zapletalová, Š., 2015, 'Models of Czech companies' internationalization,' *Journal of International Entrepreneurship*, 13 (2), pp. 153–168.

8

ENTREPRENEURSHIP DEVELOPMENT AND INTERNATIONALIZATION IN SERBIA

A case study of ComTrade and Nordeus

Sanja Marinković, Jovana Rakićević, Milica Jovanović and Jasna Petković

Introduction

The Republic of Serbia is a country in South-Eastern Europe, covering an area of 88,361 km^2 with 7.2 million inhabitants. With its excellent geographical location, at the crossroads of Central and South-Eastern Europe, Serbia is also a member of the UN, OSCE, Organization of the Black Sea Economic Cooperation, CEFTA and other organizations. As an acceding country, Serbia is currently negotiating its accession to the EU. However, comparative research and official data on competitiveness and entrepreneurship ranked Serbia very low when compared to both EU countries and countries in the ex-Yugoslavia region.

The position of Serbia on the list of Global Competitiveness Index (GCI), for example, is gradually declining (Zdravkovic, 2011). In comparison to other former Yugoslavian republics, Serbia has one of the lowest scores for the year 2016, ranking at place 94. The only country with a lower score is Bosnia and Herzegovina, with 3.7 and place 111 in the Global Competitiveness Report. The countries that ranked better are Croatia (77), Montenegro (70) and FYR of Macedonia (60), while the best ranked was Slovenia (59). Unfortunately, rankings of Serbia by other indexes are also not very encouraging. For example, according to GEI, the Global Entrepreneurship Index (previously known as the Global Entrepreneurship and Development Index), Serbia ranks at place 74 amongst 132 countries around the world. This value is again the second lowest in the region, being ahead of only Bosnia and Herzegovina (ranked 82). Furthermore, according to the Doing Business (DB) ranking, Serbia is ranked as the fifty-ninth country, amongst 190 economies worldwide, while the best country in the region is FYR of Macedonia, being in twelfth place. The results for the region, according to all three methodologies, are given in Table 8.1.

Indicators of vertical technology transfer position Serbia among the countries with the lowest investment in R&D, with a declining trend of patent and trademark

TABLE 8.1 Rankings of region countries according to the Global Competitiveness Index (GCI), the Global Entrepreneurship Index (GEI) and the Doing Business Index (DB) methodologies in 2016

Country	*GCI rank (score)*	*GEI rank (score)*	*DB rank (score)*
Serbia	94 (3.9)	74 (30.9)	59 (68.41)
Bosnia and Herzegovina	111 (3.7)	82 (28.6)	79 (63.71)
Croatia	77 (4.1)	51 (39.9)	40 (72.71)
FYR of Macedonia	60 (4.3)	57 (36.6)	12 (80.18)
Montenegro	70 (4.2)	54 (37.5)	49 (71.85)
Slovenia	59 (4.3)	31 (50.4)	29 (75.62)

Sources: GCR (2016); GEDI (2016); Doing Business (2016).

applications (Levi Jaksic *et al.*, 2014b). The causes of such a state could be traced to the slow and inefficient economic development, incomplete privatization of the public economy sector, etc. Such indicators are very much grounded in the fact that Serbia and Yugoslavia underwent a years-long isolation from the European and world economic trends, during the Yugoslav wars. Such isolation has also left a trace in exporting patterns of Serbia. The data on the export sector presented in Table 8.2 show that export mainly revolves around traditional production industries and the food industry.

The services sector in Serbia is primarily oriented towards local market needs. However, the software industry is an exception. According to recent years' data, software export reached the value of agricultural export. Currently, around 180 companies export software from Serbia and they employ around 5,500 people.

The IT industry and software exports are seen as having great potential and as a developmental opportunity for Serbia. Examples of successful companies in the field point to excellent knowledge and personal enthusiasm. It is highly important that strategies and development plans be defined in this area, and that rules of doing business are established with the help and support of the state.

TABLE 8.2 Exports structure by product categories in Serbia in 2015

Product category	*Export (in 000 USD)*
Road vehicles and ACV vehicles	1,569,097.90
Electrical machines and appliances	1,031,381.00
Fruit and vegetables	763,982.00
Grain and grain-based products	638,068.90
Non-magnetic metals	563,097.80
Metal products	532,655.50
Clothing	527,547.70
Iron and steel	488,872.60

Source: Statistical Yearbook of the Republic of Serbia (2016).

TABLE 8.3 Value of software export from Serbia in millions USD

Year	*2010*	*2011*	*2012*	*2013*	*2014*	*2015*
Export value *(mil. USD)*	139	181	242	332	354	437

Source: World Bank (2016).

In the contemporary business environment, internationalization is considered an important factor for achieving sustainable competitiveness at different levels in the economy. The Republic of Serbia has a good geographical position and cooperation with the neighbouring countries, but the economy of Serbia, which has seen gradual improvement in some ways, cannot be positively evaluated in recent years. As presented above, however, the entrepreneurship and technology ecosystem of Serbia is primarily oriented towards the local market, with low rank according to the recent Global Competitiveness Index results. In such an environment, the ICT sector is an exception, with significant achievements of companies that have found their own path to international markets. Today, ICT is one of the most productive and export-oriented industries in Serbia. The good practices from the ICT sector with two case studies of Serbian international companies will be analysed to recognize the success factors and entrepreneurial perspectives in this field. Prior to turning to the case study, however, we will provide some further information related to the development of entrepreneurship and their internationalization in Serbia.

Entrepreneurship and internationalization perspectives in Serbia

General development patterns

International business prospects for Serbian companies are directly caused by the country's economy. According to recent studies, Serbian companies often face problems such as lack of funds for export activities (Zdravkovic, 2011; Bobera *et al.*, 2014), lack of trained and highly skilled labour, lack of knowledge of foreign markets and lack of information (Zdravkovic, 2011). Further challenges include VAT on invoiced instead of realized values and taxes, and contributions on salaries (Bobera *et al.*, 2014), and poor regulatory, administrative and development policies and procedures (Radovic-Markovic, 2014; Nikolic *et al.*, 2015; Popovic *et al.*, 2016). Despite a lack of more substantial government incentives, some companies still manage to successfully internationalize driven by the evolutionary approach to internationalization, pragmatic implementation of rules, using appropriate strategies and high enthusiasm of managers (Djordjevic *et al.*, 2012).

Of course, there is some institutional support available to address the challenges mentioned above. The Serbian Chamber of Commerce with its Board of International Economic Relations supports Serbian companies on their way towards international markets. The organization provides information on business operations in a given country, provides support to Serbian companies with product placement, internationalization of business activities, defining the necessary procedures in entering the markets of particular countries and finding suitable partners. In 2016, the Development Agency of Serbia published a public invitation to tender for awarding grants through the program of support to the internationalization of commercial companies, entrepreneurs and clusters in 2016. Enterprise Europe Network (EEN) Serbia helps SMEs and all institutions (particularly clusters) who have the potential to cooperate with companies from the EEN outside of Serbia, gives them information about intellectual property protection, technological audit (technology review) or business analysis, provides and support in taking part in EU projects, etc. Still, companies in Serbia, particularly SMEs, need more assistance, training and consultancy services for managers and owners to develop more nuanced models for entering foreign markets.

Education in entrepreneurship

Education in the field of entrepreneurship in Serbia is a very popular topic in both academic and non-academic circles. However, its implementation, the content of educational programs and the results in practice are still below expected. For instance, a survey conducted by Levi Jaksic *et al.* (2014a) found that professors in the field of technology and innovation management (TIM) in Serbia perceived entrepreneurship as one of the most critical knowledge areas for companies. Statistical analysis of their response showed that this is the best-covered area in curricula (Levi Jaksic *et al.*, 2014a). Also, the survey revealed that there is a significant disparity between the opinions of professors and practitioners on the importance of the observed TIM knowledge areas. Here, practitioners often do not see entrepreneurial education as being vital for their TIM activities. Instead, they tend to place greater emphasis on the financial aspects of TIM, IT and adaptation of technology for business.

Overall, we can conclude that, on average, managers of Serbian companies are more focused on operational efficiency than innovations. On the other hand, informal education in entrepreneurship became increasingly popular in Serbia in recent years, through the activities of technology parks, hubs and startup support centres. Another study conducted in the same year in Serbia showed that informal education had become the dominant educational factor for entrepreneurial success, as results showed a positive correlation between this form of education and entrepreneurial knowledge, skills and attitudes (Milosavljevic and Benkovic, 2014). All of the aforementioned findings confirm that there is a need to rethink educational programs in entrepreneurship to prepare managers for local and international markets.

ICT and internationalization

When it comes to the ICT sector, the primary "push" factor of ICT internalization is that the Serbian market is relatively small for the potential of local ICT companies.

In recent years, the ICT sector in Serbia has been one of the fastest growing industries, and it has the potential for an even stronger growth. In 2013, the Serbian ICT industry ranked fortieth globally regarding the value of exported software. This positioned ICT as one of the most successful and export-oriented industries in Serbia. The sector's export is on the constant rise, especially export of computer and information services, i.e. software development. In 2008, the value of exported services amounted to €96 million. By 2013, it reached €265 million, which is a remarkable 165 per cent increase. The Serbian IT market was worth around €410 million in 2013, which is still far less than before the global financial crisis outbreak in 2008, when it was worth €550 million. The potential for reaching and exceeding that result is evident (SIEPA, 2015). This particularly refers to ICT services.

The potential for the development of technology entrepreneurship in Serbia has been reflected in the study by Rakićević *et al.* (2016), who use the originally designed index of Technology Entrepreneurship Development Potential (TED-pot). The index includes four World Bank indicators grouped into two pillars – ICT potential (ICT goods and ICT service exports) and entrepreneurial potential (the number of startup procedures and the time needed to start a business). The index was applied on six ex-Yugoslav countries and the EU for the time period 2009–2014. The study confirmed that Serbia's potential lies in the entrepreneurial IT sector since Serbia was ranked second according to the TED-pot values, just behind the EU average. Nonetheless, this does not make up for a significant setback of Serbia in comparison to developed European countries in this sector.

To further improve this result, the state has to invest in research and development and science, which at this point stands at 0.3 per cent of GDP (the EU average is around 2 per cent). Serbia, with its remarkable results in ICT exports, is currently investing only €60 per capita into the development of this industry, which is far less than, for example, Croatia (€200). The EU average is €800 (SIEPA, 2015). Since ICT is recognized as a priority sector by the government, greater support to this sector is expected in the following years, especially since it gives strong results in attracting investors and increasing employment.

On the other side, internationalization "pull" factors are coming from developed countries as they recognize the knowledge and enthusiasm of Serbian engineers. They are competent in a broad range of technologies and have extensive expertise in developing front-end, back-end and middle-ware components, but are also proficient in understanding client requirements and creating tailored software and systems solutions (SIEPA, 2012). Many leading global ICT companies have set up their businesses in Serbia: Cisco Systems, Motorola, Ericsson, Oracle, Hewlett Packard, SAP, IBM, Siemens, Intel, Telenor and Microsoft. IT companies from Serbia are present on the global market, mainly in the outsourcing of software development, testing software and designing websites, and providing solutions in the embedded industry. The software export share in GDP has been on the rise over the years, from 0.3 per cent in 2008 to 1 per cent in 2013 (Matijevic and Solaja, 2015). Individual initiatives, entrepreneurship and innovation of Serbian engineers resulted in a number of successful projects of IT companies.

To further develop the ICT potential, more substantial investments in education are required, including constant improvement and adjustment of the educational system to market needs. Appropriate investment in the education of IT experts, focus on IT management and entrepreneurship could lead to positioning the export of computer services and software as the most significant export economic activity of Serbia.

We can expect more government initiatives and influence on the IT market and the IT sector since these are investments in technologies which require investing in education rather than infrastructure. Most IT graduates in Serbia find employment upon graduation, with a trend of more than 1,000 new employees per year (Matijevic and Solaja, 2015). The number of ICT companies increases by 20 per cent each year (Depalov *et al.*, 2013). The success of domestic companies on the international market and employment opportunities are a crucial motivation factor resulting in a growing interest of Serbian students for ICT programs and specializations. The following case studies will support the aforesaid. In collecting the data for ComTrade and Nordeus, we used multiple sources of evidence: secondary data from available documents, web presentations and published articles and interviews with general managers. We also interviewed employees from both companies to clarify the data collected.

Case studies of ComTrade Group and Nordeus

Internationalization of ComTrade Group

The founder of ComTrade Group, Mr. Veselin Jevrosimovic, represented Serbia in athletics and was the university league champion in pole vaulting. He graduated in Management at the University of Florida and was in the management of the world's largest IT equipment distributor for five years. Upon selling his shares, he founded the ComTrade Group in 1996. Today, this is one of the leading ICT companies in South-Eastern Europe. Their portfolio of products and services is diversified and includes the development and implementation of complete ICT solutions, the distribution of ICT equipment, and the production and distribution of ComTrade computers and other brands of electronic devices. One of the products is SCOM technology for monitoring customers and their IT systems. Citrix Company from Silicon Valley bought the licence for using this technology. Another product is TESLA tablet, which is widely accepted in Serbian schools as an educational tool.

ComTrade is the largest exporter of software in Serbia present on the markets of Western Europe, the USA and the Middle East. Since the crisis in 2008 to date, the Serbian and the regional IT market marked a constant decline of around 45 per cent in comparison to 2008. However, ComTrade had the same success in 2011 as in 2008, meaning that as a company they grew much faster in crisis conditions than the declining market. Cooperation with partners from international environments significantly contributed to their success. In March 2008, ComTrade Group acquired Hermes SoftLab, which expanded the potential of ComTrade Group as the largest IT conglomerate in South-Eastern Europe. The new company was able to offer an even wider range of ICT solutions and services in 14 countries over three continents, marking the continuation of its development on a global scale (SIEPA, 2012).

In 2011, the company signed a multimillion-dollar contract with the American company Bally Technologies, a leading company in the field of advanced devices and systems for games of chance, with the stock market value of $1.82 billion. This deal meant hiring ComTrade's experts to "move" standard slot machine games to an online environment. They are one of the few companies in Eastern Europe and among a few in Western Europe with this type of licence. They currently operate in over 40 countries, including Benelux, where they sell software solutions. Also, in February 2012, ComTrade was awarded best IT company in SEE on the fourth traditional award ceremony of DISTREE-EMEA (for best IT companies in Europe, the Middle East and Africa).

Comprised of 22 enterprises that operate in 11 countries across Europe and North America, ComTrade has a well-established reputation as a reliable partner to both small and big companies. The Company's slogan is "Simplify Technology – Reduce Business Complexity with ComTrade". Innovative information technology solutions and services have contributed to a comprehensive and diverse portfolio with more than 900 satisfied clients in the public sector, government agencies, healthcare, telecommunications, automotive, finance, travel, logistics, gaming and hospitality industries. The company is considered a "pioneer in the area of near shoring and external R&D services and is a trusted developer of end-to-end technology product solutions in various industries" (ComTrade, 2015).

The company's strengths are a strong brand name and excellent reputation, and expertise in various industries (automotive, financial, energy, high-tech, gaming, public sector). The entrepreneurial culture is also developed as employees are focused on proactive innovation at the local and global level, in a large company but with a startup culture and approach when needed (Jevtic *et al.*, 2016).

ComTrade has several business focuses: software solutions engineering, system integration, distribution and media. The solutions' design is oriented towards clients worldwide and provides software and IT solutions, while the system integration works in close collaboration with governments, their agencies, ministries, and local enterprises and private companies. The media comprises of operations oriented towards the digital, Internet-based content and channels, while the distribution business involves significant and major partners locally and worldwide (more than 50 IT and consumer electronics vendors), and it effectively covers the entire process: from import to distribution, in addition to logistics, service and support, focusing on efficient stock optimization and improvement of inventory rates. ComTrade develops sophisticated software solutions for companies such as HP, IBM, Vodafone, DisneyWorld, Yahoo and many others. The company has an invaluable and large customer base for its distribution business: retail, telco, system integrators, value added and Internet-based resellers, as well as PC assemblers. Main product categories include consumer electronics, mobile phones and information technology. ComTrade is a member of the World Economic Forum with the status of Global Growth Company. In 2015, the company became an associate member of CERN open-lab.

TABLE 8.4 ComTrade Solutions Engineering, 2013–2015

Year	Number of employees	Revenue from sales	Net profit	Revenue from exports	% of revenue from exports from total revenue
2013	92	240,236	2,228	231,075	99.88
2014	118	402,304	1,915	387,703	98.89
2015	164	700,732	286	683,025	100.00

Source: SBRA (2017).

The organization's vision is to become a world leader in delivering high-value end-to-end technology solutions, products and services while reducing business complexity with technology solutions for storage, enterprise application management and gaming technology. As ComTrade strives to achieve its mission, it is focusing on creating a culture of innovation that is focused on valuing knowledge, professionalism, passion for high-quality work, accountability, entrepreneurship and mutual trust and respect.

According to Jevrosimović:

> The Group's strategy is based on development and expansion into new markets, and we will continue to strengthen our position in the fast developing ICT solutions segment through high-end technological competencies. Our company also intends to remain one of the most stimulating places to work in the region. For current shareholders it means a good value exit, and for our clients it means that they can expect a wider range of improved services.
>
> (SIEPA, 2012)

Entrepreneurship in Nordeus

The company Nordeus was founded in Belgrade in 2010 by three friends, Branko Milutinovic, Milan Jovovic and Ivan Stojisavljevic, who returned to Serbia from Sweden, where they had worked in Microsoft for around a year and a half. They joined their ideas about the gaming industry and developed a cross-platform-based gaming concept, Top Eleven Football Manager, which was remarkably successful. In 2012 and 2013, the company was among the 15 fastest growing European hi-tech companies. Today, Top Eleven has around 12 million active users a month on web, Android and iOS devices in more than 150 countries in the world. It is the most played online sports game in the world, with more than 100 million registered users.

Today, Nordeus is one of the largest software and Internet business companies in Serbia, with more than 100 employees. In just several years, as an award-winning European game developer and officially the best European gaming startup of 2011, the company became one of the most important Facebook partners. For several years in a row (2012–2015), they have held the title of best employer in Serbia and

TABLE 8.5 Nordeus company data, 2010–2015

Year	*Number of employees*	*Revenue from sales*	*Net profit*	*Revenue from exports*	*% of revenue from exports from total revenue*
2010	5	41,241	18,260	NA	NA
2011	19	690,684	330,437	NA	NA
2012	57	2,610,838	135,595	NA	NA
2013	88	7,344,694	56,087	7,335,781	99.88
2014	122	968,030	403,354	957,271	98.89
2015	129	1,170,890	38,257	1,170,890	100.00

Source: SBRA (2017).

the region. Apart from Belgrade, Nordeus has offices in San Francisco, Dublin, London and Skopje.

Along with experts in software development, the company employs artists and experts in finances, marketing and communications, of whom 15 are foreign nationals. With the slogan "Work and Play", a mentorship system and access to latest technologies, the employees have excellent working conditions. It is worth noting that the company is one of the top three social gaming companies in Europe and among the world's top companies, with no investment or external support, in the Balkans.

The company provides an innovative and inspiring working environment, offers flexible working hours and encourages employees to reach their goals and explore different fields, attend conferences and work on self-improvement. The work space in the company is designed to meet the everyday needs of employees, with ergonomic office furniture, food, car wash and sports activities, with Nordeus often being compared to Google. This approach brings the company high-quality and loyal staff, which is particularly important in modern circumstances with a high demand for experts in software design both in Serbia and internationally.

Nordeus has received many awards (SIEPA, 2015): ranking among the 25 Hottest European Hi-Tech Companies at Techtour, 2011, The Best Gaming Startup at Europas Awards, 2011, The Best Facebook Application at Web Fest, 2011 and People's Choice Award – The Best Startup at London Web Summit, 2012.

Asked about whether it would have been easier for Nordeus if it were in London or Berlin instead of Serbia, Branko Milutinovic said:

> I think it would have been equally hard and there are pros and cons. Serbia and Eastern European countries have started to receive tax incentives when it comes to fundraising, which is good for companies established there. But I do see a lot of pros when it comes to building from Serbia: excellent talent, less expensive, less competition from other companies and thus that talent will be more passionate and involved in the company, etc.
>
> *(Tech EU, 2014)*

Conclusions

The indicators of competitiveness of Serbia in comparison to the neighbouring countries are not satisfactory. However, entrepreneurial activities and the results of individual companies on international markets point to a significant potential. While there has been much historical turbulence in the region, Serbia has companies that can be globally competitive (Depalov *et al.*, 2013). In modern business terms, with resources available to everyone, yet still limited, knowledge-rich industries are becoming an opportunity for less developed countries. IT has become a developmental opportunity for Serbia in the last few decades, owing to high-quality education and entrepreneurial ideas of trained IT experts. Despite a steady growth of brain drain, particularly with the younger generation, IT companies can succeed based in Serbia with the help of new forms of communication. An example of this is the two companies presented in this paper.

ComTrade, as one of the most successful businesses in Serbia, owes its success to knowledge and exceptional managerial skills of the people who run it. They primarily recognize new trends and market needs and find key strategic partners to work together towards innovative solutions. Partnerships with leading international companies enabled expansion to a global market while maintaining quality and reputation.

The example of Nordeus, however, showed the success and internationalization of a small enterprise based on knowledge and innovation of its founders, who, based in a small country, make social games free and accessible to a wide range of people. Their young teams put all of their talents into making five-star games, and every day millions of people worldwide enjoy what they have created. High standards in working conditions and the employee selection procedure help attract the best candidates to a company which was awarded best employer in the country.

The cases show that intuition, expertise and managerial skills of leaders were the common success factor in both companies, followed by successful strategic partnerships and employment strategies. Since the ICT industry is seen as a developmental potential for Serbia, with demand exceeding the offer, and since 2016 was the Year of Entrepreneurship, the next important steps should be to provide institutional support and more IT educational programs in years to come.

References

Bobera, D., Lekovic, B. and Berber, N., 2014, "Comparative analysis of entrepreneurship barriers: Findings from Serbia and Montenegro", *Engineering Economics*, 25 (2), pp. 167–176.

ComTrade, 2015, "Simplify technology". Available at www.comtrade.com/. Accessed 1 May 2017.

Depalov, V.R., Todorovic, M. and Marinkovic, S., 2013, "Hidden Champions of Serbia", in P. McKiernan and D. Purg, eds., *Hidden Champions in CEE and Turkey*, Heidelberg: Springer, pp. 307–330.

Djordjevic, M., Sapic, S. and Marinkovic, V., 2012, "How companies enter international markets: Presentation and analysis of the empirical research", *Actual Problems of Economics*, 7, pp. 331–342.

Doing Business, 2016, *Doing Business Report 2016*. Available at www.doingbusiness.org/reports/global-reports/doing-business-2016. Accessed 1 May 2017.

GCR, 2016, *Global Competitiveness Report 2015–2016*. Available at http://reports.weforum.org/global-competitiveness-report-2015-2016/competitiveness-rankings/. Accessed 7 June 2017.

GEDI, 2016, *Global Entrepreneurship Index Powered by GEDI 2016*. Available at http://thegedi.org/2016-global-entrepreneurship-index/. Accessed 5 June 2017.

Jevtic, M., Demirovic, R. and Marinkovic, S., 2016, "Evaluation and selection of technology strategies using quantitative strategic planning matrix", *SYMORG 2016 – Symposium Proceedings*, Belgrade, Faculty of Organizational Sciences, pp. 1465–1473.

Levi Jaksic, M.L., Marinkovic, S. and Kojic, J., 2014a, "Technology and innovation management education in Serbia", in M. Levi Jaksic, S.B. Rakocevic and M.Martic, eds., *Innovative Management and Firm Performance*, London: Palgrave Macmillan, pp. 37–67.

Levi Jaksic, M.L., Marinkovic, S. and Rakicevic, J., 2014b, "Sustainable technology entrepreneurship and development – the case of Serbia", *Management*, 70, pp. 65–73.

Matijevic, M. and Solaja, M., 2015, *ICT in Serbia – At a Glance*, Novi Sad: Vojvodina ICT Cluster.

Milosavljevic, M. and Benkovic, S., 2014, "Education as a driver of entrepreneurship among graduates in Serbia", *Актуальні проблеми економіки*, 2, pp. 79–86.

Nikolic, M., Despotovic, D. and Cvetanovic, D., 2015, "Barriers to innovation in SMEs in the republic of Serbia", *Ekonomika*, 61 (4), pp. 89–96.

Popovic, J., Radic, V., Radic, N. and Vukadinovic, S., 2016, "Rating the relevant factors of business conditions for entrepreneurs in Serbia", *EuroEconomica*, *35* (1), pp. 7–25.

Radovic-Markovic, M., 2014, "Unleashing the potential of the small and medium enterprise sector in Serbia", *Economic Research-Ekonomska Istraživanja*, 27 (1), pp. 700–712.

Rakićević, J., Levi Jakšić, M. and Jovanović, M., 2016, "Index of potential for technology entrepreneurship development: Practice from Serbia", *Proceedings of the XV International symposium SymOrg 2015: Reshaping the Future through Sustainable Business Development and Entrepreneurship*, FON, Zlatibor, 10–13 June 2016.

SBRA, 2017, *Serbian Business Registry Agency*. Available at www.apr.gov.rs/eng/Registers/Companies/Search.aspx. Accessed 2 June 2017.

SIEPA, 2012, *Serbia ICT Smart Solution*. Available at http://siepa.gov.rs/files/pdf2010/ICT_Serbia%20Smart%20Solution.pdf. Accessed 2 June 2017.

SIEPA, 2015, *ICT Industry in Serbia*. Available at http://ras.gov.rs/uploads/2016/02/ict-industry-in-serbia.pdf. Accessed 2 June 2017.

Statistical Yearbook of the Republic of Serbia, 2016, Available at http://webrzs.stat.gov.rs/. Accessed 7 July 2017.

Tech EU, 2014, "The Serbian hit: How Nordeus became one of Europe's most successful gaming companies without raising a dime in funding". Available at http://tech.eu/features/3417/branko-milutinovic-nordeus-interview-leweb/. Accessed 4 May 2017.

World Bank, 2016, *World Bank Open Data*. Available at http://data.worldbank.org/. Accessed 6 June 2017.

Zdravkovic, B., 2011, "International business prospects of small and medium enterprises in Serbia", *International Journal of Economics and Law*, 1, pp. 159–168.

9

BUSINESS INTERNATIONALISATION

A case study of Telegrafia from Slovakia

Peter Džupka and Miriam Šebová

Introduction

Slovakia's economy is small and open. Slovakia is a member of the European Union with a population of 5.4 million, located in Central Europe. The volume of Slovakia's foreign trade accounts for almost 190 per cent of its GDP (2013) as one of the most open economies in the EU.[1] The Slovak economy is significantly interlinked with countries of the Eurozone and especially with the biggest trade partner, Germany. The Ministry of Economy has estimated that the openness will continue to increase up to 250 per cent by 2020 (Ministry of Economy, 2014).

Although a high level of economic openness is a typical feature of small developed economies, the level in Slovakia is higher than some of the neighbouring countries – for example, the Czech Republic and Hungary. The economic openness is rooted in several reasons, such as the low capacity of the small domestic market, limited natural resources and a high number of foreign direct investments (FDI), amongst others. This increased rapidly between 2001 and 2008, driven by a strong inflow of FDI into new green-field projects which were dominantly export oriented. These investments, however, did not come to Slovakia in order to sell them in its domestic market but to utilise Slovakia's advantages, especially its location and the good qualifications-to-cost ratio of the labour force, for the establishment of their new export-oriented facilities (Liptáková, 2014).

The high level of openness means that almost all companies are directly or indirectly linked to foreign trade in Slovakia. From this point of view, the internationalisation determines the vitality and profitability of Slovak companies and thus also the growth of the Slovak economy. For this reason, the objective of the current chapter is to provide a comprehensive overview of the business internationalisation in Slovakia and derive conclusions and recommendations from it. This chapter is organised as follows.

The first part of the chapter presents the state of the art in the field of business internationalisation in Slovakia. Different sources of data are used, such as statistics about export provided by the Statistical Office of Slovakia, academic surveys about business internationalisation and Eurobarometer data. The second part of the chapter introduces a case study of a medium-sized company called Telegrafia, which operates in the field of warning systems worldwide. The final section concludes the chapter.

Macroeconomic perspective – export figures

From a macroeconomic point of view, business internationalisation is shown through the intensity of foreign trade. The recent business internationalisation has been influenced by two milestones: Slovakia entering the European Union in 2004 and adoption of the euro in 2009.

Based on trade statistics, exports have accounted for about 44.8 per cent of the total economic output of Slovakia (IMF, 2015). The exports from Slovakia amounted to approximately 630 million euros in 2015, increasing by 19.5 per cent from 2011 to 2015. Imports were nearly 600 million euros in 2015. From a continental perspective, around 90 per cent of Slovak exports by value were delivered to Europe while nearly 5 per cent were sold to Asia. Around 3 per cent of exports were sold to customers in North America and 1 per cent to Africa in 2015 (Statistical Office of Slovak Republic, 2015). Figure 9.1 shows the most important export countries according to the share of total export. The most important export territories are Germany (23 per cent share in 2015) and the neighbouring countries of the Czech Republic, Poland, Austria, Hungary, etc.

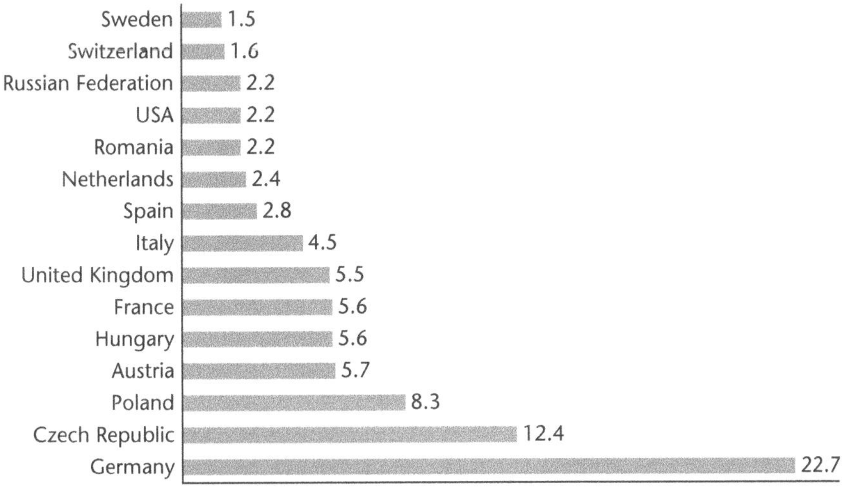

FIGURE 9.1 Share of total export (%).

Source: Statistical Office of the Slovak Republic (2015).

A closer look at exports from the industrial perspective (Figure 9.2) shows the top export industries to be the production of machinery, electrical and vehicles equipment with nearly a 60 per cent share of the total export in 2014. The exports are led by cars, which represent approximately 18 per cent of the total exports, followed by video displays, which account for 8 per cent.

The property structure of companies operating in Slovakia shows an openness towards direct foreign investment in the country. The Slovak Statistical Office (2015) provides data about the geographical origin of owners. Based on a statistical survey, foreign companies are defined as companies established and controlled by a foreign owner. International companies have Slovak and foreign owners. As can be seen from Figure 9.3, the total amount of foreign companies has rapidly increased in Slovakia since 2005 after joining the European Union while the amount of international firms has remained at the same level. The flow of FDI per capita in Slovakia is comparable to that in neighbouring Hungary and the Czech Republic.

From the regional perspective, the increasing number of foreign companies has mainly been located in the region of the capital city, Bratislava, and Nitra region in Western Slovakia. The localisation of foreign companies predominately in the western part of the country strengthens the regional disparities in the country. The next figure (Figure 9.4) shows the relationship between the localisation of foreign companies in different Slovak regions and distance from the capital city and regional GPD per capita.

While explaining the propensity to export between firms, the former political position should be taken into account. According to (Cieślik *et al.*, 2014), the highest share of exporting firms has been reported for the countries that emerged from former Yugoslavia. This could be explained by the fact that those countries were

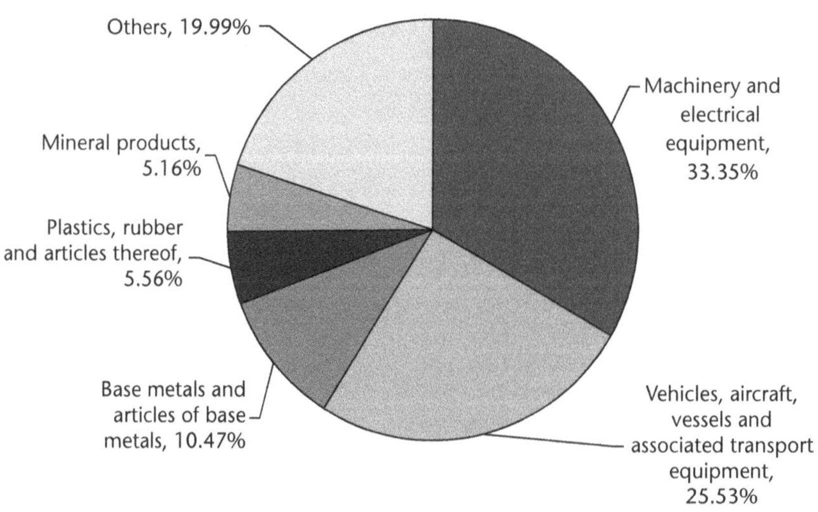

FIGURE 9.2 Share of total export according to economic sectors, 2014.

Source: Statistical Office of the Slovak Republic (2015).

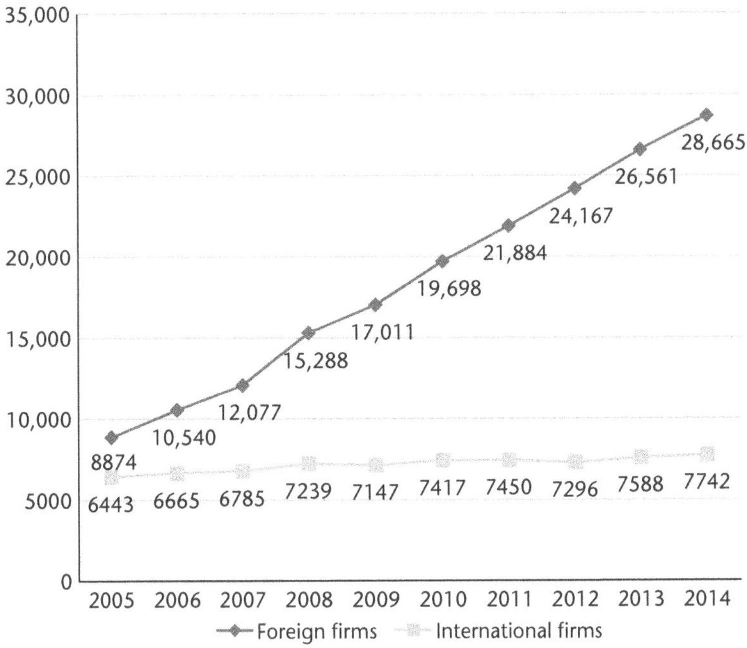

FIGURE 9.3 Number of foreign and international companies in Slovakia.

Source: Statistical Office of the Slovak Republic (2015).

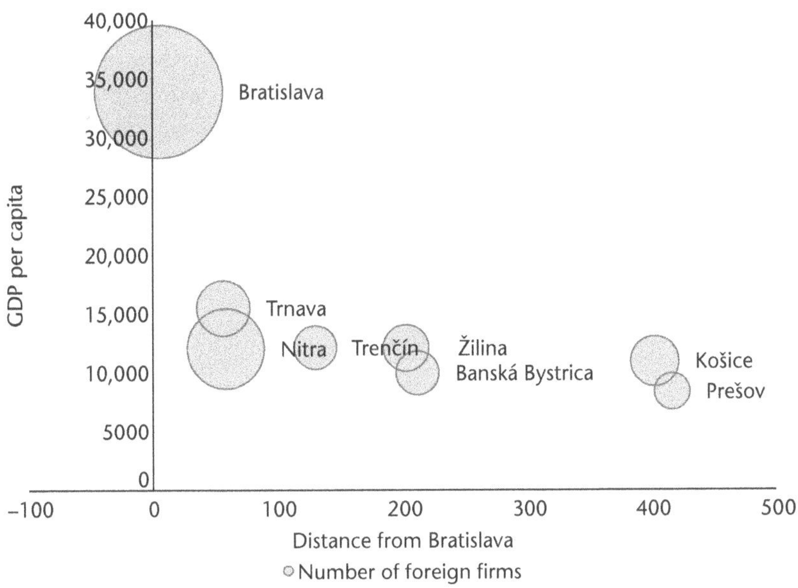

FIGURE 9.4 Regional localisation of foreign firms.

Source: Statistical Office of the Slovak Republic (2015).

traditionally more market-oriented and had more liberal trade regimes in the past compared to other post-communist countries. The Visegrad countries are located in the upper-middle of the group, with the exception of Poland, which has the biggest internal market compared to the remaining Visegrad countries (Cieślik *et al.*, 2014). Slovakia has been calculated to have the highest propensity to export (Cieślik *et al.*, 2014). The export performance is determined not only by country characteristics but also by firm-level characteristics which are outlined in the next section.

Microeconomic perspective – patterns of business internalisation

The Statistical Office only provides aggregate data, which limits the understanding of the behaviour of enterprises against the challenges they face in their internalisation process. Unfortunately, there hasn't been a national survey focused on internalisation to collect data about Slovak enterprises. There have been several academic surveys carried out in this field by Slovak researchers (Magdolenová, 2010; Horská and Gálová, 2014; Ubrežiová *et al.*, 2014). While the academic surveys are not representative, their results still allow a deeper insight into the motives and obstacles of the internalisation of Slovak companies.

The highest number of firms involved in a survey (Horská and Gálová, 2014) was conducted within a common research project among V4 countries in 2013–2014. The research sample consisted of 143 enterprises differing in size, economic activity, year of establishment (Table 9.1), etc. in Slovakia. This research fulfilled the conditions of reliability.

The results show the following internationalisation patterns of Slovak companies (Horská and Gálová, 2014). Almost half of the companies (49 per cent) started with their first international activity after 2004 (when Slovakia joined the EU). The integration process was the most important stimulus to foster the internalisation of Slovak companies (Ubrežiová *et al.*, 2014). Following the Uppsala model of internationalisation[2] in most cases the internalisation was part of the traditional business development process. Companies mostly stated that they had first operated in the domestic market before they entered foreign markets (Gálová and Horská, 2012). Most Slovak companies seem to be in the second phase of the Uppsala model, which is exporting to other countries (Magdolenová, 2010).

TABLE 9.1 Characteristics of surveyed companies in research about internationalisation patterns in Slovakia

Establishment year	*Share %*	*Size of the firm*	*Share %*
Before 1993	16.8	Large	9.1
1993–2003	44.1	Medium	21.7
2004–2013	39.2	Small	33.6
		Micro	35.7

Source: Excerpt from Horská and Gálová (2014).

According to the territorial dimension of international activities, 32 per cent of the surveyed firms only operate in the domestic market, 12 per cent only in neighbouring countries, 27 per cent only within EU markets and 30 per cent in global markets within and outside of the EU. The territorial focus is strongly connected to the firm's size. Micro and small-sized companies enter closer markets – mainly in V4 countries and CEEC (Central and Eastern Europe) countries. The global markets are only entered by 16 per cent of micro firms, 30 per cent of small firms, 45 per cent of medium-sized firms and 54 per cent of large firms.

The survey included questions about their available resources related to the internationalisation process (Figure 9.5). Firms had to evaluate the quality of their financial resources (e.g. own capital, approach to credit, venture capital), human resources (e.g. staff speaking a foreign language, staff with experience from abroad), physical resources (equipment, know-how, innovation) and information resources (information about international markets). The companies stated that they have particularly low human resources to foster internationalisation activities. They presented sufficient information about business opportunities and the characteristics of foreign markets.

The next insight was into the timeframe of the internationalisation. The companies internationalised quite rapidly, with 75 per cent of the surveyed companies starting with internationalisation within three years after their establishment (Horská and Gálová, 2014). The timeframe of internationalisation is influenced by the industry. The high-tech industry companies internationalised faster than firms from other industries. According to the results, the companies from high-tech industries were internationalised on average within a period of 2.06 years, while in low-tech industries it took 4.41 years to go international.

The internationalisation process seems to only be partially formalised. Only 22 per cent of firms stated that they had developed a written strategy for their

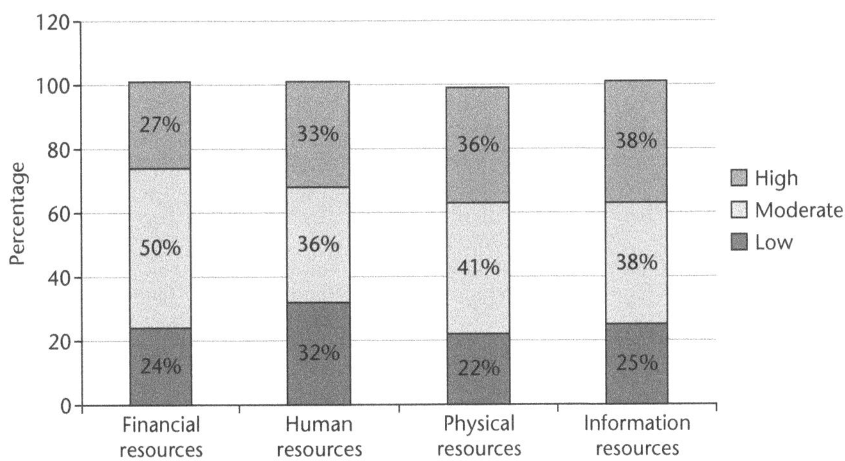

FIGURE 9.5 Evaluation of firm's resources linked to internationalisation.

Source: V4 survey (Horská and Gálová, 2014).

internationalisation. According to the EPG model[3] (Perlmutter, 1969), Slovak companies prefer ethnocentric and regiocentric strategies over polycentric and geocentric strategies. The ethnocentric strategy means that they use the same marketing and management activities in international markets as in domestic markets, while the regiocentric strategy means the use of different strategies for a couple of international markets with similar marketing and management conditions. According to the survey, the Slovak firms use much less territorial specialised marketing and management strategies (Horská and Gálová, 2014). This finding is probably correlated with the territorial targeting of their international activities. Slovak companies mainly operate in EU markets with similar market conditions.

In terms of the entry modes of the surveyed firms (Table 9.2), most Slovak firms use contractual modes (especially subcontracting) and direct exporting (mainly foreign distributors). The more advanced entry modes (contractual and investment) were used by firms from high-tech industries in comparison with other industries (Horská and Gálová, 2014). Of the respondents, 53 per cent provided some kind of contractual modes and also 24 per cent some kind of investment modes (Table 9.2).

The survey resulted in an interesting finding about the key role of management in the fostering of the internationalisation process in a company. The knowledge and experience of the manager directly influences the internationalisation progress of the company. The study found a correlation between the level of knowledge and experience of the manager and the use of advanced entry modes (Horská and Gálová, 2014). Moreover, the more informed and motivated the manager was, the more advanced the modes of internationalisation were in the company.

Internationalisation of SMEs in Slovakia – Eurobarometer findings

As many empirical results have confirmed (Olejnik and Swoboda, 2012), there is a direct link between the level of internationalisation and the size of a company. Big companies enter foreign markets far more easily. The challenge is also to involve small and medium-sized enterprises (SMEs) in the internationalisation process. There are several policy documents and proposals about how to support the entrance of Slovak SMEs into foreign markets. The support is initially coordinated by the Slovak Business Agency (SBA), which is a member of the Enterprise Europe Network. The SBA was established by the Slovak government in cooperation with European communities

TABLE 9.2 Modes of internationalisation process

Entry modes	*Frequency of answers*	*Share of surveyed companies*
Indirect export	59	41.26
Direct export	74	51.75
Cooperative export	40	27.97
Contractual modes	76	53.15
Investment modes	34	23.78

Source: Horská and Gálová (2014).

in 1993 (SBA, 2015). The supporting activities for fostering of business internationalisation provides plenty of other institutions – for example, Slovak Investment and Trade Development Agency (SARIO), Business and Innovations Centres (BIC), Slovak Chamber of Commerce and Industry, Regional Advisory and Information Centres, etc. In 1997, a so-called Export-Import Bank of the Slovak Republic was established, which provides banking products for Slovak exporters. The institutional framework is well developed in Slovakia. The question is whether companies are able to benefit from this institutional supporting system.

Eurobarometer data were used to show the position of Slovak SMEs in internationalisation. There have been several Eurobarometer surveys about the internationalisation of European SMEs – for example, in 2009 and 2015 (EC, 2010, 2015). In the Eurobarometer, the internationalisation does not only refer to exports but to all activities that put SMEs into a meaningful business relationship with a foreign partner: exports, imports, foreign direct investment, international subcontracting and international technical cooperation. The data from the Eurobarometer were based on a survey with 500 SMEs in Slovakia.

Slovak companies were found to be less likely to have conducted business activities outside the EU (Figure 9.6). Twenty-five per cent of Slovak companies have

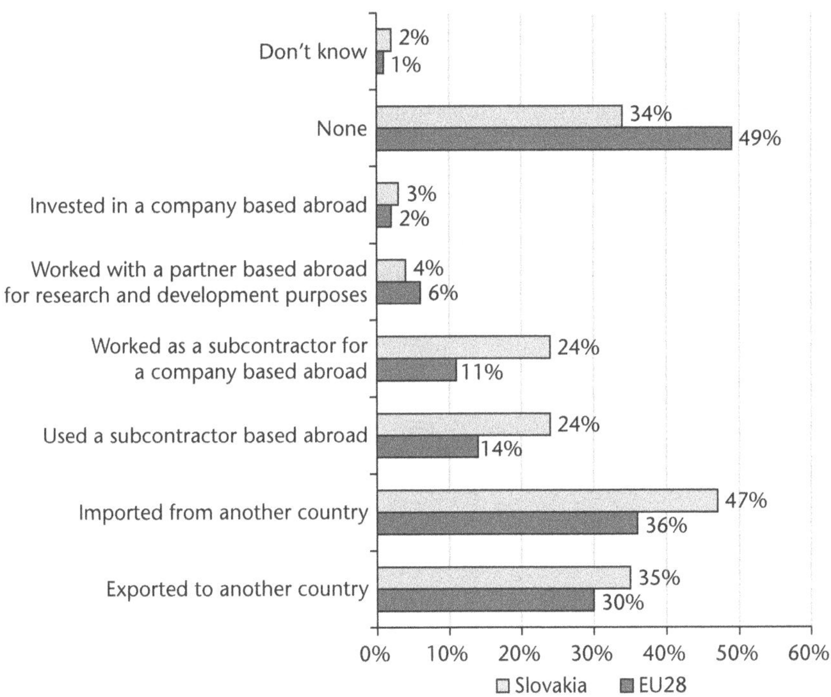

FIGURE 9.6 In the last three years, has your company done any of the following activities inside the EU?

Source: EC (2015).

experience with internationalisation outside the EU compared to 31 per cent of EU28 companies. Sixty-six per cent of Slovak companies provide experienced internationalisation activity in the EU market.

Slovak companies prefer to cooperate with business partners in European countries more than the average of the EU28 and their tendency to carry out international activity outside the EU is lower than the average of the EU28 (Figure 9.7). The prevailing internationalisation activities of Slovak SMEs are import and export as in other EU states.

The Eurobarometer results showed lower imports from China compared to other European countries. Companies in Finland (32 per cent), Malta, Germany, Poland (all 26 per cent) and Cyprus (24 per cent) are the most likely to have imported from China, particularly when compared to those in Bulgaria and Slovakia (both 6 per cent) (EC, 2015). Slovak companies deal with similar problems with exporting as other European companies. The biggest problems were seen as high financial costs, difficulties resolving cross-border complaints and the lack of specialised staff (EC, 2015).

There is a high percentage of SMEs with FDI just above 40 per cent in Slovakia. It was the third highest score among EU countries in 2009 (EC, 2010). On the

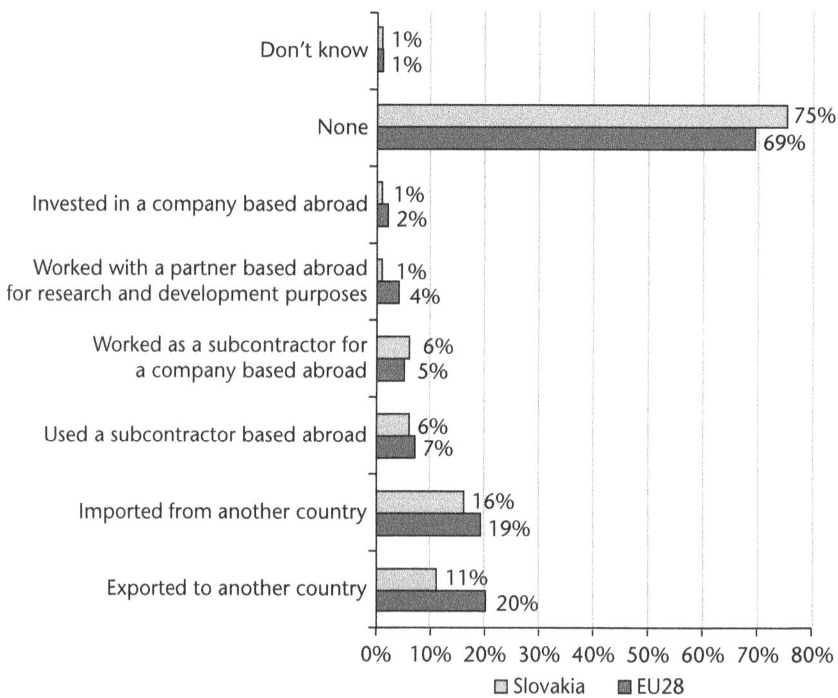

FIGURE 9.7 In the last three years, has your company done any of the following activities outside the EU?

Source: EC (2015).

other hand, the use of financial and non-financial support for internationalisation by the internationally active enterprises was low. Financial support was reported by only 9 per cent of respondents and non-financial only by 1 per cent. Slovak companies used the support programmes at a lower level in comparison with other European countries in 2009 (EC, 2010). Unfortunately, this question wasn't included in the Eurobarometer in 2014.

In 2014, companies were asked about their preferred measures which could help them engage in business abroad (Figure 9.8). For Slovak companies, financial measures would help the most, as is usual in other countries. Surprisingly, Slovak companies demand more information about foreign markets. Twelve per cent of Slovak companies have heard of the Enterprise Europe Network (the average of the EU28 was 8 per cent). These findings indicate that the information flow from the national and regional supporting institution is not effective and should be revised.

Case study: Telegrafia

A number of sources were used in the case study. The main data were gathered from three semi-formal interviews with managers and employees of the company. In order

FIGURE 9.8 Which of the following measures would help your company the most to engage in business abroad?

Source: EC (2015).

to reduce the risk of informant bias, more than one interview was conducted. During the interviews, questions were asked about the motives of the company to enter foreign markets, the problems behind this decision, how the process of foreign market entry started and what the milestones were, about the strategy and marketing approach, etc. The other sources of information were the company's website, annual reports of the company and relevant professional websites.

Characteristics of Telegrafia

Telegrafia a. s. is a manufacturer and supplier of cutting-edge products and technological solutions in the field of early warning and notification systems. It is located in the second biggest Slovak city, Košice (250,000 inhabitants) in the east of Slovakia. The flagship products of Telegrafia's production are its electronic sirens (e.g. PAVIAN), evacuation radios and specialised software for dispatching centres. Telegrafia was the first company to introduce the innovative modular product line aSCADA® to the global market. This provides a cost-effective creation of professional solutions in the field of indoor and outdoor sound systems. The products and solutions in the field of early warnings and notifications have already been implemented in more than 50 countries from French Polynesia through to Asian and European countries and South America.[4]

The high quality and technological standard of the products and solutions was gained through gradual innovation processes in the company. Telegrafia provides its own research and development in this area, which is targeted on the innovation and competitiveness of the products. There are 13 people working in the research department, mainly in the ICT field.

Telegrafia is a certified partner of large global companies such as Microsoft® and Hewlett Packard® and runs an IT education and training centre in Slovakia. This cooperation became a source of additional knowledge in the field of management and marketing for the company.

Background of Telegrafia

Telegrafia was established in the former Czechoslovak Republic in 1919. Originally it focused on the development and production of telephones and communication infrastructural devices. Later, production also included home radios and other electrical appliances. After the Second World War, during the Communist era, the company was renamed Tesla Pardubice and produced military products, including the world-famous passive radio locators Tamara. There was a branch of Tesla established in eastern Slovakia. After 1990 this branch was closed. Consequently, the current Telegrafia company was founded by five co-founders in 1991. Two of them had worked in a branch of Tesla Pardubice before. The founders chose the name Telegrafia for the new company because they had been inspired by the knowledge gained during their time at Tesla in radio communication.

Telegrafia was one of the first companies that introduced personal computers to the free market in Slovakia at the time. The managers were able to find the market niche and utilise it. Subsequently, the company started with the development of radio communications technological devices, which were soon supplemented with acoustic early warning devices and the company's own outdoor electronic sirens. Today, Telegrafia is a technological leader in the field of early warning and emergency notification systems (EWANS®). Nowadays the company employs around 70 people and its turnover was 9 million euros in 2015 (Telegrafia, 2016).

The internationalisation of the company was the key moment in its development. The company exports all over the world, including Australia, Chile, the Maldives, Malaysia, Indonesia, Ecuador, etc., and in four continents (Australia, South Africa, Asia, America). It only imports a few electronic parts from China (a small amount), and it prefers suppliers from Slovakia or from neighbouring countries. The company established its subsidiary in Romania in 2000, but would like to close it soon.

The geographical structure of export changes according to the current projects of the company and is increasing continuously every year (Figure 9.9). There is no special position of neighbouring countries and the share of V4 countries is small.

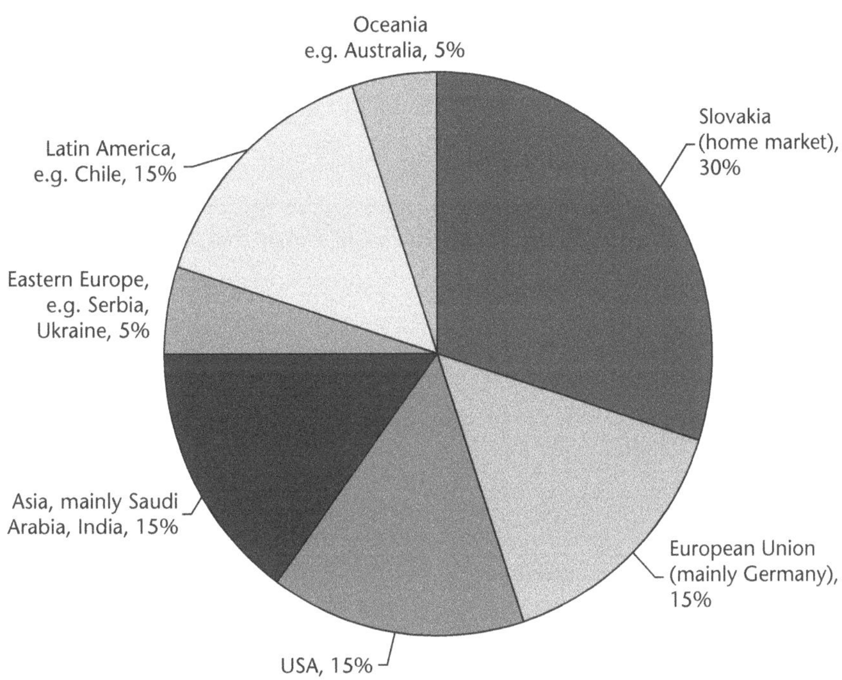

FIGURE 9.9 The geographical structure of export of products in 2016.

Source: Interview with the manager of Telegrafia (30 November 2016).

The evolution of the internationalisation of Telegrafia[5]

The evolution of the internationalisation of Telegrafia is outlined. In the first few years, the company seems to have followed gradual internationalisation as proposed by the Uppsala model. After 2007, it changed its strategy and a radical increase of export activities started. Therefore, it can be assumed that the company could be designated as a so-called "born-again global" (Olejnik and Swoboda, 2012).

1991–1999

The company operated in the Slovak market for ten years. It entered foreign markets after it had had enough experience in the domestic market. During this period, it had continuously improved its products. It developed a first generation of electronic sirens and implemented them in the Slovak Republic (national warning system). As mentioned above, this gradual approach seems to be similar to the traditional Uppsala internationalisation model (UIM).

2000–2002

First steps

Around the year 2000, the company started to think about internationalisation and started cooperating with a partner from Romania. The main incentive to export was the limited growth of the company in the domestic market. "Slovak producer is judged to export…" (manager of Telegrafia). The first export activity was pushed by a foreign partner. The company regularly took part in international forums about civil protection in Slovakia. After one of these forums the company was contacted by a client from Romania and carried out its first imports to Romania. The company established its subsidiary in Romania in 2000, but would like to close it now.

2002–2006

Slow start

The period 2002–2006 was characterised by small individual projects to mainly neighbouring countries. The breakthrough came with a substantial tender acquired in the German city of Dresden. Telegrafia was the main subcontractor in the biggest tender for the local warning system in Germany. They won the tender with the best technical parameters of the product. This project changed the strategy about internationalisation in the company. The management started to think conceptually about internationalisation, which became the source of the firm's growth.

When asked about the impact of the entry of Slovakia into the EU, the manager answered:

> It wasn't a dramatic change for us. It enabled the travelling and customs procedures to be done more easily, especially in countries of the EU (Germany). Now they can send the spare parts in the post; before it was necessary to travel.

The adoption of the euro made the pricing and price list easier. The membership to the EU and euro is especially valuable for clients outside the EU because foreign partners value the company as more credible.

2007–2011

New internationalisation strategy adoption

In the period 2007–2011, a new strategy for penetrating foreign markets was developed.

> We had a lot of internal discussion in the company about how to do it. We realised that there is no chance to communicate with clients from Spain, Italy or France in English. We understood that we had to overcome the language barrier.

The company started with a proactive approach. It redesigned the webpage and built its own coherent marketing strategy about how to overcome language barriers and simplify the first contact with clients. At the same time, they enhanced their knowledge in the field of management, marketing and communication. They started with agile project management inspired by partners from Microsoft.

From 2008, Telegrafia started cooperating with AIESEC and regularly offered internships for international students who visited the Technical University in Košice. The job description of trainees was to analyse the market in their home countries (law, demand, competitors) and to translate the webpage of Telegrafia into their native language. During this time a lot of international students worked in the company. "We had 12 trainees working on market research in the company at the same time. [...] This has changed our view on how to communicate with foreign customers."

The other big project, which created crucial references, came from French Polynesia in the field of tsunami siren systems in 2007. There were about 190 Pavian sirens installed in the French Pacific. The specific climate conditions led to several product innovations which have enhanced the utilisation of sirens.

In the Slovak ranking of ICT companies, Telegrafia was placed eleventh as one of the most rapidly growing ICT companies in Slovakia in 2009. Telegrafia increased the added value of 132.4 per cent and more than doubled their profits (TREND, 2010).

Since 2012

Thriving export

The next milestone was building a platform to communicate online with customers. The managers indicated that an online platform and the optimisation of web searches were important factors. Telegrafia decreased participation at professional exhibitions as the manager said "the exhibitions are dead matter in our business" and invested in high-quality online presentations.

Since 2011, the company has actively searched and contacted foreign partners. However, this position has changed since 2012 where foreign customers have started to seek the company out by themselves. It resulted in orders of individual sirens by customers from around 20 different countries in 2013. In 2014–2015, Telegrafia was involved in several small and medium-sized international projects. Since 2016, Telegrafia has worked as a key subcontractor in a big international project in the field of warning and notification systems in India.

In 2016, the company developed a new software application called Acusticus, which was the next step in simplifying online communication with clients. The software simulates coverage of any environment with a warning signal. It is compatible with Google Maps. Thanks to this software, clients can adjust the warning system to their requirements and needs. The application is free and it is available in all language versions on the Telegrafia webpage. The application enables the detailed specification of the product.

The successful internationalisation strategy helped Telegrafia to overcome the economic crisis after 2008. Telegrafia worked on contracted projects (e.g. in French Polynesia) during this period. After the projects finished, Telegrafia felt the consequences of the crisis (decreased demand) with a delay in 2013 (Table 9.3). Concurrently, they started negotiations on new foreign projects and were able to increase their turnover and penetrate new markets.

Nowadays the company operates a small "sales department". The company employs four sales managers (two Slovak, one Polish, one Ukraine) with perfect language skills. The company cooperates with more than 50 partners worldwide.

The phase of new market searches and translating webpages is finished and they no longer hire foreign students. They have improved the content of the online platform, which is their crucial marketing tool. Telegrafia lends several samples of sirens to their sale partners if they want to exhibit at their local exhibitions. The

TABLE 9.3 Revenues and costs of Telegrafia, 2011–2015, in million euro

	2012	*2013*	*2014*	*2015*
Revenues	5.19	4.71	9.23	8.05
Costs	5.16	4.12	8.83	7.1

Source: Telegrafia (2016).

approach to samples has changed. Before, they gave the samples for free to prospective clients. This strategy was cost demanding and not successful. Now they offer samples for half price and invite prospective clients to the newly built company headquarters in Košice. The company invests a lot of resources into the training of employees. It is inspired by its partners (e.g. Microsoft), who are examples of how to manage the partnership chain.

During the interviews, questions were asked about recommendations for Slovak support policy. In the early phases of foreign market penetration, the company asked for cooperation of the Slovak embassies in different countries. The embassies were too slow and not well enough informed to help them. Information about foreign markets is still important and the Internet has made it much easier for exporting companies to obtain information. That is why Slovak supporting policy should be more focused on financial tools rather than information activities. According to the managers at Telegrafia, financial support could be helpful in overcoming the excessive allowances related to export activities. The managers did not acknowledge the Enterprise Europe Network and did not cooperate with any supporting institution in Slovakia.[6]

The crucial factors of the successful export activities of Telegrafia can be summarised as follows:

- a high-quality product which is regularly innovated (60 per cent of the product costs are related to the research and development)
- active searching of customers and coherent online presentation (redesign of the webpage, optimisation of search engines)
- building of the internalised platform of online communication with the customer (webpage and manuals in different language versions, software application Acusticus, etc.)
- educated and motivated sales managers and competent managers
- understanding of the specifics of foreign markets (e.g. slow tenders in India, closed Polish market).

Conclusions

The challenge of a highly open economy is to maintain competitive business conditions for local businesses as well as offering an attractive environment for investments. Slovak companies are dependent on internationalisation. Their recent business internationalisation has been influenced by two milestones: Slovakia entering the European Union in 2004 and adoption of the euro in 2009. The main internationalisation activities of Slovak companies are export and import. Slovak business is characterised by a high propensity to export and a high share of FDI. The same Slovak companies prefer to cooperate with business partners in European countries more than the average EU28 and their tendency to carry out international activity outside the EU is lower than the average EU28. The main export partners for them are the geographically closest neighbouring countries (especially Germany).

There have been several academic surveys conducted about business internationalisation by Slovak researchers (Magdolenová, 2010; Horská and Gálová, 2014; Ubrežiová *et al.*, 2014). Unfortunately, there has been no national survey carried out with comparable longitudinal data. Therefore, it is not possible to objectively evaluate the specifics of the internationalisation patterns in Slovak business in general. However, some information about the behaviour of SMEs could be found in the findings from the Eurobarometer. Despite similar macroeconomic conditions (as compared to the situation in the EU), it seems that Slovakia's SME sector is impeded to become fairly internationalised. The biggest problems were considered to be the high financial costs, complications of resolving cross-border complaints and the lack of specialised staff (EC, 2015). There are several national support programs and institutions in the field of internationalisation. It seems, however, that they need to be promoted further to Slovak companies because a low use of information and financial instruments was detected.

The case study highlights some factors of a successful internationalisation of a technological company. The proactive approach in the internationalisation strategy has shifted the paradigm of the company from the traditional UIM approach to "born-again global" status. The movers of internationalisation in the company were open-minded and innovative managers. The cooperation with international technological leaders was the source of knowledge in the field of management, marketing and product innovation. This knowledge has shaped the internationalisation process of Telegrafia. The case study has validated the importance of a formulated internationalisation strategy aimed at deeply exploring foreign markets. The cooperation with foreign students could be a valuable inspiration for similar SMEs with limited personal and financial sources for internationalisation. In addition, the perfectly mastered online communication with customers points to the crucial factors of success in a global business environment.

Despite its limitations, the chapter contributes to the discussion about business internationalisation in Slovakia. Certainly, further empirical research drawing on a larger company sample will be necessary to develop reliable insights into the whole complexity of the determinants of business internationalisation development in Slovakia. It would be useful to improve the statistics about business internationalisation at the national level and to organise regular national surveys to capture the internationalisation patterns.

Notes

1 In 2013, higher openness was calculated only for Ireland and Luxembourg.
2 The Uppsala internalisation model distinguishes four different steps of entering the international market (Johanson and Vahlne, 1977).
3 The EPG model explains the dimensions of the international business model: ethnocentric, polycentric and geocentric.
4 Official website: Telegrafia.
5 Source of information: interview with the manager of Telegrafia, 30 November 2016.
6 Interview with the manager of Telegrafia, 30 November 2016.

References

Cieślik, A., Michałek, J. and Michałek, T., 2014, "Firm characteristics and export performance in Post-Communist countries", in N. Daszkiewicz and K. Wach, eds., *Firm-level Internalisation and its Business Environment. Knowledge-based and Entrepreneurial Approach*, Gdańsk: Gdańsk University of Technology, pp. 34–44.

EC, 2010, *Internationalisation of European SMEs. Final Report*, Brussels: Entrepreneurship Unit Directorate-General for Enterprise and Industry European Commission.

EC, 2015, *Flash Eurobarometer 421. Internalisation of Small and Medium-sized Enterprises. Report*, Brussels: European Commission.

Gálová, J. and Horská, E., 2012, "Business internationalisation and the choice of international strategy in case of Slovak companies", *Quaestus Multidisciplinary Research Journal*, 2, pp. 81–93.

Horská, E. and Gálová, J., 2014, "Patterns of business internationalisation in Slovakia: Empirical results from the V4 Survey", in A. Durendéz and K. Wach, eds., *Patterns of Business Internationalisation in Visegrad Countries – In Search for Regional Specifics*, Cartagena: Universidad Politécnica de Cartagena, pp. 103–124.

IMF, 2015, *World Economic Outlook: Adjusting to Lower Commodity Prices*, Washington, DC: International Monetary Fund.

Johanson, J. and Vahlne, J.E., 1977, "The internationalization process of the firm: A model of knowledge development and increasing foreign market commitment", *Journal of International Business Studies*, 8 (1), pp. 23–32.

Liptáková, J., 2014, "Exports are key to economic growth", *The Slovak Spectator*. Available at https://spectator.sme.sk/c/20049697/exports-are-key-to-economic-growth.html. Accessed 27 August 2017.

Magdolenová, J., 2010, "Analysis of selected factors of Slovak companies' internationalization", *Journal of Competitiveness*, 2, pp. 86–98.

Ministry of Economy, 2014, *The Strategy of External Economic Relations of the Slovak Republic for 2014–2020*, Bratislava: Ministry of Economy.

Olejnik, E. and Swoboda, B., 2012, "SMEs' internalisation patterns: Descriptives, dynamics and determinants", *International Marketing Review*, 29 (5), pp. 466–495.

Perlmutter, H., 1969, "The tortuous evolution of multinational enterprises", *Columbia Journal of World Business*, 4 (1), pp. 9–18.

SBA, 2015, *Small Business Act. Fact Sheet Slovakia*, Brussels: European Commission Enterprise and Industry.

Statistical Office of Slovak Republic, 2015, *Trade Statistics*, Bratislava: Statistical Office of Slovak Republic.

Telegrafia, 2016, *Annual Report 2015*, Košice: Telegrafia.

TREND, 2010, *Slovak National Ranking of ICT Companies 2009*, Bratislava: News and Media Holding.

Ubrežiová, I., Mura, L. and Kozáková, J., 2014, "Position of SMEs in the context of business internationalization in Slovakia", *Trendy v podnikání – Business Trends*, 3, pp. 31–39.

PART IV

Entrepreneurs-innovators going international

10

THE INTERNATIONALISATION OF RICHTER GEDEON, THE HUNGARIAN PHARMACEUTICAL COMPANY, AND ENTREPRENEURSHIP IN HUNGARY

Katalin Antalóczy and Magdolna Sass

Introduction

Hungary is a relatively small, open economy in Central and Eastern Europe (CEE) with a population of 10 million and it was among the first CEE countries to start rebuilding its market economy after more than 40 years of operation as a planned economy. It became a member of the OECD in 1996 and of the European Union in 2004. GDP per capita of Hungary was 27,596 USD in 2016, thus it is a mid-developed country. Hungary is also amongst those CEE countries that had built up a functioning market economy relying to a great extent on foreign direct investment (FDI).

In this short company case study, we analyse whether and how the internationalisation of one leading Hungarian company, Richter Gedeon, had an impact on developments in entrepreneurship in the country. Entrepreneurship is perceived as the establishment of new enterprises and the growth of already existing enterprises. We first present the main characteristics of the entrepreneurial ecosystem in Hungary. Second, the general picture of outward foreign direct investments originating from Hungary is provided. Then we show the history of and facts about the internationalisation of Richter Gedeon. In the next section, we give details about the sources of information and data used and the methodology applied. The following section analyses the factors of internationalisation of the company. Next, we describe the simple conceptual framework used to trace the impact of the internationalisation of Richter Gedeon on local entrepreneurship and analyse the impact relying on this framework. The final section concludes.

The entrepreneurship ecosystem in Hungary

In Hungary, entrepreneurship has increasingly been a scarcity. Hungary has long been in the middle of the Global Entrepreneurship Index rankings (Szerb, 2015), but the development of entrepreneurship in Hungary remains below what can be expected based on the development trends of the country (Horváth and Szerb, 2015). For instance, both the share and the performance of the SME sector are not significantly better in Hungary than in other less developed European Union member countries (Kállay, 2010). In addition, forced entrepreneurship, for example, to avoid unemployment or to be paid through "economising" on taxes for a workplace, is still prevalent in Hungary, similar to other former transition economies (Soós, 2012).

The aforementioned characteristics should be considered when analysing the entrepreneurial ecosystem in Hungary in detail. For this reason, we use an analytical framework that draws on Koltai and Company's 6+6 model[1] (Figure 10.1). The model comprises six fundamental actions which are required to build a successful entrepreneurial ecosystem: Identify, Train, Connect and Sustain, Fund, Enable, and Celebrate entrepreneurs. In that respect, its main factors are Policy (Enable and Fund), Human Capital (Identify and Train), Support (Connect and Sustain) and Culture (Celebrate) (Aspen Network of Development Entrepreneurs, 2013). We proceed by shortly analysing each of these aspects, and rely on various sources, with strong emphasis on the Global Entrepreneurship Monitor.[2]

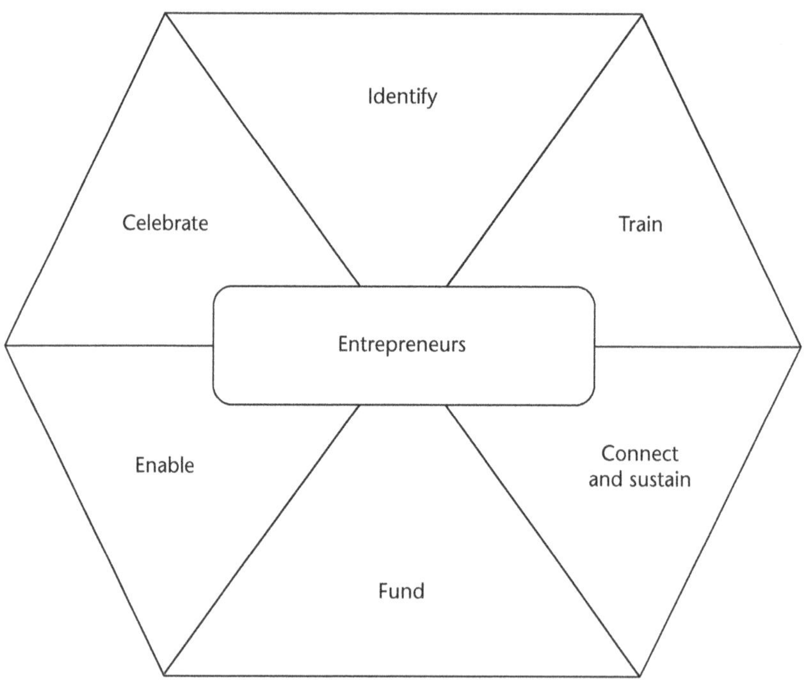

FIGURE 10.1 The 6 + 6 model of the entrepreneurship ecosystem.

Note
Figure 10.1 is a reproduction of Steven Koltai's original model (http://koltai.co/) by the authors.

In the *Policy and Support* areas, the Hungarian entrepreneurial ecosystem has deteriorated significantly recently, due to changes in government policy (Szerb, 2015). Overall, in this "illiberal era", the role of the state and government regulations and direct state intervention are strengthened, while market forces are weakened. There are more and more discretionary measures introduced by policymakers aiming at benefitting or punishing certain sectors, industries, regions, groups of entrepreneurs or even individual companies. According to Szerb (2015, p. 1):

> Under the name of "unorthodox" economic policy the Hungarian government has comprehensively centralized the administration, increased state ownership, levied new, selective taxes, begun to regulate utility prices heavily, and introduced discriminatory rules in many industries. At the same time education, the health system and social security support has been declining.

Furthermore, this new approach negatively affects overall entrepreneurship through not leaving the assessment of the various entrepreneurial projects to market forces. Entrepreneurs are thus more inclined to bribe bureaucrats or politicians in order to get into a better market position through hindering competition, softening budget constraints or getting access to (overpaid) government contracts or to extra cash free of charge or with favourable terms (e.g. from EU or Hungarian funds). These funds and financial resources, however, are quite abundant compared to the previous years, though not in comparison with other OECD countries, and they are not efficient (OECD, 2016). In the area of fostering linkages between companies, either in the form of supplier programmes or in the form of supporting clusters, there have been numerous government programmes in operation with rather varying results (Horváth *et al.*, 2013).

In the *Human Capital* area, Hungarian entrepreneurial inclinations can be explained well by demographic features and personal dispositions in the country in international comparison (Kuczi and Lengyel, 2001). According to data presented by the Global Entrepreneurship Monitor, one of the key challenges lay in personal characteristics and attitudes. Namely, Hungary has continuously been among the least entrepreneurial countries of CEE both during the crisis period and afterwards (Horváth and Szerb, 2015). (At the same time, many other countries in the region could improve their entrepreneurial positions.) When regional disparities in entrepreneurship are taken into account, Central Hungary (the region with the capital city, Budapest) shows relatively good results for entrepreneurial attitudes and abilities, while the other six regions perform poorly. Thus these latter regions are especially weak in entrepreneurial attitudes and aspirations (Szerb *et al.*, 2013). Furthermore, entrepreneurship training does not really fulfil the needs of (potential) entrepreneurs (Gubik and Farkas, 2016); hence, substantial improvements cannot be awaited.

In terms of *Culture*, lack of respect for entrepreneurs is largely present in Hungary in international comparison. Among the analysed CEE countries, the media presents by far the least positive picture of entrepreneurs in Hungary (Horváth and Szerb, 2015). This can partly be attributed to the relatively large share of forced entrepreneurship and the relatively high inclination of local entrepreneurs to avoid taxes – even in illegal ways.

It is interesting to note that the *Internationalisation* sub-pillar of entrepreneurial aspirations is the only area where Hungary exhibits higher indicators than the CEE or European Union average. This leads us to the analysis of the main features of the internationalisation of Hungarian enterprises. Here we concentrate on two distinct forms of internationalisation: foreign trade (mainly exporting) and foreign direct investments (FDI).[3] Data are only sporadically available separately for Hungarian micro companies and SMEs. In exporting, the share of small and medium-sized companies of all ownership structures is considerably lower in total exports than the European Union average (Némethné Gál, 2010); it is estimated to fluctuate around 30 per cent (Mikesy, 2013) and their main export market is the European Union (NGM, 2013).

Interestingly enough, microenterprises have a higher export/sales ratio (above 20 per cent) than small (around 13 per cent) and medium-sized companies (around 17 per cent) (Kállay, 2010). However, within the group of microenterprises and SMEs, foreign-owned ones are the most successful exporters (Kazainé Ónodi, 2014). Indeed, other survey-based (Szerb *et al.*, 2014; Gubik and Farkas, 2016) data also indicate that Hungarian-owned SMEs have a relatively low inclination to export: only every fourth does that. On the other hand, they improved their position according to the export/sales indicator starting out from a lower level, but reaching a close to EU average value by 2013. The main reason can be a push factor: recession in the domestic economy (Szerb *et al.*, 2014). Overall, exporting Hungarian-owned SMEs perform better in job creation, profitability and capital formation than their non-exporting counterparts (Mikesy, 2013) and they have a higher incidence of being among high growth enterprises (Békés and Muraközy, 2012). Exporting SMEs are operating mainly in manufacturing (Mikesy, 2013).

Outward foreign direct investments from Hungary

In terms of foreign direct investments, Hungary has been among the leading countries in the CEE region both in the stock of and in per capita outward FDI (Sass *et al.*, 2014). According to data published by the Hungarian National Bank,[4] the stock of outward FDI at the end of 2015 stood at 32 billion euros. A considerable part of that can be attributed to outward foreign investments by subsidiaries of foreign multinational companies operating in Hungary. However, there are important Hungarian multinationals as well (Sass *et al.*, 2012). Statistics are not available about the composition of outward FDI, in terms of either FDI realised by Hungarian subsidiaries of foreign multinationals on the one hand and FDI realised by Hungarian companies on the other hand or outward FDI by SMEs.

Here we can rely on the surveys prepared in the framework of the EMGP project,[5] where Hungarian-owned and controlled companies are analysed separately (Sass and Kovács, 2015).

In 2013, the top 20 Hungarian-owned or controlled foreign investor companies are estimated to be responsible for more than half of the outward FDI stock. Based on their total employment, we can find three small and eight medium-sized companies among these firms. Based on their Hungarian employment only, there are one micro, three small and nine medium-sized companies among the leading Hungarian-owned or controlled foreign investors based on their foreign assets. These foreign investor SMEs are operating mainly in IT-related services (three companies) and in research activities (three companies). Nine are services and four are manufacturing companies (Sass and Kovács, 2015). Thus, while overall the level of internationalisation of Hungarian firms is relatively low in international and regional comparison, we can still find a few successful exporters and foreign investors among micro-firms and SMEs.

On the other hand, there are a few large local firms dominating outward FDI, such as the petrol company MOL, OTP Bank and the electronics company Videoton. Furthermore, our case study firm, Richter Gedeon, is also among the top investors (Sass and Kovács, 2015). The following section presents in detail the company, its history, main characteristics and internationalisation.

Case study of Richter Gedeon

Introduction to Richter Gedeon and to its industry

Richter Gedeon is a Hungarian pharmaceutical firm with a very long tradition. It(s predecessor) was established in 1901. It is a highly innovative company, being responsible for the highest share in Hungarian R&D and registering a large number of patents. Richter Gedeon's main activities are research, development, manufacturing and marketing of pharmaceutical products. After being nationalised in 1948, the firm maintained its important position and market share in Hungary (and the [former] CMEA – Council for Mutual Economic Assistance[6] countries) and has been one of the leading companies of the country. Richter Gedeon was privatised through the introduction of its shares on the Budapest stock exchange in three tranches between 1994 and 1999 (Antalóczy, 2008). At present, it has three production units in Hungary: in Budapest (the oldest), Dorog and Debrecen (operating since 2012).

The company operates in the pharmaceutical industry, which is at present in the process of undergoing significant changes. The industry is moving towards a new model, where first, profits are significantly lower than in the previous era, and second, there is an ongoing consolidation, mainly through mergers and acquisitions (M&As). The link between these two phenomena can be traced to the previously high prices based on the exceedingly high costs of product (molecule) development. With the expiry of previous patents (and the appearance of new competitors with generic products), companies strive to find new molecules, which is increasingly costly. That is why firms increasingly rely on new strategies: they either outsource basic R&D or try to find small firms with potentially successful molecules. In these new circumstances, pharma companies from "mid-developed" countries, such as Hungary, cannot really compete with Big Pharma (leading pharma companies of developed countries) because of their limited resources in terms of both capital and human resources.

On the other hand, for pharma firms coming from "mid-developed" countries, competing with emerging pharma multinationals is also problematic because these latter have a significant cost advantage due to labour costs and economies of scale. In these circumstances, Richter Gedeon decided to move into the "specialty pharma" direction: specialty pharma companies usually concentrate on the dispensation of specialty pharma drugs. Specialty drugs are specialised, high-cost products which are part of therapies for complex diseases and should be administered in a special way: they require special handling, distribution and administration. This is a high growth area for pharmaceutical firms and may constitute a good way to remain competitive for those firms that cannot rely on cost advantages in production or on large scale-economies and brand names as those belonging to Big Pharma (Pharmavoice, 2014). Richter Gedeon specialised on the one hand in gynaecological pharmaceuticals and, on the other hand, in psychotic drugs, due to its new development: cariprazine, an antipsychotic drug under clinical trials, and previous discoveries in this area.

The pharma industry has another specialty: because of its highly innovative nature and because of producing a product for which quality and health security issues are of paramount importance, a large part of the value chain (that is, the various production, R&D and sales-related activities) is "kept" within the companies. Thus, its backward and forward linkages are very few compared to other industries (Medina *et al.*, 2017). A further important characteristic of the industry is that the market is still highly fragmented due to the national systems of registering and financing pharmaceutical products.

Richter Gedeon, during its long history, has witnessed many changes in its industry and business environment and has adapted its strategy accordingly, when it was needed. This flexibility explains its long existence. An important part of the strategy change is connected to the internationalisation of the company.

The history of internationalisation of Richter Gedeon

Richter Gedeon has a very long internationalisation history: some of its products were already exported at the time of its establishment, with quick growth afterwards. As for foreign direct investment, Richter Gedeon turned into a company limited by shares in 1923, and soon afterwards it established two foreign affiliates in Bucharest, Romania and Warsaw, Poland. Before the Second World War, it had ten foreign subsidiaries and 40 foreign representative offices, and it was one of the top exporters of the country.[7] After the Second World War, the company could maintain its exports, now mainly towards CMEA countries, with some sales in developed markets, especially starting from the 1970s (Antalóczy, 2008).

After the transition process started, the company had to adapt and change its internationalisation strategy at least three times.[8] First, with the collapse of regional trade, former CMEA markets became more risky and less solvent. However, while Richter Gedeon's brand and products were well known in the former CMEA countries, the company decided to maintain its market position in this region. That is why Richter Gedeon acquired, together with another Hungarian pharma company, Egis, the specialised foreign trade agency for pharma products, Medimpex,[9] with its foreign representative offices. From these, Richter Gedeon became parent to the non-CMEA offices and it established its own network of offices in former CMEA countries soon afterwards. Then the 1998 Russian and Asian crisis reinforced the problems of the former CMEA region. As a reaction, the company targeted new foreign markets (especially in the Americas and in emerging Asia).

The second strategy change occurred, when, after around 2004–7, negative developments in the domestic market together with industry developments globally induced another change in company strategy. As a result, foreign markets, as opposed to the domestic one, and thus exports and FDI became even more important.

The third strategy change was introduced after 2010, as a reaction to new developments due mainly to the global financial crisis. The top management took the decision to become a specialty pharma company. That brought over changes in the main destinations of especially FDI: acquisitions of pharma and biotech firms in developed European countries (Germany and Switzerland).

A highly internationalised company

At present, the company has a very high export/sales ratio (89 per cent in 2016), which has never gone below 60 per cent in the last two and a half decades, and since 2007, it has been permanently above 80 per cent. In terms of FDI, Richter Gedeon has a wide geographic outreach: it is present mainly with representative offices and with three production units in former CMEA countries (Poland, Romania and Russia). Furthermore, it is present in Western European countries in almost all EU member states with trading affiliates and with two production units in Germany and Switzerland. Another important focus of foreign expansion is Asia, where there are two production units in the form of joint ventures in China and India, as well as numerous trade representative offices. The fourth main locus of foreign expansion is the Americas, where the firm is present mainly through trading affiliates and trading joint ventures (Sass and Kovács, 2012).

The Transnationality Index (TNI)[10] of UNCTAD shows the highly internationalised nature of the company and the fact that this is mainly due to exports (Table 10.1). The foreign assets/total assets ratio is the lowest, while every third employee works abroad.

TABLE 10.1 Elements of the Transnationality Index of Richter Gedeon (2013)

Element		*Foreign/total (%)*
Assets abroad (million USD)	743	22.4
Total assets (million USD)	3314	
Foreign sales (million USD)	1480	91.0
Total sales (million USD)	1626	
Foreign employment (number)	4299	37.6
Total employment (number)	11,446	
TNI		51

Source: Authors, based on Sass and Kovács (2015).

The owners of Richter Gedeon

As for the ownership structure, the Hungarian National Asset Management Inc. is the largest owner, with 25.25 per cent of the shares of the company. The only other share-owner with more than 5 per cent of the shares is a foreign financial investor company, Aberdeen Asset Management Plc, based in the United Kingdom. Numerous other foreign and domestic owners are present in the ownership structure of Richter Gedeon, with the combined share of foreigners exceeding 60 per cent (Richter Gedeon, 2016). Thus, its ownership structure has been dispersed since its privatisation on the Budapest stock exchange, with no majority owner and thus with no controlling owner.

An interesting question in connection with Richter Gedeon is whether the state as the biggest owner intervenes in any way into the activities of the company. In another paper (Antalóczy and Sass, 2016), we analysed in detail that question, and found that the state as owner never intervened into the operation of the company. On the other hand, the state as regulator created a business and regulatory environment after 2007, which is rather detrimental for Richter Gedeon, and that acted as a push factor from the point of view of the internationalisation of the company, in terms of both exports and FDI (that we identified here as the second strategy change of the company).

Another question emerges in connection with the majority foreign ownership in the firm. Because of that, the firm can be evaluated as indirect foreign investor (UNCTAD, 1998; Altzinger *et al.*, 2003; Andreff, 2003; Kalotay, 2012), that is, a non-indigenous company using the Hungarian subsidiary as a "mediator" in its foreign expansion in third countries. However, in the case of Richter Gedeon, foreign majority ownership does not equal foreign control. There are no major foreign owners with more than 10 per cent of the shares. Thus, the ownership structure of Richter Gedeon is highly dispersed. That is why Sass *et al.* (2012) introduced the notion of "virtual indirect" investor, where there is majority foreign ownership but no foreign control. The main reason for distinguishing indirect and virtual indirect investors is that their characteristics are different: virtual indirect investors behave actually similarly to direct investors. Richter Gedeon's case is obviously supporting this statement.

The impact of Richter Gedeon on entrepreneurship development in Hungary: theoretical background and methodology

We analyse the entrepreneurial impact of Richter Gedeon in the framework of "corporate entrepreneurship". Conceptually, we rely on the definition provided by Wolcott and Lippitz, according to which "corporate entrepreneurship is the process by which teams within an established company conceive, foster, launch and manage a new business that is distinct from the parent company but leverages the parent's assets, market position, capabilities or other resources" (2007, p. 1). In particular, Wolcott and Lippitz (2007) distinguish among four types of corporate entrepreneurship: the enabler, the producer, the opportunist and the advocate.[11] In our understanding, besides strengthening the competitive position of the firm in question, corporate entrepreneurship may "spill over" to entrepreneurs in the environment of the firm and have a beneficial impact on entrepreneurship in general. We try to determine and analyse the channels through which corporate entrepreneurship in Richter Gedeon spills over to its business environment and enhances entrepreneurship.

Empirically, we draw on multiple sources of information. The most important sources were eight anonymous semi-structured, questionnaire-based interviews conducted with various leading representatives of the company in 2016, including the head of R&D, the head of PR and government relations, and the medical director of the company. We also conducted a semi-structured interview with the representative of the company in Pharmapolis. With some representatives of the company we had multiple appointments. The interviews were between 55 and 95 minutes' long. Furthermore, we conducted interviews with other companies that are in business contact or in cooperation with the analysed firm. As a second source of information, we extensively used the annual reports of Richter Gedeon, various other reports, press releases and communications published by the company. Third, we used various statistical sources for macrodata and company ranks.

These various sources of quantitative and qualitative information supplement each other well and relying on multiple sources helps us to handle the problems of bias and subjectivity, while providing a good basis for analysis in the framework of a company case study.

In the following sections, we will present details about the success factors in the internationalisation of the analysed company. We underline the importance of innovativeness and R&D and the role of the CEO and the top management. After identifying the possible channels of the impact of the successful internationalisation of the firm on entrepreneurship in the domestic economy, we analyse these one by one based on the information we obtained from the company interviews.

Factors of success in and obstacles to internationalisation

The most important factor for the internationalisation success of Richter Gedeon is obviously the innovative and highly R&D intensive nature of its activities. The company has a strong tradition in R&D. Its R&D is centred on the development of generic drugs; however, there are certain new molecules as well invented by the researchers of the company. Most recently, the antipsychotic drug cariprazine obtained the permission to be marketed in the US in 2015.[12] This is a substantial success, as the FDA approves around 30 new medicines per year.[13] As for the size of R&D at Richter Gedeon, it is illustrative that the company is responsible for almost 10 per cent of total Hungarian R&D (2014, own calculations based on the data of Hungarian Central Statistical Office and Richter Gedeon). The company represents the majority of Hungarian R&D in the pharmaceutical industry: 55.5 per cent in 2014 (based on the information of MAGYOSZ: Association of Hungarian Pharmaceutical Companies).

The R&D performance of Richter Gedeon is comparable to other EU companies: in 2015, according to the EU R&D Scoreboard, Richter Gedeon stood in 178th place with regards to its R&D spending. In the list of the companies of the ten new member states of the EU, Richter Gedeon was first according to R&D spending in 2014 and sixteenth according to turnover in 2015. The company registered 1415 patents since 1927 and 129 in the period between 2010 and 2014, both of which are the highest numbers among Hungarian pharmaceutical firms, including foreign-owned subsidiaries (Rugraff and Sass, 2016). It is important to note that, more recently, certain strategic-asset seeking FDI served the further strengthening of the innovative activities of the company: the acquisition of the Swiss PregLem in 2010 and the German Strathmann Biotech (2007), as well as the most recent acquisition of the Swiss biotech holding Finox, are strategic asset seeking.

One must note also another factor of success in the former CMEA markets: Richter Gedeon and its products were well-known in these markets, and the company could capitalise on that "fame" after the collapse of the CMEA.[14] In 2015, the share of the CIS markets (mainly Russia) amounted to 33 per cent in total sales, and the share of former CMEA without CIS was 27 per cent, thus the former CMEA markets (excluding Hungary) have a 60 per cent share in total sales.

The role of well-grounded strategies, including on internationalisation, should be further emphasised as it guided the activities of Richter Gedeon. Obviously, implementation of these strategies was shaped by the CEO of the company – Erik Bogsch.

Erik Bogsch has been the CEO of Richter Gedeon since 1992. He seems to be the main "engine" behind the strategy, image and overall behaviour of the company. Mr Bogsch's commitment to the company is clearly presented by that fact that he has dedicated his entire professional career to the development of Richter Gedeon and the Hungarian pharma industry. Besides being talented in chemical engineering and managing a pharma firm, at the start of the transition process he already had international market economy experience[15] of the pharmaceutical industry and market. That is a unique combination among the Hungarian pharmaceutical CEOs (Antalóczy, 2008). The CEO put together his own management team: he started to work with his trusted colleagues. Mr Bogsch has also always emphasised the importance of teamwork in managing the company. During our interviews, we found that there exists a "Richter heart", to which workers of the company are very loyal.

An important area connected to the role and personality of the CEO and of the top management team is the internationalisation of the company. The top management elaborated and determined the internationalisation strategy and changes in it, as was described in detail on page 000. First, after the transition process started, the company acquired a large part of the foreign offices of Medimpex, realising how important that is in order to keep their presence on the (former) CMEA markets. Second, after 2008, when the domestic environment became less advantageous (even disadvantageous) for the company, and there was a substantial decrease in its domestic market share, the company increased its presence in foreign markets (Antalóczy, 2008). Third, a little later, the company moved into the "specialty pharma direction". One of the most important ways for doing that was the acquisition of Western European companies, the pharma and molecule portfolio of which fitted well with that of Richter Gedeon. The CEO and the top management team elaborated and implemented this strategy.

It is important to emphasise that the success factors for the internationalisation of Richter Gedeon have changed considerably between the periods connected to the different strategy changes. A common success factor is the intense innovative and R&D activity of the company; however, its intensity and importance came to the forefront after the first strategy change. Own R&D was "supplemented" and boosted by foreign acquisitions with at least partly a strategic asset seeking motive. Furthermore, another common success factor has been the thorough and flexible, in certain cases pro-active, strategy-building activities of the CEO and the top management team. In the first, immediate post-transition phase, after the first strategy change, an important success factor was the inherited network of personal and business links and the internationally (or at least in the countries of the former CMEA) still well-known and remembered "Richter brand". In the second phase, following the second strategy change, which – as we have shown – was forced by losses in the domestic market share, pro-actively positioning the company on developed markets was successful. In the third phase – that is, after the third strategy change – the decision to move in the specialty pharma direction can be evaluated as important.

The internationalisation of Richter Gedeon and local entrepreneurship

Richter Gedeon can be viewed as an "opportunist" corporate entrepreneur company: there is no designated organisational ownership or resources for corporate entrepreneurship; it proceeds mainly due to the activities of certain people in the top (or mid-) management (Wolcott and Lippitz, 2007) In that respect, we already called the attention to the important role of the CEO and other members of the top management team. Their new ideas, including the strategy of internationalisation and in connection with that setting up new links and forms of cooperation with other local companies, economic and noneconomic actors resulted in direct and indirect impacts on their business environment.

We constructed a simple framework for the analysis of the impact of the internationalisation of Richter Gedeon on entrepreneurship in Hungary (Figure 10.2).

The internationalisation of Richter Gedeon has had both direct and indirect impacts on Hungarian SMEs and entrepreneurship. The direct impact was exercised on one hand through the increased demand for supply from already supplying firms and from potential suppliers. In that respect, the characteristics of the pharmaceutical industry – that is, the fact that a much larger share of the value chain is "kept" in the companies, as compared to other industries – reduce significantly the size of this impact. Indeed, we found that only medium to large-sized packaging and labelling companies, suppliers of Richter Gedeon, could benefit from the increase of sales due to the internationalisation of our case study firm.

However, even this impact was limited, because Richter's foreign subsidiaries relied mainly on local suppliers. Thus, in that case, export and foreign direct investment acted more as substitutes to each other.

On the other hand, the highly innovative nature of the company poses new challenges for research and development. In that area, the direct impact in the form of outsourcing certain activities to other firms and acquiring prospective biotechnology companies is significant, according to one interview. Thus, Richter Gedeon relies increasingly on outsourcing of certain (usually standardised) R&D related activities to local (and foreign) small biotechnology companies, and this type of R&D supply has grown considerably. Sometimes Richter Gedeon acquires small

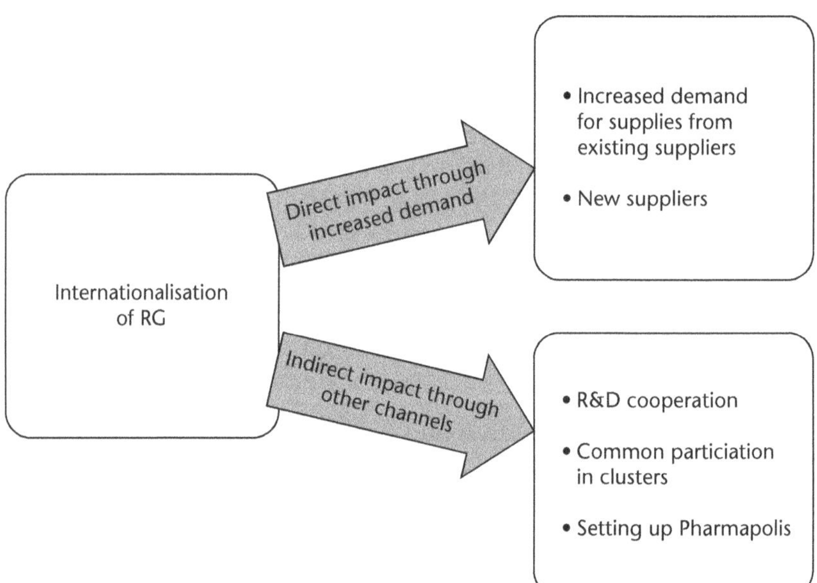

FIGURE 10.1 The 6 + 6 model of the entrepreneurship ecosystem.

Note

Figure 10.1 is a reproduction of Steven Koltai's original model (http://koltai.co/) by the authors.

local or foreign companies with half-ready molecules or promising research results. Spin-off and startup biotechnology companies, related mainly to the university centres in Hungary (especially in Budapest, Debrecen and Szeged), play an important role in that. This contributes obviously to the increase in entrepreneurial activities in Hungary, especially in innovative activities.

As for the indirect entrepreneurial impact of Richter Gedeon, we identified three main channels. The first channel is the more intense cooperation of Richter Gedeon in R&D; in which universities (mainly in the above-mentioned university towns) and research institutes (private and public, connected to the Hungarian Academy of Sciences) are the main partners in basic research. In applied research (development) the company cooperates with industry partners. However, the local impact is limited due to the fact that Richter Gedeon's top industry research partners come from abroad – these are Japanese, Finnish and US companies. But among smaller partners and basic research partners, Hungarian firms and institutions are also present.[16] Thus through this channel the company contributes to domestic entrepreneurship, as small companies are set up and become partners of Richter Gedeon. A few such instances were found during the interviews, pointing to an existing, though relatively limited, entrepreneurial impact of the company in this respect.

Another channel of the indirect impact and a more interesting case is that of the Pharmapolis Pharmaceutical Science Park Ltd (see Box 10.1). This has been set up in one of the less developed (in terms of per capita GDP) eastern counties of Hungary. This region, however, has a long scientific tradition and strong scientific base in the form of a large university and public research institutes. In spite of the attractive features described in Box 10.1 and the intense advertising and promotion of the park for potentially interested domestic and foreign parties, at present Richter Gedeon itself has been renting 75–80 per cent of available space. This share is expected to go up to close to 100 per cent by 2017–18. At present, besides Richter Gedeon, there is only one small company present with an office space of negligible size.[17] According to one of the interviews, there were negotiations taking place with a few dozen firms, including SMEs; however, almost all of them retreated from concluding an agreement with the management of the science park. The main reason seems to be the parallel existence of a non-market based supply of similar services from local universities and research institutes using public assets.[18] Thus, in the absence of regulatory changes, the expected impact on SMEs could not be realised; in spite of the fact that this would have been especially important in the analysed region, which is among the least entrepreneurial ones in Hungary.

The third channel is connected to the other local activity of Richter Gedeon in Debrecen, which is a cluster (see Box 10.1), in which our case study company plays the leading, even dominating role: it represents the overwhelming majority of total sales, exports and employment. According to one analysis, Richter Gedeon's share has not changed substantially throughout the operation of the cluster (MAG Zrt, 2012). We have collected data to extend the timeframe of the previous evaluation

BOX 10.1 PHARMAPOLIS PHARMACEUTICAL SCIENCE PARK LTD AND PHARMAPOLIS ACCREDITED CLUSTER

Pharmapolis Ltd was founded by the Debrecen Asset Management Company, the Hajdú-Bihar County Chamber of Commerce and Industry and Gedeon Richter Plc in 2009. The centre was financed from public and private funds. It was opened in July 2012 in the immediate vicinity of the Biotechnology Plant of Richter Gedeon, opened in April 2012. The 3300 m^2 science park contains a state-of-the-art biotechnology research base and offers related technological and business services for pharma and biotechnology firms, including SMEs. A further attractive feature of the science park is the vicinity of the plant of Richter Gedeon, the University of Debrecen and the Institute for Nuclear Research of HAS, all providing significant scope for scientific cooperation for entrepreneurs and SMEs.

Pharmapolis innovative pharmaceutical cluster

The cluster was established in 2007 with ten founding members, including Richter Gedeon. It is one of the leading accredited clusters in Hungary. At present, there are 24 members, among them Richter Gedeon and the science park. Debrecen University and a local hospital are also among the members. Sixteen members are SMEs, many of them owned and managed by university professors from Debrecen and other leading Hungarian universities in the research field affected (mainly Szeged) – thus they can be considered as university-related spin-off or startup companies. Focus areas of the cluster are innovative therapeutic products, functional imaging, in vitro technological platforms, education and biotechnology. Research areas include radioimaging, diseases of the central nervous system and metabolic diseases, immunological disorders and cancer. The role of Richter Gedeon is determining in the cluster. The most important activities of the cluster are centred around common R&D projects and R&D cooperation of the members.

Sources: Interviews conducted in the framework of the research project; MAG Zrt. (2012); http://pharmapolis-hungary.eu/;http://ec.europa.eu/regional_policy/hu/projects/hungary/pharmaceutical-research-development-and-innovation-centre-provides-tailor-made-technological-services.

of MAG Zrt (2012). We found, that the share of Richter Gedeon has even slightly increased in the cluster's total sales between 2010 and 2015, from 89.3 to 90.4 per cent. However, total sales of the cluster members have grown by 31 per cent during that period, and even without Richter Gedeon, there is 18 per cent growth. Notwithstanding, this growth is not distributed equally among the cluster members: there are seven companies with substantial (above 20 per cent) growth rates, but sales of six companies actually declined between 2010 and

2015.[19] Thus, the results are quite mixed; seven companies (two middle-sized and five small-sized) could use the opportunities provided by being in one cluster with Richter Gedeon, while in the case of 12 companies we could not trace any positive impact.

Thus, this cluster provides another opportunity for cooperation, and local entrepreneurs (mainly small-sized companies set up by employees of the local university and research institutes) are quite active in it. However, up until now the positive impact of Richter Gedeon – in spite of the efforts of the firm itself – could materialise only partially, as it is still the dominating participant. The mixed results show the persistently low entrepreneurial inclinations of the countryside region, where even the regulatory framework takes its toll on local entrepreneurship by preferring non-market solutions. Richter Gedeon in itself could not change significantly the local situation. As the Hungarian saying goes: one swallow does not make a summer…

Key conclusions

Richter Gedeon is one of the leading Hungarian controlled companies with a long history of internationalisation through exports, FDI and R&D. It is present worldwide, with both production units and representative offices. Export represents more than nine-tenths of total sales. Its main export markets are the former CMEA markets; however, it is present increasingly in Asia, in Western Europe and in the Americas as well. Besides exports, foreign direct investments of Richter Gedeon are also to be found in these locations. The company's CEO and top management have had a determining role in the successful survival and operation of the company, and initiated and carried out at least three important strategy changes after the start of the transition process. These were of outstanding importance in the success of the company. At present the company defines itself as a specialty pharma firm, specialising in gynaecological products and anti-psychotic drugs. The other factor of success of the firm is its intensive R&D activity resulting in a high number (the highest in Hungary) of patents.

We found that the impact of internationalisation of the firm on local entrepreneurship can be connected to the intensive R&D activity, while through increased foreign sales and thus production, the local entrepreneurial impact is limited due to industry specificities. On one hand, directly, through increased demand for local supplies of R&D, partly through outsourcing certain non-core R&D activities to already existing local SMEs. On the other hand, indirectly, when R&D cooperation with local universities and research institutes and to a much lesser extent with SMEs results in the birth of new firms or quick growth of existing SMEs. Interestingly enough, those two organisations (science park and cluster) in which Richter Gedeon plays a leading role and offers the opportunity for local SMEs, entrepreneurs and experts to get into a closer business relationship with it could not result in a substantial increase in local entrepreneurship, in spite of the substantial efforts of the company. Thus, the company could not initiate a substantial change in the low entrepreneurial inclination characterising Hungary.

Notes

1 For more details, see http://koltai.co/.
2 In the Global Entrepreneurship Monitor (see www.gemconsortium.org/about/gem), the analysis of data is based on three main pillars: Entrepreneurial Activity, Entrepreneurial Aspirations and Entrepreneurial Attitudes. Within the main pillars, there are 14 "sub-pillars". Internationalisation is one of the five sub-pillars of Entrepreneurial Aspirations. The indicators are presented for numerous countries, thus enabling international comparison.
3 FDI is analysed separately, in the next section.
4 www.mnb.hu/en/statistics/statistical-data-and-information/statistical-time-series/viii-balance-of-payments-foreign-direct-investment-international-investment-position/foreign-direct-investments.
5 For more details, see http://ccsi.columbia.edu/publications/emgp/.
6 The economic organisation comprising of planned economies under the leadership for the Soviet Union, functioning between 1949 and 1991.
7 For more details, see www.richter.hu/en-US/about-us/Pages/corporate-history.aspx.
8 This analysis is based on the interviews conducted with the representatives of the company.
9 In the planned economy, foreign trade was conducted through specialised foreign trade agencies, organised on a sectoral or industry basis.
10 The Transnationality Index is a composite index measuring the level of internationalisation of a multinational firm. It is an arithmetic mean of the ratio of foreign assets to total assets, foreign sales to total sales and foreign employment to total employment.
11 The enabler: the company provides funding and senior executive attention to the project. The producer: the company establishes and supports a full-service group with a mandate for corporate entrepreneurship. The opportunist: the firm has no deliberate approach to corporate entrepreneurship. Internal and external networks drive concept selection and resource allocation. The advocate: the firm strongly evangelises for corporate entrepreneurship, but business units provide the primary funding (Wolcott and Lippitz, 2007).
12 www.drugs.com/newdrugs/fda-approves-vraylar-cariprazine-schizophrenia-bipolar-disorder-4264.html.
13 Interview with the head of R&D.
14 Interview with the head of public relations.
15 Between 1977 and 1983 he worked in Mexico and between 1988 and 1992 in the United Kingdom as head of local representative offices of Medimpex. See www.richter.hu/en-US/about-us/management/Pages/executive-board.aspx.
16 Information from the interviews with the representatives of the company.
17 Information from the interview conducted with the representative of Pharmapolis.
18 According to the interviews, this is not a Hungarian specificity; in Europe, many of the universities provide similarly low-priced services.
19 Five cluster members are non-profit organisations and thus they do not have a balance sheet.

References

Altzinger, W., Bellak, C., Jaklic, A. and Rojec, M., 2003, "Direct versus indirect foreign investment from transition economies: Is there a difference in parent company/home country impact?", in M. Svetlicic and M. Rojec, eds., *Facilitating Transition by Internationalization. Outward Direct Investment from Central European Economies in Transition*, Aldershot, UK: Ashgate, pp. 91–108.

Andreff, W., 2003, "The newly emerging TNCs from economies in transition: A comparison with Third World outward FDI", *Transnational Corporations*, 12 (2), pp. 73–118.

Antalóczy, K., 2008, "Állami piacteremtés – nemzeti bajnok teremtése: A Richter Gedeon NyRt. esete" ("Creation of market by the state – creation of national champions: The case of Richter Gedeon"), *Külgazdaság*, 52 (7–8), pp. 41–80.

Antalóczy, K. and Sass, M., 2016, "Internationalisation of a minority state-owned company: The case of the Hungarian Richter Gedeon", Paper prepared for the first EIBA workshop, Corvinus University, Budapest, 12 October 2016.

Aspen Network of Development Entrepreneurs, 2013, *Entrepreneurial Ecosystem Diagnostic Toolkit*. December 2013. Available at https://assets.aspeninstitute.org/content/uploads/files/content/docs/pubs/FINAL%20Ecosystem%20Toolkit%20Draft_print%20version.pdf. Accessed 3 May 2017.

Békés, G. and Muraközy, B., 2012, "Magyar gazellák. A gyors növekedésű vállalatok jellemzői és kialakulásuk elemzése" ("Hungarian gazelles. Characteristics and origin of high growth companies"), *Közgazdasági Szemle*, 59 (3), pp. 233–262.

Gubik, S.A. and Farkas, Sz., 2016, "Student entrepreneurship in Hungary: Selected results based on GUESSS survey", *Entrepreneurial Business and Economic Review*, 4 (4), pp. 123–139.

Horváth, K. and Szerb, L., 2015, *GEM 2015 Magyarország: Vállalkozások és vállalkozói ökoszisztéma helyzete 2015-ben* (*GEM 2015 Hungary: Enterprises and Entrepreneurial Ecosystem in 2015*), London; Pécs: Global Entrepreneurship Monitor; University of Pécs.

Horváth M., Kerekes I. and Patik R., 2013, "Elemzés a magyar klaszterfejlesztés elmúlt 4 évéről" ("Analysis of the last four years of Hungarian cluster development"), MAG Zrt, Budapest, 30 April. Available at www.klaszterfejlesztes.hu/content/cont_51d4102c8c68e4.02287351/elemzes_a_magyar_klaszterfejlesztes_elmult__4_everol.pdf. Accessed 1 March 2017.

Kállay L., 2010, "KKV-szektor: versenyképesség, munkahelyteremtés, szerkezetátalakítás" ("The SME sector: Competitiveness, job creation and restructuring"), Working paper prepared in the framework of Competitiveness Research at the Competitiveness Research Centre of the Corvinus University, Budapest. Available at www.szolidaritas.org/files/1/3/kkv_versenykepesseg_-_tanulmany_-_kl_2012_03__.pdf. Accessed 25 January 2017.

Kalotay, K., 2012, "Indirect FDI", *Journal of World Investment and Trade*, 13, pp. 542–555.

Kazainé Ónodi, A., 2014, "Export performance clusters of the Hungarian enterprises: What factors are behind the successful export activities?", *Entrepreneurial Business and Economics Review*, 2 (4), pp. 9–29.

Kuczi, T. and Lengyel, Gy., 2001, "The spread of entrepreneurship in Eastern Europe", in P. Meusburger and H. Jöns, eds., *Transformations in Hungary. Essays in Economy and Society*, Berlin; Heidelberg: Springer Verlag, pp. 157–172.

MAG Zrt., 2012, "A magyar klaszteresedés elmúlt 3 éve az akkreditált innovációs klaszterek példáján keresztül" ("The last three years of Hungarian clustering on the basis of the accredited innovation clusters"), MAG Zrt, Budapest. Available at www.mvfportal.hu/data/regio/20/news/Klaszterek_elemzese_2012.pdf. Accessed 1 February 2017.

Medina, A., Thompson, D., Spinoglio, M., Magalhães, H., Pinho, F., Rocha, F., Esteves, S., Bilsen, V., Debergh, P., Greeven, S., Kretz, D., Stehrer, R., Hanzl-Weiss, D., Siedschlag, I., Di Ubaldo, M., Szalavetz, A. and Sass, M., 2017, *Study on Investment Needs and Obstacles Along Industrial Value Chains*, SPI, IDEA, WIIW, ESRI, IWE, Manuscript.

Mikesy, Á., 2013, "A magyarországi mikro-, kis- és középvállalatok nemzetköziesedése és a külföldi értékesítést nehezítő akadályok" ("The internationalisation of Hungarian micro enterprises and SMEs and obstacles to foreign sales"), *Külgazdaság*, 52 (1–2), pp. 92–120.

Némethné Gál, A., 2010, "A kis- és középvállalatok versenyképessége – egy lehetséges elemzési keretrendszer" ("The competitiveness of small- and medium-sized enterprises") *Közgazdasági Szemle*, 57 (2), pp. 181–193.

NGM, 2013, *Kis- és középvállalkozások stratégiája, 2014–2020* (*Strategy of Small- and Medium-sized Enterprises, 2014–2020*), Budapest: Ministry of National Economy.

OECD, 2016, *Hungary Policy Brief. Finance. Improving SMEs' Access to Finance.* Available at www.oecd.org/hungary/hungary-improving-SME-access-to-finance_EN.pdf. Accessed 12 March 2017.

Pharmavoice, 2014, "Specialty pharma on the rise", November/December. Available at www.sas.com/content/dam/SAS/en_us/doc/other2/pharmavoice-specialty-pharma.pdf. Accessed 12 October 2016.

Richter Gedeon, 2016, *Gedeon Richter Annual Report 2016.* Available at www.richter.hu/en-US/investors/company-reports/Company%20report/Richter-Gedeon-Annual-Report-2016.pdf. Accessed 3 May 2017.

Rugraff, E. and Sass, M., 2016, *Indigenous Technological Development Through Subcontracting Linkages from Multinationals: Evidence from the Hungarian Pharmaceutical and Biopharmaceutical Industry*, Manuscript.

Sass, M. and Kovács, O., 2012, *MOL Group, the Petrol Company, Continues to Lead the Ranking of Hungarian Multinationals*, New York: Columbia Center on Sustainable Investment, A Joint Center of Columbia Law School and the Earth Institute, Columbia University.

Sass, M. and Kovács, O., 2015, *Hungarian Multinationals in 2013 – A Slow Recovery After the Crisis?* New York: Columbia Center on Sustainable Investment, A Joint Center of Columbia Law School and the Earth Institute, Columbia University.

Sass, M., Antalóczy, K. and Éltető, A., 2012, "Emerging multinationals and the role of virtual indirect investors: The case of Hungary", *Eastern European Economics*, 50 (2), pp. 41–58.

Sass, M., Antalóczy, K. and Éltető, A., 2014, "Outward FDI from Hungary: The emergence of Hungarian multinationals", *Entrepreneurial Business and Economics Review*, 2 (3), pp. 47–61.

Soós, K.A., 2012, "Polish and Hungarian SMEs facing the crisis", in B. Dallago and Ch. Guglielmettied, eds., *The Consequences of the International Crisis for European SMEs. Vulnerability and Resilience*, London and New York: Routledge, pp. 154–174.

Szerb, L., 2015, "Entrepreneurship in an illiberal, unorthodox country: The case of Hungary". Available at: https://thegedi.org/entrepreneurship-in-an-illiberal-unorthodox-country-the-case-of-hungary/. Accessed 12 November 2017.

Szerb, L., Komlósi, É., Ács, Z.J. and Ortega-Argilés, R., 2013, "Regional entrepreneurship in Hungary based on the Regional Entrepreneurship and Development Index (REDI) methodology". Paper presented at the 35th DRUID Celebration Conference 2013, Barcelona, Spain, 17–19 June. Available at http://druid8.sit.aau.dk/acc_papers/lim19j8lbffgon8n99kxif03are7.pdf. Accessed 5 June 2017.

Szerb, L., Márkus, G. and Csapi, V., 2014, "Versenyképesség és nemzetköziesedés a magyar kisvállalatok körében" ("Competitiveness and internationalisation of Hungarian SMEs"), *Külgazdaság*, 58 (11–12), pp. 53–75.

UNCTAD, 1998, *World Investment Report 1998: Trends and Determinants*, New York; Geneva: UNCTAD.

Wolcott, R.C. and Lippitz M.J., 2007, "The four models of corporate entrepreneurship", *MIT Sloan Management Review*, 49 (1), pp. 75–82.

11

ENTREPRENEURSHIP AND THE INTERNATIONALIZATION PROCESS OF HIDRIA – A HIDDEN CHAMPION COMPANY FROM SLOVENIA

Danica Purg, Iztok Seljak, and Alenka Braček Lalić

Introduction

Entrepreneurship and internationalization are two distinct, yet related processes, both very important for Slovenia's economy. This article explains the development of entrepreneurship in Slovenia's economy through the lens of internationalization. It traces both processes in Slovenia's historical context. Then, it provides a case study of Slovenian company Hidria, one of the Hidden Champions of Central and Eastern Europe, according to Hermann Simon's methodology. The company is one of the world's leaders in the field of automotive and industrial technologies and one of the most innovative companies in Europe (in 2012–2013, it won the prestigious European Business Award for the most innovative company in Europe among 15,000 European companies). It employs more than 2,000 people in its subsidiaries located in Slovenia, Germany, Hungary, and China, and sells its products in more than 80 countries. Because of Hidria's high international profile and commitment to innovation, the case study focuses on the company's internationalization pathways. It identifies challenges, obstacles, achievements, and internal and external implications, as well as how these relate to the entrepreneurship process within Hidria. Besides the focus on the entrepreneurial and international aspect, the case study places significant emphasis on Hidria's innovativeness, which is an important characteristic of the company.

Entrepreneurship and the development of internationalization – the Slovene context

According to Rebernik *et al.* (2016), "we cannot learn about entrepreneurship by merely counting the number of businesses and entrepreneurs. We can learn about entrepreneurship by examining the entrepreneurship ecosystem, fundamental characteristics of entrepreneurship activities, as well as motivations and ambitions of entrepreneurs" (Rebernik *et al.*, 2016, p. 19). The same applies to the internationalization process, which should be studied from the perspective of the economic, cultural, and social development of a particular country and its essential political and historical features. Taking into consideration both assumptions, we start this chapter by explaining the entrepreneurship process in Slovenian companies and their innovation endeavors through the lens of the internationalization development of the Slovenian economy. By exploring main developments associated with both concepts, we lay the groundwork for the case study of Hidria, which is one of the leading global companies in the field of automotive technologies and industrial technologies, and one of the most innovative companies in Europe.

Welter and Smallbone (2011) write that Slovenia developed its own entrepreneurship and small and medium-sized enterprise policies after it gained its independence from Yugoslavia in 1991. "The Enterprise Law (1988) from ex-Yugoslavia initiated the first spontaneous entrepreneurial wave" (Glas *et al.*, 2000, p. 3) "when many firms started as a result of administrative deregulation" (Drnovšek, 2004, p. 185). After gaining its independence, Slovenia moved from a socialist self-management system toward a market economy. Jaklič and Svetličič (2010, p. 3) indicate that "the loss of markets in former Yugoslavia put Slovenian companies in a very difficult position." According to Glas *et al.* (1999), besides losing markets in parts of former Yugoslavia, Slovenian companies lost their market share in other former COMECON countries. In the transition period, Slovene companies were faced with severe business challenges that required new internationalization and innovation strategies.

> the small business sector contributed disproportionately to net employment growth rates over the period 1989 to 1998 in Slovenia. The small business sector created many new jobs through the opening of new enterprises. … During this period, many firms restructured from production-oriented activities to service activities, which were underdeveloped before 1990.
>
> *(Drnovšek, 2004, pp. 185–186)*

"The number of registered incorporated firms increased from 2,500 to over 23,000 in three years with 52,000 being in existence at the end of 1996" (Glas *et al.*, 1999, p. 3). Slovenia has, in less than two decades, "made remarkable progress in entrepreneurship" (Širec and Rebernik, 2009, p. 7).

With regard to redefining the internationalization process, Jaklič and Svetličič (2010) identified four stages in the internationalization development from 1990 to 2009:

1. Early transition stage (1990–1993) – the first wave of internationalization – marked by a rapid increase of outward investment on one hand, and divestments and restructuring on the other.
2. Consolidation phase in the mid-nineties (1994–1998) characterized by slow progress in outward investment activity that was mostly carried out by existing multinational companies, which consolidated and strengthened their foreign affiliates' network.

3. A new wave of internationalization at the end of the decade (from 1999–2008) that speeded up the outward investments of existing multinationals and newcomers in terms of broadening and strengthening their foreign affiliate networks and rapid expansion to the former Yugoslav markets.
4. "Consolidation, diversification and slowing down internationalization plans (2009–??)" (Jaklič and Svetličič, 2010, p. 3).

Following increased outward investments and a rapid expansion into the former Yugoslav markets, "the period of 2002 to 2007 in Slovenia reflected a steady growth in the number of enterprises and is perceived as the momentum for entrepreneurship development" (Rangus and Drnovšek, 2009, p. 7). Širec and Rebernik (2009) also confirm that the 2002–2007 period was very positive in terms of development of entrepreneurship in Slovenia. Based on data of the Statistical Office of the Republic of Slovenia, in the 1999–2007 period, the growth index of micro companies (from 0 to 9 employees) was 114. Small enterprises (from 10 to 49 employees) had the highest growth index in this period: 140. According to Rant (2010):

> Slovenia successfully avoided the economic slowdown in Europe in 2001–2003, but was less fortunate during the 2008–2009 recession. Before 2008, Slovenia's annual GDP growth exceeded the EU's average by two percentage points, while after 2008 it was two percentage points below that average. GDP per person shrank by 8.7 percent in 2009, which was the steepest fall in the European Union after that of the Baltic countries and Finland. The drop of Slovenia's competitiveness was also steep. In the IMD's 2010 global competitiveness ranking, Slovenia plummeted from number 32 to 52. In the World Economic Forum competitiveness ranking for the same year, Slovenia's drop was less severe, yet still significant: from 37 to 45.
>
> *(Rant, 2010, p. 359)*

TABLE 11.1 Core economic indicators

	2011	*2012*	*2013*	*2014*	*2015*	*2016*
GDP per capita growth (annual %)[1]	0.44	(2.89)	(1.22)	3.00	2.22	2.50
Foreign direct investment, net inflows (% of GDP)[2]	1.70	0.07	0.21	2.05	3.92	2.45
Competitiveness index: (rank/score)[3]	51/56.88	51/52.96	52/51.00	55/46.25	49/56.76	43/64.87
Ease of doing business index[4]	37	31	33	35	30	30

Source: World Bank website database (1,2); IMD World Competitiveness Center (3); Trading Economics (4).

Jaklič and Svetličič (2010, p. 9) indicate that "the first reaction to crises was cost-cutting and increasing sales activity. Long term investment has been postponed, investment in R&D and marketing reduced." Slovenia needed several years (2008–2013) to recover from the financial recession. The first positive results in terms of GDP per person growth were visible only in 2014. The same applies to net inflows of foreign direct investment.

Table 11.1 shows that by 2014 Slovenia's economic indicators had recovered from the 2008–2009 recession. GDP-per-person growth improved significantly after 2011 and the competitiveness index increased (in 2016 it was 43/64.7). In terms of ease of doing business, Slovenia was ranked thirtieth in 2016 (the same as in 2015), whereas in previous years it had been ranked higher. Since 2014, Slovenia's GDP has been rising again. The main GDP growth factor is export. In 2015, the trade balance was positive. Table 11.2 shows trade statistics for Slovenian companies.

Among prospering Slovenian companies (see Table 11.3), the strongest international positions are held by pharmaceutical companies and those specialized in mid to high-tech automotive and industrial equipment manufacturing. These companies were able to grow and gain market share even during the period of the global recession. According to Jaklič and Svetličič (2010):

TABLE 11.2 Trade statistics for Slovenia in 2015

Category	*Statistic/result*
Total exports in 2015	$26,586,979,271
Total imports (2015)	$25,870,229,469
Trade balance (2015)	$716,749,802
Exports of goods and services (% of GDP) (2015)	77.94%
Imports of goods and services (% of GDP) (2015)	68.82%
Top four trade exports partners (2015)	Germany Italy Austria Croatia
Top four trade import partners (2015)	Germany Italy Austria China
Top four export goods (2015)	Motor vehicles and parts Electrical machinery Industrial machinery Pharmaceuticals
Top four import goods (2015)	Motor vehicles and parts Oil and mineral fuels Industrial machinery Electrical machinery

Source: globalEDGE (https://globaledge.msu.edu/countries/slovenia/tradestats).

TABLE 11.3 Top ten Slovenian exporters in 2014 (exports in euro, thousands)

Company	*Total exports*	*Share of exports over sales (%)*	*Exports to the EU*	*Exports to the states of former Yugoslavia*
KRKA GROUP	1,113,585	93	616,725	51,947
GORENJE GROUP	1,063,153	85	649,951	133,648
LEK GROUP	982,003	96	398,503	25,690
REVOZ D.D.	837,165	99	836,901	0
SIJ GROUP	610,308	86	486,349	19,220
IMPOL GROUP	464,013	95	410,208	10,541
KOLEKTOR GROUP	274,657	84	163,650	18,928
BSH HISNI APARATI D.O.O.	245,658	91	234,755	10,903
JULON	227,777	97	227,499	145
HIDRIA GROUP	220,000	89	181,000	9,000

Source: Slovenian Public Agency for Entrepreneurship, Internationalization, Foreign Investment, and Technology (www.investslovenia.org/business-environment/trade/).

> none of the top MNEs has withdrawn from the foreign market, but on the contrary they increased international economic cooperation. Strategic alliances, international R&D cooperation, outsourcing and captive offshoring have been identified as the most promising escape from the crisis and expected to be used more in the future.
>
> (*Jaklič and Svetličič, 2010, p. 10*)

As for entrepreneurship development in Slovenia, regardless of the recession there was a positive trend in terms of newly established companies (especially micro). One of the reasons for that could be the financial recession, which resulted in redundancies and cut labor costs.

Table 11.4 shows a significant increase in the number of micro companies from 2008 to 2015 (when the growth index was 128). The number of employees in micro companies also grew (see Table 11.5). In 2015, the number of employees in micro companies was 247,960, whereas the number of employees in large companies was 251,607. The data suggest two trends: increasing numbers of employees in micro companies and declining numbers in large companies. In 2015, 29.6 percent of all employees in Slovenia worked for micro companies, 16.8 percent were employed in small companies, 23.6 percent were in medium companies, and 30 percent worked for large companies. Micro and SMEs employed 69.9 percent or 585,847 employees.

Rebernik *et al.* state that "entrepreneurship does not mean simply establishing, owning, and operating a business. It primarily means creating something new. To do so, one needs creativity, innovativeness, and an entrepreneurial mindset" (2016, p. 19). Furthermore, Pšeničny *et al.* state that:

> entrepreneurship cannot be automatically equated with, or restricted to, small business only, or to the creation of new enterprises. The growth of the most

TABLE 11.4 Number of companies from 2008 to 2015

	2008	*2009*	*2010*	*2011*	*2012*	*2013*	*2014*	*2015*	*Index (2008–2015)*
Micro enterprise (0–9)	142,283	150,916	156,305	159,986	164,115	172,983	177,235	182,454	128
Small enterprise (10–49)	7,661	7,500	7,181	6,950	6,815	6,788	6,897	7,081	92
Medium enterprise (50–249)	2,212	2,152	2,129	2,082	2,031	1,988	1,971	2,002	91
Large enterprise (250+)	385	363	344	342	344	330	330	326	85
Total	152,541	160,931	165,959	169,360	173,305	182,089	186,433	191,863	126

Source: Statistical Office of Republic of Slovenia.

TABLE 11.5 Number of employees from 2008 to 2015 by type of the company

	2008	*2009*	*2010*	*2011*	*2012*	*2013*	*2014*	*2015*	*Index (2008–2015)*
Micro enterprise (0–9)	217,874	226,638	227,225	226,997	229,771	235,900	240,123	247,960	114
Small enterprise (10–49)	154,166	151,011	144,449	139,586	136,706	136,185	138,355	140,510	91
Medium enterprise (50–249)	216,745	210,375	209,482	203,572	199,151	194,698	193,571	197,377	91
Large enterprise (250+)	292,813	276,323	261,003	252,213	251,114	250,675	255,351	251,607	86
Total	881,598	864,347	842,159	822,368	816,742	817,458	827,400	837,454	95

Source: Statistical Office of Republic of Slovenia.

> dynamic enterprises contributes crucially to the growth of national economies, social prosperity, job creation, technological progress and development, and also creates the highest added value.
>
> *(2014, pp. 63–64)*

At the same time, entrepreneurship can be associated with, and connected to, large companies where, based on literature reviews, the entrepreneurship process is understood in terms of research and development and innovation (product or process) or by the term intrapreneurship.

The following section explains the internationalization and entrepreneurship processes (especially in terms of innovation) at Hidria, one of the top ten Slovenian exporters and, according to Hermann Simon's methodology, a Central and Eastern European Hidden Champion in terms of niche market leadership.

A case study of internationalization and entrepreneurship processes at a Slovene Hidden Champion company

Overview – historical highlights

Hidria started as Rotomatika in the small Slovenian town of Spodnja Idrija as a part of Iskra Group in 1971, at a time when the Yugoslav economy was developing successfully. It was founded by the local authorities in an attempt to ensure economic activity and jobs in the region of Idrija after the decline of the region's mercury mine almost 500 years after the start of its operations in 1490. At the time of its foundation, Rotomatika was a member of the former Iskra Group, and produced small electric motors for household appliances. Hidria grew during the 1970s by developing larger electric motors for refrigerator compressors. It operated in the wider environment of the Yugoslav economy, specializing in custom-designed electric motors. Around half of its sales were generated by the internal market, whereas the other half of its products were exported already in those early stages of the company's development, mainly to Western Europe. Due to a lack of foreign currency for imports, the federal government helped exporting companies with different measures.

In the 1980s, Rotomatika had a new, ambitious young management team with high goals and aspirations for the company. The team first executed an upward vertical integration in rotors and lamination as components of electric motors. As a first step, it covered the internal demand for these components, and, at the end of the 1980s, it started to sell these components to other producers of electric motors. In parallel, links were established with US buyers of electric motors for air-conditioning compressors, and exports to the US reached one third of total sales by the end of the 1980s.

At the start of the 1990s, Hidria was first affected by Slovenia's exit from Yugoslavia and then by the consequent loss of the Yugoslav markets, losing approximately one third of its overall turnover. The period from 1991 to 1995 was thus marked by an intensive further repositioning toward exports (primarily to the EU), as the small Slovenian market did not offer any opportunities for counter-balancing such a large market loss. As some important customers had started to make their own motors in the early 1990s, lamination, and stator and rotor stacks became Hidria's new core business. The company sold these components to other producers of electric motors in Europe and globally. In parallel, Hidria entered a joint venture with Alcatel SEL of Germany (originally of France) in 1994, based on its original program of small motors in Spodnja Idrija. This joint venture was followed by another one in 1996, with Alussuise (of Switzerland), producing ALU casted parts for the automotive industry, and by a joint venture manufacturing external rotor motor fans with Elco (of Italy) in Spodnja Idrija in 1998. The first joint venture ended when the minority share was sold to partner EMB, which meanwhile acquired Alcatel SEL's share. After originally being a minority shareholder in second and third joint ventures, Hidria became their sole owner through buying the majority shareholders out. After Hidria split from Iskra in 1989, and after Slovenia split from Yugoslavia in 1991, Hidria managed to continue to play the role of a highly advanced high-tech company in Slovenia. Later, it became a leader in selected automotive segments and developed into one of the high-tech leaders in Slovenia, exporting over 90 percent of its products.

After the consolidation, achieved by rising exports to Germany, Italy, France, and other European countries, the second half of the 1990s was marked by objectives by the management team and employees, and by further successful development. Even in the period of so-called social ownership and self-management until 1990, the management team acted with responsibility as if it owned the company. This was an additional boost for Hidria's further development in the 1990s. Management and employees became Hidria's owners and achieved intense diversification and organic growth through acquisitions of a power tool company, a diesel cold-start systems company, and a professional air-conditioning, ventilation, and heating solutions providing company.

In the last ten years, Hidria has again been re-positioning itself by concentrating on two core businesses – automotive and climate technologies – by divesting or closing non-core businesses, by growing naturally or through acquisitions, and by strengthening its management board and making it international.

In the 2004–2005 period, Hidria profoundly analyzed its existing positions and competences and defined where these could represent an asset and an advantage. It was a crucial period, as Hidria set up automotive and industrial divisions. In 2015, IMP Klima and the climate business were divested and all efforts concentrated on mainly quickly growing automotive segments. Most important, knowledge and innovation as values were defined as a core competitive advantage and Hidria started to build related competences over several phases. Based on the Hidria Innovation Center foundation, Hidria started to deal with internal technological innovation in products, materials, and processes. It then took Hidria only a couple of years to understand that it would never have, and does not need to have, all of the best relevant knowledge on its own pay-roll. Hidria understood quickly that it is rather the company's ability to link such best knowledge available anywhere on the globe that really matters and that open innovation principles and partnerships would help Hidria achieve its targets in the most efficient way.

In 2006–2007, Hidria began to broaden the scope of innovation to include also business model innovation. By that time, this had become an important focus of the company's strategy. As Hidria deepened its familiarity with, and understanding of, the phenomena of business model innovation, the company expanded its efforts from technological innovation to examining possibilities for innovation across the value-added chain. In these processes, Hidria considered all aspects of the value chain, including those not under its control, in search of collateral competitive advantages for itself and its partners.

By 2010–2011, results from business model innovation and technological innovation clearly started to provide important value added to Hidria's customers, strengthened the company's advantages over its competitors, and considerably contributed to its performance. At that point, Hidria integrated business model innovation into its business development planning process. This was an addition of business model innovation to the existing technological innovation focus in Hidria's annual planning process, which takes into account both ten-year strategic views and three-year operative views. By doing so, Hidria assured that business model innovation became a systematic preoccupation of the management of each of its strategic business units, i.e. of its core businesses, including all employees, and that business model innovation represented an additional support for the launch and success of Hidria's innovative new products, processes, and technologies.

> In a world obsessed with technology, the idea that the real source of your competitive advantage comes from a business model (and not technological innovation!) is nothing less of revolutionary. You might have the best technology in the world, but if you fail to continuously reinvent the way to monetize its benefits, the true value of this technology is near zero.
>
> *(Seljak, 2016)*

Consequently, with breakthrough technological innovation, hand-in-hand with business model innovation, Hidria developed into a European and global leader in its selected niches and further internationalized its activities with high speed.

Core steps of Hidria's internationalization process

In the 1970s and 1980s, internationalization was driven by a focus on electric motors and development of European and US markets with significant government support. In the 1990s, the loss of the Yugoslav markets strengthened the company's orientation toward EU markets, including the establishment of three joint ventures in Slovenia and learning from them. After defining a new focused vision and strategy in 2004–2005, Hidria developed into a global market leader in selected specific automotive niches and acquired companies abroad. Hidria's mission became to provide innovative breakthrough solutions for assuring sustainable green mobility and sustainable indoor well-being. As a result of the successful implementation of that vision and strategy since 2004, boosted by Slovenia's accession to the EU, Hidria is today one of the global leaders in diesel cold-start systems and lamination for electric power trains for hybrid and electrical vehicles. In accordance with the company's strategic directions, Hidria set up several institutes, technological centers, and international production facilities. The company has grown organically and through acquisitions in, among other countries, Germany, Hungary, and China.

Hidria has been recognized many times for its innovations. Among other distinctions, it was named one of the four most innovative companies in Slovenia in 2009 by AT Kearney and Europe's most innovative company for 2012–2013 by the European Business Awards (EBA). Hidria provided the best eco innovation in the European automotive industry by CLEPA in 2016 – a pressure-sensing diesel engine cold-start technology, slashing down emissions in modern diesel engines by as much as 30 percent.

Core factors influencing Hidria's internationalization activities

The core factors that influenced Hidria's internationalization steps were external and internal. One of the external factors was Yugoslavia's support for export-oriented companies, which played an important role in the company's early stage. Afterwards, the collapse of the country and its domestic market, the small size of the Slovene market, and the transition from a planned socialist economy to capitalism boosted Hidria's entrepreneurship and internationalization. A similar effect was created by Slovenia's accession to the EU and the euro zone, as well as the globally changing paradigm from seemingly unlimited natural resources to the carbon-free economy and green mobility of the future. Idrija's 500-year tradition of technological innovation in mercury mining also played an important role.

There were several internal factors, as well. The quality and ambition of the management team, who took over in 1980, were crucial. It was later upgraded by the presence of West European members of the management board. They were ambitious, internationally-oriented, charismatic leaders, providing a focused vision and strategy. They implemented innovation as a core value and a competitive advantage enabled global innovation in technology, business models, and social engagement. The company's customers – large globally positioned transnationals – also exerted a positive influence as they required their partners and suppliers to boost their international activities. The joint ventures with Alusuisse Alcatel and Elco between 1994 and 2000 contributed significantly to the development of entrepreneurship and the internationalization of Hidria, followed by acquisitions of companies in different countries.

Good practices – strategic business development process

By involving international management board members by the early 2000s, Hidria launched its Business Development Process (BDP), requiring each business unit in the April–June period of each year to take a ten-year view into the future. This necessitates a profound understanding of all core trends and factors that will influence the future, envisaging such a future, and turning dreams into reality by creating a Product and Technology Road Map of Hidria – targeted breakthrough innovation projects that should create that future. Each of the projects has a budget for the necessary human, financial, and other resources, including an open innovation approach to the best available knowledge providers worldwide. In the fall of each year, the ten-year strategic development plan is strengthened by a three-year operative plan, containing details about new products, targeted customers, market shares, capital expenditure, and cash flow. As a result of the BDP process, Hidria quickly moved from using and integrating the knowledge of others to understanding that we live in an age so accelerated that the existing knowledge is becoming obsolete more quickly than ever before. To stay a step ahead, Hidria needed to create breakthrough new knowledge by and within itself. Such endeavors reconfirmed the wider need for individuals, organizations, and societies to challenge themselves to the point of profoundly understanding that the best way to cope with an uncertain future is to realize that it is not there yet. Hidria co-creates it through its own actions. Hidria dreams of that better future for our civilization and our planet while developing capabilities to convert these dreams into solid and clear visions, missions, and strategies, as well as capabilities to execute them.

The case of internationalization – acquisition of Dr. Karl Bausch

Having some limited presence in Bosch and other core strategic German customers, Hidria decided to acquire Dr. Karl Bausch's company in Stuttgart in 2010, so as to strengthen its overall production presence in Germany, and specifically to build a long-term partnership with Bosch and other core customers. It all started with some cooperation between the two companies on some projects and a successful common integrated approach to an important hybrid power train project. Neither company would have been able to compete alone in that domain, yet they achieved good synergy by pooling their strengths. By integrating Hidria and Dr. Karl Bausch's Bosch business and relations, Hidria soon became a preferred Bosch supplier and enhanced its previous business with Bosch and other targeted customers. With over 230 employees in Germany and a subsidiary with 60 employees in Hungary, Hidria Bausch today represents an important pillar of Hidria in its attempt to further internationalize and globalize its lamination business, including a wide global production presence.

Cases of innovation – linked internationalization

A team developing a mild-hybrid stop-start system – an auxiliary electric power train platform for a premium motorcycle producer – moved from only developing the innovative technological solution for the original equipment manufacturer (OEM) to upgrading this offering by engaging with a partner PR agency to develop a complete innovative PR campaign for that solution for the final customer, as if Hidria were the OEM, dealing with the end-user. This approach included top state-of-the-art brochures addressing final customers in such a convincing way that it also persuaded the OEM to proceed with the project. This transition from just technological innovation to an innovative approach also in the related sales and marketing field showed to the OEM that the practicality of the new technical solution provided real added value to the end user. Had Hidria not taken this wider approach to the issue, the OEM would not have decided to proceed with the project. It quickly launched the prototype phase along with substantial coverage of R&D costs by the customer.

Hidria's climate technologies division developed a new software model to manage all core variables influencing the optimal design of solar power plants. This design enabled our teams in renewable solar energy to provide customers not just with solar panels, but with complete turn-key solutions for solar power plants on the spot during the first introductory discussion with customers. This impacted our time and speed to market positively and significantly. As time to market depends on continually changing subvention conditions and is crucial for investment decisions, it is one of the key success factors. Therefore, this approach resulted in a considerable competitive advantage for Hidria.

In a broader spectrum, Hidria led a new initiative in the construction world with the creation of a consortium of companies from Southeast Europe (SEE), named Feniks. This is a group of 45 former competitors employing 35,000 people, with collective revenues of more than five billion euros annually. These small and medium enterprises within the SEE construction industry were for some time fighting each other and losing value in an increasingly shrinking market. Seeing this unproductive positioning, Hidria championed the Feniks initiative, seeking to unite the competences and capabilities of these companies and create a critical mass to be able to handle large turn-key projects outside of the SEE region. Today Feniks is executing projects in Russia, Ukraine, Belarus, Kazakhstan, Azerbaijan, and markets in the Middle East and North Africa (MENA). Within this consortium, Hidria provides and integrates its proprietary indoor well-being solutions. It represents a successful move from a competition to co-opetition business model.

As a core integrator in a global partnership based on an open innovation principle, Hidria developed a pressure sensor glow plug, revolutionizing the cold-start systems for diesel engines, enabling a so-called "closed loop combustion system." Hidria's pressure sensor glow plug measures cylinder pressure 110,000 times per second and converts the data into a signal sent through smart microelectronics to an engine control unit in a common rail injection system, optimizing the injection of fuel in the cylinder according to a specially developed algorithm. The result of this digital innovation is a 30 percent lower consumption and thus a 30 percent decrease in harmful emissions and a relevant contribution to future green mobility.

Overview of internationalization of the economy

Hidria has thus developed spectacularly from a small electric motor producer, and later a follower in the automotive industry, to a globally leading company in selected automotive applications.

In the period from 2004 to 2007, Hidria was entering the business of car components in their final stage of production (fourth to seventh year of certain models) to reduce the cost of what had been previously sourced from other suppliers. Hidria then moved to a development supplier position in 2007. In 2012, Hidria started to develop components for vehicles that were expected to be launched within two or three years. After 2010, Hidria managed to move further to a positon of a pre-development conceptual supplier, and started proactively to provide breakthrough innovative conceptual solutions to car producers so that they could consider applying them to future models. Hidria thus developed its automotive turnover from 10 million euros in 2005 to over 170 million in 2015. As a result, it became a European and global market leader (20 percent of European core ALU parts for steering systems, 40 percent of the European market for stators and rotors for electric steering systems, 40 percent of the European market for semi-hermetic motors for refrigeration compressors, 20 percent of the global market for diesel cold-start systems). Hidria received EBA's 2012–2013 award for the most innovative company in Europe and CLEPA's 2016 award for the best eco innovation in the European automotive supply industry.

Hidria's vision today is to be a leader in providing customized innovative solutions for selected automotive and industrial applications by using state-of-the-art manufacturing processes. It achieves this by creating an inspiring environment, developing employees' competencies through the Hidria Leadership System and being a reliable development partner, responsibly creating value and building long-term partnerships. It is obvious that the world around Hidria has been changing intensively in the last four decades. Hidria was a follower in the first two decades and was constantly worried that it might not be able to cope with the uncertain future. All this changed by 2004–2005, when Hidria profoundly realized that it had the critical mass of human resource quality, competence, knowledge, and capabilities, as well as the desire to lead and create the future by itself. All that is reflected in Hidria's inspiring slogan launched in 2005: "We have the vision. We know the way."

Conclusions and implications

Hidria was challenged by Yugoslavia's disintegration and the specifics of Slovenia's transition, as well as by the profound changes in the global environment and its specific industries. A particularly tough challenge was the recent complete paradigm shift from taking natural resources for granted and as unlimited to understanding the need to preserve them and enable a sustainable carbon-free economy of the future.

However, the external factors that affect the development and entrepreneurship and internationalization processes and practices were largely similar for all companies in Slovenia, whereas the global context was the same for all global companies. Nevertheless, just a few managed to perform as brilliantly as Hidria. Many underperformed or even completely disappeared from the scene.

What really differentiates Hidria from others and constitutes the core foundations of its success is its perspicacious decision not only to embrace the ongoing and accelerating change, but also to co-create that change. It is viewed as creative destruction in its basic form that few companies are capable of dealing with. This capability allowed Hidria to achieve the transition from follower to leader. Focusing on technological and business model innovation as a core value is only a natural consequence of the mind shift that the company was able to achieve, based on its decades-long experience. As a result, Hidria re-invented itself in 2004–2005 and grew into what it is today. Consequently, the culture of global-level innovation for the benefit of the planet and its whole population is a vital characteristic of Hidria, reflected in its proactive effort to address the ongoing challenge of turning the automotive industry into a holistic mobility provider.

Naturally, Hidria's development largely mirrors that of the regional and global context. Yet, it was its own decision, declaration, and commitment to achieve global leadership and global breakthrough innovation that pre-destined Hidria's internationalization and globalization process as a natural consequence of that fundamental underlying strategic decision. The company made a conscious decision not to accept to be just a small collateral part of the transition story of a specific country, but to attempt to become a global leader.

What if one of the countries in transition in Central and Eastern Europe decided not just to be one of the countries in transition, but rather attempt to achieve global leadership by all means at its disposal, yet primarily with a clear vision, strategy, and dedication to work for the common good? This would make Central and Eastern Europe, just like the world of Hidria today, look completely different. Like many other globally successful Slovenian high-tech companies, Hidria delivered on its high aspirations far above the existing standards. These success stories have had a profound impact on government policies and ambitions and on public opinion, teaching a clear lesson: "Yes, it can be done." This lesson continues to be a role model for the economy and the whole society.

References

Drnovšek, M., 2004, "Job creation process in a transition economy," *Small Business Economics*, 23, pp. 179–188.

Glas, M., Drnovšek, M., and Mirtic, D., 2000, "Problems faced by new entrepreneurs: Slovenia and Croatia – a comparison," The University of Ljubljana, Faculty of Economics. Available at: webv3ef.ef.uni-lj.si/_documents/wp/GlasDrnovsek%20Mirtic_final.doc. Accessed February 25, 2017.

Glas, M., Hisrich, R.D., Vahčič, A., and Antončič, B., 1999, "The internationalization of SMEs in transition economies: Evidence from Slovenia," The University of Ljubljana,

Faculty of Economics. Available at: webv1ef.ef.uni-lj.si/dokumenti/wp/glas4.doc. Accessed February 25, 2017.

globalEDGE, 2015, *Slovenia: Trade Statistics*. Available at: https://globaledge.msu.edu/countries/slovenia/tradestats. Accessed March 25, 2017.

IMD World Competitiveness Center. *Rankings*. Available at: www.imd.org/wcc/world-competitiveness-center/. Accessed March 25, 2017.

Jaklič, A. and Svetličič. M., 2010, "Multinationals from Slovenia – nano size, but giga important," The University of Ljubljana. Available at: http://gdex.dk/ofdi10/Andreja%20Jaklic%20-%20Slo%20MNE%20-%20Nano%20size,%20Giga%20important.pdf. Accessed February 23, 2017.

Pšeničny, V., Jakopin, E., Vukčević, Z., and Ćorić, G., 2014, "Dynamic entrepreneurship – generator of sustainable economic growth and competitiveness," *Journal of Contemporary Management Issues*, 19 (1), pp. 61–92.

Rangus, K. and Drnovšek, M., 2009, "Study of the innovative potential of Slovenia. South East Europe." Available at: www.southeast-europe.net/document.cmt?id=109. Accessed February 23, 2017.

Rant, M., 2010, "Hidden Champions of Slovenia," in P. McKiernan and D. Purg, eds., *Hidden Champions in CEE and Turkey. Carving Out a Global Niche*, Berlin, Heidelberg: Springer, pp. 357–381.

Rebernik, M., Tominc, P., Crnogaj, K., Širec, K., Bradač Hojnik, B., and Rus, M., 2016, "Podjetništvo med priložnostjo in nujo: GEM Slovenija 2015," The University of Maribor, Faculty of Economics and Business. Available at: www.spiritslovenia.si/resources/files/doc/publikacije/GEM_Slovenija_2015.pdf. Accessed February 23, 2017.

Republic of Slovenia Statistical Office RS, 2016, *Number of Enterprises*. Available at: http://pxweb.stat.si/pxweb/Database/Economy/14_business_subjects/01_14188_Enterprises/01_14188_Enterprises.asp. Accessed March 15, 2017.

Seljak, I., 2016, *Embedded Business Model Innovation in the European Automotive Industry: Business Model Innovation as Dynamic Capabilities within a Moderately Dynamic Industry*. IEDC – Bled School of Management postgraduate studies, Doctoral dissertation series, Vol. 1.

Širec, K. and Rebernik, M., eds., *Dynamics of Slovenian Entrepreneurship*, Slovenian Entrepreneurship Observatory 2008, The University of Maribor, Faculty of Economics and Business. Available at: www.epfip.uni-mb.si/raziskovanje/slovenski-podjetniski-observatorij/spo-monografije/. Accessed February 25, 2017.

Slovenian Public Agency for Entrepreneurship, Internationalization, Foreign Investment, and Technology, 2015, *Trade*. Available at: www.investslovenia.org/business-environment/trade/. Accessed March 25, 2017.

Trading Economics, 2016. *Ease of Doing Business in Slovenia*. Available at: www.tradingeconomics.com/slovenia/ease-of-doing-business. Accessed March 25, 2017.

Welter, F. and Smallbone, D., eds., *Handbook of Research on Entrepreneurship Policies in Central and Eastern Europe*, Cheltenham: Edward Elgar Publishing Limited.

World Bank, 2016, *Slovenia*. Available at: https://data.worldbank.org/country/Slovenia. Accessed March 25, 2017.

12

ENTREPRENEURSHIP AND DENTAL INDUSTRY DEVELOPMENT IN UKRAINE

The case of dental clinic Apollonia entering international markets

Iryna Tykhomyrova, Nataliya Golovkina and Mykola Radlinskyy

Introduction

As in other ex-Soviet Union countries, entrepreneurship development in Ukraine started with economic transformation and evolution of a market economy in the late 1980s. By then, the Soviet command economy in Ukraine was in terminal decline and considerable changes in the economy took place that steadily encouraged the emerging private sector. This was also the start of the cooperative movement and the time when most of the formal institutions that should enable private entrepreneurship activity – laws and regulations – were established. Newly founded cooperatives mostly focused on providing personal services, manufacturing and selling groceries or fast-moving consumer goods (FMCG).

In 1991, after Ukraine proclaimed its independence, the country faced a major challenge to develop its market economy rooted in private ownership. The state seemed to understand the role of entrepreneurship and small and medium business. Thus, not surprisingly, since 1991, entrepreneurs have been the drivers of the Ukrainian economy. The number of entrepreneurs grew by 148–191 percent annually during the period of 1991–96. In 1996–2003 growth slowed, though still reaching an impressive 114–117 percent. Since 2004, however, the growth rate of entrepreneur numbers has been decreasing.

According to the Statistic Reference Book (2015), 343,400 companies were registered in 2015. Only 423, or less than 0.1 percent of them, with more than 250 employees and more than 50 million euros of annual turnover, qualified as large businesses. Thus, the majority of domestic businesses are small- and medium-sized companies. In fact, 82.8 percent of those firms are considered micro-businesses, since they employ fewer than ten persons and have an annual turnover less than 2 million euros. Medium-sized companies, however, account for just 4.4 percent of the private sector in Ukraine.

In 2015, there were around 2,290,300 self-employed persons in Ukraine. In the same year, 71 percent of the 5.9 million people employed by domestic businesses worked for medium and small companies (44.2 percent and 26.8 percent, respectively). Small and medium enterprises (SMEs) were mostly active in wholesale and retail trading and auto maintenance (27 percent of all SMEs). Trade was the main activity for 56.2 percent of private entrepreneurs. Of all private sectors, only SMEs render services in education and healthcare. Finally, it should be noted, however, that the above numbers only reflect the official sector of the economy of Ukraine. According to the research by Omelchuk and Khachatryan (2010), 4.3 million of those aged 15–70, or as much as 26.4 percent of the total workforce, are employed in the unofficial economy.

Support for the SME sector is one of the top priorities of the current national economic policy. The results of these policies are arguably reflected by positive trends in "Doing Business" rankings over 2008–17 (see Table 12.1).

With the launch of a market economy in Ukraine, Apollonia Dental Clinic – the case study further addressed in this chapter – evolved from an entrepreneurial startup to its current form. Before presenting the story of Apollonia Dental Clinic, we will describe the context, i.e., the development of dental markets within the Commonwealth of Independent States (CIS).

Business and technology development at Apollonia

Development of Apollonia and first results on the Ukraine market

Mykola Radlinskyy, head of the Business Development department for the Apollonia Group, tells his story of the Apollonia clinic.

> My father (Sergii Radlinskyy) started his business in 1991. It was a very special time in Ukraine. My parents often call that period "interesting." On the one hand, people were breathing freely for the first time in many years and opportunities seemed boundless. On the other hand, everyday life looked gloomy as people lacked everything. The old economic model was crumbling. Many doctors, teachers, nurses and other healthcare professionals engaged in trading smuggled food or fast moving consumer goods just to put food on the table.
>
> In this situation, my father took the very bold step to start a technology-based business in healthcare. At the beginning, he applied composites and polymers that were similar to natural teeth in durability and color, which were technologies dating from the late 1970s for polymeric teeth filling as were available in Ukraine. Later, he expanded the application of composites to other dental activities and called this wider application "restoration" (Radlinskyy, 1997a, 2001). However, at that time, composites were imported and so not available to most dental practitioners.

TABLE 12.1 Doing Business: Ukraine's rankings in 2008–17

	2008	*2009*	*2010*	*2011*	*2012*	*2013*	*2014*	*2015*	*2016*	*2017*
Ease of doing business overall score	139	145	147	149	152	140	112	96	81	80
Key indicators:										
Starting a business	109	128	136	118	116	50	69	76	24	20
Registering property	138	140	160	165	168	158	88	59	62	63
Paying taxes	177	180	181	181	183	168	157	108	83	84
Access to electricity	n/a	n/a	n/a	169	170	170	182	185	140	130
Enforcing contracts	46	48	43	44	44	45	44	43	93	81
Resolving insolvency	140	143	145	158	158	157	141	142	148	150
Access to credit	68	28	30	21	23	24	14	17	19	20
Trading across borders	120	121	139	136	144	148	153	154	110	115
Dealing with construction permits	174	179	181	182	182	186	68	70	137	140
Protecting minority investors	141	142	108	108	114	127	107	109	101	70

Source: World Bank (2016).

> In the late 1990s, my father started a training line of his business. He founded CompoDent, Ltd, a training center for dental professionals. It was the result of his visit to a big dentistry fair in Moscow. At that fair he learned that Dentsply International (USA) together with the Soviet Union Scientific Industrial Association Stomatiologia (Dentistry) had founded the Stomadent joint venture in Kharkiv, a city located very close to Poltava. The venture manufactured cutting-edge composites. The enterprise employed the latest management practices and quality assurance systems.

It was a mutually beneficial undertaking, as the American company followed the "sales through training" approach. They created a good market whereby Ukrainian dentistry practitioners and academics received access to the latest research, supplies and equipment and learnt how to run customer-oriented healthcare and training businesses. As Dentsply International was very active not only in Ukraine but in all CIS and Baltic countries, CompoDent operated as an international venture from the very beginning, despite the fact that it was headquartered in a provincial city.

From the start, the company maintained two lines of business: Dentsply International supplied application training and clinical activities rooted in techniques developed by CompoDent. CompoDent launched a number of regular training opportunities, especially its annual international seminar "Teeth Restoration with Dentsply Supplies," weekly five-day training sessions for DDSs (Doctors of Dental Surgery) and launched the annual "Best Teeth Restoration" competition. In 2009, the international training center was renovated and conference facilities and a hotel were added to its operations.

The dental business, like many other knowledge-based services, depends on people, their competences and skills. Therefore, it is only natural that it was decided to keep it a family business and to let it grow naturally. In 1999, CompoDent was transformed into Apollonia, a dental clinic and training center, thus combining the two core businesses.

Apollonia's business is based on science and supported by dental research, including original research by Apollonia. In addition to expert usage of new dental composites, unique procedures are utilized to fully replicate the anatomy and color of the natural tooth. For example, practitioners typically utilize standard colors from commercially available choices, but the methods employed by Apollonia better match original tooth color by mixing five colors to create an identical natural color to the original tooth. In addition, the clinic developed a special dental adhesive with unique restoration properties.

Particular emphasis at Apollonia is placed on biomimetic dentistry, a method of tooth restoration that emulates the physical, biomechanical and functional properties of natural teeth.[1]

Collectively the methodologies are oriented on natural simulation of the original tooth and have received popular acclaim both in Ukraine and in the region.

In 2010–12, even though Apollonia's market share was small, the operating rate was high enough to keep the business sustainable. The lowest operating rate was in 2009 and 2014, the reason being public sentiment to cut expenses.

BOX 12.1 BIOMIMETIC TECHNOLOGY

Biomimetic comes from two words: "biology," the science of life or of living things, and "mimic," to copy or imitate. Biomimetic means the treatment of a tooth that allows it to behave like – or mimic – a natural tooth. Biomimetic dentistry treats weak, fractured and decayed teeth in a way that restores their strength and seals them from bacterial invasion. Careful sealing against infection removes the need for aggressively cutting down teeth for crowns and drastically reduces the need for root canals. Biomimetic dentistry takes advantage of advanced ceramics and adhesives. These technologies allow dentists to use small onlays that work like the original teeth rather than applying large caps/crowns. Old techniques can cause teeth to eventually crack and leak, allowing bacteria to rot the teeth from the inside. Biomimetic dentistry locks out the bacteria for safer, more durable dental work. Think of it as "tooth conserving dentistry," for that is the goal and the properties for restoration (Radlinskyy, 1997b).

Assessing potential for international expansion

The current economic situation in Ukraine limits Apollonia's growth. Therefore, international expansion seems only natural. The company has decided to look both East (CIS and Central Asian countries and China) and West (Europe). CIS markets are considered to be more attractive based on the history of training sessions provided to dentists from these countries during the past 20 years. It is hypothesized that a market exists for Apollonia's training delivered in the home countries of participating dentists.

The CIS population excluding Ukraine is 209 million, serviced by 104,360 dentistry professionals, making a ratio of 0.5 dentistry professionals per 1,000 people. This ratio ranges from 0.1 per 1,000 in Tajikistan to 1.9 per 1,000 in Armenia (Table 12.2).

An increase of market capacity as measured by the number of visits to a dentist was observed during the period 2010–13, driven by overall aging of the population, an increased understanding that dentists need to be visited twice a year and the necessity for prophylactic care. In 2014, visits declined by 0.6 percent to 243.9 million due to the deteriorating economic situation. This trend is continued in 2015–16, as the number of visits to dentist practitioners was expected to drop to 228.4 million visits due to the worsening of the economies in Kazakhstan and Russia. Because of the reduction of purchasing power, clients will seek dental professionals only in cases of acute pain.

In 2010–14, the CIS market size in dollar terms from dentistry services increased by 77.6 percent to US$11.8 billion. The growth was driven primarily by an increase in prices. The pricing of dentistry services is based on dental products and anesthesia

TABLE 12.2 CIS dental markets overview, 2014

Country	*Population (thousands of people)*	*Number of dentists*	*Number of dentists per 1,000 capita*
Azerbaijan	9,417	2,761	0.3
Belarus	9,460	4,132	0.4
Armenia	3,238	6,103	1.9
Georgia	4,477	785	0.2
Kazakhstan	16,422	4,342	0.3
Kyrgyzstan	5,482	865	0.2
Moldova	3,560	1,618	0.5
Russia	142,905	81,213	0.6
Tajikistan	6,743	764	0.1
Turkmenistan	5,176	1,223	0.2
Uzbekistan	3,024	554	0.2
Ukraine	45,745	20,244	0.4
Total:	255,649	124,604	0.5
Total without Ukraine:	209,904	104,360	0.5

Source: The Interstate Statistical Committee of the Commonwealth of Independent States (2015).

costs, practitioners' salaries, cost of equipment and rental of premises. At the same time, since 2010 the number of healthcare employees has declined due to market optimization processes. Dentistry was also affected by reforms. Lack of skilled dental professionals is one of the worst problems in CIS healthcare. Tertiary dentistry educational institutions do not have their own clinics. The supply of new equipment and dental products is scarce. Therefore, dentistry school graduates cannot be well-trained in the latest technologies for patient care, and restoration approaches in particular.

Furthermore, DDSs are not liable for the quality of their services. Although dentistry services are subject to licensing, there is no mechanism of license revocation. Countries outside the CIS often deal with poor quality services by market mechanisms. For example, insurance companies will not cover DDSs if they make one to three verified mistakes a year.

In 2010–14, the number of dental clinic employees in the CIS followed the reduction in the number of dental facilities.[2] In 2012–14, the number of employed dentistry professionals declined by 5.4 percent to 104,300 in 2014. CIS statistics compared to those in Western Europe reveal a potential market that is unfulfilled.[3] As of 2013, the average ratio of dental professionals to the general population was: 7.2/10,000 in France, 8.8/10,000 in Denmark, 8.5/10,000 in Greece and 8.9/10,000 in Norway. Meanwhile, the ratios were 3.26/10,000 in the Russian Federation, with 5.95/10,000 in St. Petersburg and 5.47/10,000 in Moscow. In Belarus, the ratio ranged from 3.7/10,000 in Vitebsk and Mogilev to 11.5/10,000 in Minsk.

Dentistry is high-tech, equipment and dental product-driven, which requires constant updating and continuing education for dental practitioners to remain state of the art. CIS dentistry needs overall critical reforms, including reform of education and training. Of course, there are different models of dentistry education.[4] For example, purely commercial systems function in the USA and South Korea, whereas such countries as France, Germany, the UK and Turkey have government-paid systems. Russia and Ukraine have mixed systems. Dentistry school tuition fees vary from US$25,000 per year in the USA to US$6,000 per year in South Korea. The program length is six years. Because of its knowledge-based and technology-driven nature, education is expensive.

Dental health is greatly affected by dentistry professionals' skills. Thus, the role of education cannot be overestimated together with the efficiently in the utilization of dentistry professionals.

CIS dentistry markets proved that DDSs working for commercial clinics have to keep up with new technologies and new dental products more than those who work for state-owned or municipal clinics. Moreover, those who work in the public sector have to follow obsolete procedures and render outdated services because the sector is not flexible enough to adjust to new developments in a timely manner. The analysis showed that dentistry professionals from commercial and public clinics require general skills training, because certification and licensing depend on that. Moreover, all skills upgrading establishments in the CIS are state-owned and tailored to the needs of specific countries.

Training dentists from Russian, Kazakhstan and Kyrgyzstan (Table 12.3) in 2010–15 revealed that opportunities exist in CIS countries, especially due to inherited Russian language capabilities and a common approach to dental protocols and insurance. However, the potential and future of these markets are difficult to quantify. Programs for international markets should be designed with a wider scope than for CIS countries, with particular emphasis on Eastern European neighbors, followed by the Chinese and Indian markets. The services offered to international markets focus on the training of dentistry professionals.

Western European markets are not the best-suited because most dental services are paid by either insurance companies or mutual funds which have their own

TABLE 12.3 Apollonia's training participants per country of origin, 2010–15

Participants	*2010*	*2011*	*2013*	*2014*	*2015*
Ukraine	97	55	78	66	88
Russia	86	89	95	17	1
Other	84	64	115	8	6
Total	268	208	288	91	95
Revenue $	214,000	177,000	232,000	45,500	57,000
Courses in Moscow				110	67
Revenue $				61,000	44,000

Source: Company's own data.

clinical protocols. In order to enter this market, insurance companies would have to understand the risks associated with the procedure, and patients may have to bear additional costs. However, in Eastern Europe the rules and patient habits in Slovakia, Czech Republic, Croatia, Bulgaria and Romania are still impacted by the Soviet period, thus the procedures are similar.

The Deep and Comprehensive Free Trade Area Agreement (DCFTA) opened European markets, both Eastern and Western. Apollonia can offer a combination of dental therapy and dental training to MDs and nurses from the European market. New long-distance learning technologies allow for the implementation of innovative training programs, allowing participants to study at the most convenient time and place.

In order to meet this market, a number of developmental challenges exist, including: brand management and brand positioning, identification of new target audiences and segments, elaboration of renewed offering, assessment of the need and role of customer service as a part of a new offering and development of a new promotion strategy.

The above discussion suggests that an unfulfilled need exists for the training offered by Apollonia.

Internationalization strategies of Apollonia

Entry strategy

Due to its reputation, long-time experience and impeccable reputation, Apollonia Training Center is still dominant in the teeth direct restoration segment on the professional development market in the CIS and is slowly becoming known on the EU market.

Dentistry is a fast-developing medical area. It is also a business. Its nursing staff and doctors are critical for competitiveness and growth. Skilled dentistry professionals are in high demand. At the same time, medical school graduates do not want to start their careers in state-owned healthcare institutions because of poor pay. So, many combine dental practice with entrepreneurship as a practical necessity.

Since 2006, Apollonia has started its training program for intern DDSs. Top students from dental schools are recruited and offered positions in the Apollonia clinic. This situation is beneficial for both parties, as the clinic has planned an expansion for 2016–20 with the growth of the domestic market.

In the CIS, the number of DDSs has been declining. Furthermore, most DDSs need post-graduate education and advanced training. According to Apollonia's research, more than 56 percent of CIS dentistry professionals require further in-service education. Of them, 67 percent need specialized courses in general dentistry first of all.

Career enhancement heavily depends on improving professional skills. The World Health Organization (WHO) officially recognized the need for life-long learning as early as 1971. Life-long in-service education starts right after graduation and lasts the entire career of healthcare professionals.

Apollonia's core business creates expertise and capacity that can service new markets outside Ukraine, markets that require life-long learning. To implement the strategy of entering markets of rendering life-long learning services outside Ukraine, the following activities have been selected:

- launch of training center network in the CIS – franchising model is viewed as promising;
- development of distance learning system;
- establishment of system of training aimed at creating a mid-term program which could be bought on a per module basis rather than selling short-term workshops.

Apollonia's chances on external markets look very strong, especially in Europe, which will open to Ukrainian companies after the Deep and Comprehensive Free Trade Area (DCFTA) and other agreements come into effect.

In particular, distance learning instruments have been introduced, as they saved costs, and simplified logistics, administration and compliance issues. Apollonia started its distance learning program in 2015 by:

1. holding free and paid webinars for DDSs from Ukraine and CIS; and
2. master-class recording for either Video on Demand (VOD) dissemination or selling them directly.

In 2015, Apollonia lecturers conducted approximately ten webinars in Russian and Ukrainian. Dentsply Sirona, the world's largest manufacturer of dentistry products and equipment, partnered with Apollonia Training Center to support marketing programs and equipment sales. More than 400 DDSs attended. Also in 2015, Dr. Serhiy Radlinskyy, Apollonia's top lecturer, recorded more than 24 hours of lectures for DDSs who could not attend classes in person.

The videos were marketed in the following way:

> An agreement on VOD dissemination was concluded with vimeo.com, a popular international provider of these services. The agreement included uploading, storage, dissemination and technical support for produced videos. In addition, vimeo.com organizes payment on PayPal.com. To obtain a training video, a DDS simply registers with vimeo.com, selects a training video and arranges payment from a credit card. The selected video will be accessible on any computer for one calendar year. Apollonia Training Center pays a 20% commission for vimeo.com's service. More than 100 subscriptions were sold. Training center sales people had to cope with DDSs' bias against new online technologies, especially those who are over 45 years old from the CIS. DVDs were created to facilitate the acceptance of this new idea.

In addition to online lectures, five DVDs containing Serhiy Radlinskyy lectures have been released. Approximately 1,600 disks have been sold in Ukraine and the CIS. In 2015–16, the turnover exceeded 60,000 euros.

DVD sales resulted in the following advantages:

1 If a DDS bought a DVD before attending the class in person, the effectiveness of the class increased because the student came to the class ready and the lecture reinforced skills and increased practical questions.
2 If a DVD was bought after the practical class, it assisted in reinforcement of knowledge and skills, and to clarify issues.

The distance learning format suits the English-speaking markets of the EU, the US, China and Australia. As a fair share of distance learning is realized via the Internet, the online format is preferable.

Training heavy in practical components is another area of Apollonia activity in CIS markets because the training format is in high demand in the CIS. For example, training for endodontic treatments includes both a theoretical part and coaching to master the manual skills. In-person training usually lasts 2–3 days, for 8–10 hours per day. It includes group work led by 1–2 trainers. Groups of 12–15 persons are optimal as it allows all students to participate and receive feedback from trainers and peers.

Promotional activity

The current competitive environment for professional dental training calls for new approaches to curricula, delivery mechanisms (in person or online), quality assurance and promotional activities. Apollonia's communications fall into two categories. First, the company's selected services are advertised and, second, management aims at developing and managing Apollonia's reputation as an inventor and teacher of dentistry methods and techniques. Traditional advertising in media, specialized publications and the Internet is complemented by participation in dedicated industry exhibitions and fairs promoting Apollonia's offerings outside the domestic market. Apollonia's promotional activities include advertising in specialized industry publications, sites targeting international customers and domestic business press. In 2015, Apollonia spent 88 percent of its advertising budget allocated to external markets on commercial advertising and only 12 percent on institutional advertising.

Apollonia's sales force working with external markets has had to deal with a limited number of very well-informed customers. Therefore, customer relationship management is given special attention. To promote its educational services, Apollonia has started an aggressive policy to further penetrate its target audience and inform it about the company's new services.

Conclusions

The first results of 2017 have been calculated. In the first quarter, 15 groups of seven persons each from Bulgaria (two groups), Lithuania (one group), Kazakhstan (three groups), Russia (four groups), Belarus (four groups) and Uzbekistan took their training. Altogether, 775 dental professionals took courses at Apollonia Training Center in the first quarter of 2017. As of May 1, the training center's revenues were 170,000 euros out of a targeted 400,000 euros for 2017. Over the same period, Apollonia's dental clinics revenues were 300,000 euros out of a targeted 700,000 euros for 2017.

Development of the online training market, and with sites such as CoursEra.com, creates new opportunities. So far, the CIS market has been challenging. The EU and North America are more comfortable with online training. In the last two years, the number of services for online courses has been growing. CourseYard.com is an example developed by Ukrainian entrepreneurs. This service helps design websites that open access to videos, audios and texts after appropriate fees have been paid. After studying those materials, users can take a test and if passed successfully receive the electronic certificate of completion. Such online courses are aimed at sharing quality products, attracting pioneers and launching sales in groups with opinion leaders who make decisions quickly. Social media and professional groups in those media are the main communication channels.

Apollonia has also started developing a training and certification model to franchise training centers and clinics. Currently, it is negotiating the launch of certified training centers under the Apollonia brand in Kazakhstan and the UK. It is critical to guarantee high-quality service identical to the original when rights to render services are transferred. It is challenging to develop performance measurement criteria in education and medicine, thus this task is supposed to be accomplished by early 2017. By this time, training and certification of trainers and dentists is expected to be completed. The use of local marketing firms for franchise marketing looks to be the best solution.

It is possible to scale clinics' activities and enter external markets; however, domestic markets still have lots of potential. Kyiv is the target market because the lion's share of the national purchasing power is located in Kyiv, Kharkiv and Lviv. Kyiv is the most attractive because, regardless of the saturated dentistry market, it has the largest capacity. This is because:

- Average salary: if the market is segmented by salary, Kyiv is the largest in Ukraine.
- The fast pace of life and better oral care increases demand for total teeth reconstruction due to dental abrasion rather than bacterial effects on gums and teeth. Direct restoration is a cheaper alternative to restoration.
- Serhiy Radlinskyy's dental clinic is a brand well-known to Kyivites for its high quality. Activation of the current customer base makes a 60 percent occupancy rate of clinics possible.

Therefore, the opening of a clinic with three dental chairs and one training class in Kyiv is scheduled for 2018. Furthermore, the Kyiv clinic will be instrumental for improving logistics for customers from central, southern and western Ukraine. A chair profitability rate of 10,000 euros is planned. The transportation hub with its two international airports and railway terminal improves international logistics.

Notes

1 See Academy of Biomimetic Dentistry: www.academyofbiomimeticdent.org/about-biomimetic-dentistry/our-mission-and-values.html.

2 See Business Insider: www.businessinsider.com/which-countries-have-the-most-dentists-per-capita-2011-2.

3 For more information, see OECD. Health at a Glance 2009. Available at http://dx.doi.org/10.1787/health_glance-2009-en.

4 For more information, see www.ncbi.nlm.nih.gov/pmc/articles/PMC2647952/.

References

Interstate Statistical Committee of the Commonwealth of Independent States, 2015, *Healthcare*. Available at www.cisstat.com/eng/frame_cis.htm. Accessed September 13, 2017.

Omelchuk, A. and Khachatryan, V., 2010, *Розвиток підприємництва в Україні* (*Entrepreneurship Development in Ukraine*). Available at www.rusnauka.com. Accessed September 13, 2017.

Radlinskyy, S., 1997a, "Биомиметическое направление в реставрации зубов," *DentArt*, 3, pp. 34–40.

Radlinskyy, S., 1997b, "Управление прозрачностью реставрационных конструкций," *DentArt*, 4, pp. 30–37.

Radlinskyy, S., 2001, "Опаковость оттенков в реставрационной консфункции," *DentArt*, 2, pp. 35–40.

Statistic Reference Book, 2015, *State Statistics Service of Ukraine*. Available at http://ukrstat.gov.ua. Accessed February 5, 2016.

World Bank, 2016, *Doing Business: Measuring Business Regulations*. Available at www.doingbusiness.org/data/exploreeconomies/ukraine. Accessed February 5, 2016.

PART V

Conclusions and implications

13

TWENTY-FIVE YEARS OF TRANSITION

Entrepreneurial activities from homeland to borderless opportunities

Tõnis Mets

Introduction

Countries of CEE were in the very beginning of transition when Porter published his *The Competitive Advantage of Nations* (1990). They had just come from the socialist system of *planned*, or *command*, economy and Porter didn't even have a model to describe their competitiveness in comparison with a traditional capitalist society. This comparison became possible after reforms towards a market economy. But even in the newest situation, the CEE countries have a different position, partly as a legacy of history, partly influenced by the trajectory of transition, which is a combination of political and entrepreneurial agenda.

The firms for case studies in this book are selected by authors as experts of entrepreneurship in their countries of origin. Although these post-communist countries started the transition towards market economy practically at the same time, at the end of the 1980s and during the 1990s, starting points were partly different (Varblane and Mets, 2010; Smallbone and Welter, 2001). The case companies represent four different types of countries regarding their historical background. Entrepreneurship was most restrictive in the Soviet Union, less so in the Central European "democratic republics" and former Yugoslavia. As belonging to the Soviet Union has a different history, post-Soviet countries are divided into two groups, depicted below.

Ukraine and Belarus, now former associated member and member of the Commonwealth of Independent States (CIS), belong to the first group, for which Russia has had or still has the leading role. Private business in these countries was suppressed for about 70 years. Transition in these countries has been hard and reforms not entirely applied (Filatotchev *et al.*, 1999). This caused an "orange revolution" in Ukraine, but not in Belarus, which kept a higher GDP and standard of living (CIA, 2017). Developments in Ukraine are suppressed because of the ongoing Russian military intervention, which started in late February 2014 (Jones and Whitworth, 2014). Problems in Ukraine are corruption and a low level of welfare (Karatnycky, 2005). Ukraine became a member of the WTO in 2008; Belarus is still applying for membership (WTO, 2017). Partial indicators of the entrepreneurship ecosystem have improved in these countries in just the last few years, as shown in Chapters 5 and 12.

The second group is the Baltic States: Estonia, Latvia, and Lithuania, being annexed by the Soviet Union for about 50 years (although occupation started in 1940, nationalization of the property there was implemented fully after the Second World War). People in these countries had a more social memory about private business. Besides, since the 1960s, Estonians have been able to watch Finnish TV, getting a better understanding of the market economy. Partly, at the beginning of the transition, Estonia was a good example of societal reforms for the destiny's companion-countries. All three Baltic States had an orientation to the West; they were successful reformers and accessed the European Union (EU) and NATO in 2004.

Hungary, Poland, and Slovakia belong to the third group of post-socialist countries – former "democratic republics." They had some level of private ownership in small business, mainly in the service sector in socialist times. They reshaped their economy much faster than members of the CIS. Poland and Hungary joined NATO in 1999; Slovakia in 2004. They all accessed the EU in 2004, together with the Baltic States.

The fourth group of countries is represented by Slovenia and Serbia, republics of the former Socialist Federal Republic of Yugoslavia (SFRY). In these countries, private ownership was allowed more widely, as well as employee ownership of companies; also, free movement of labor was allowed between SFRY and the neighboring Western countries (Varblane and Mets, 2010). Since 1991, after a military conflict with Yugoslavia, Slovenia announced independence and joined EU and NATO in 2004. Serbia, as the leader of the former Yugoslavia, had several war conflicts with separating republics in the 1990s; the process continued on the political level in the first decade of the twenty-first century. Serbia is still an observer in the WTO (2017) and a candidate to access the EU (CIA, 2017).

This chapter aims to compare development trajectories of entrepreneurship in the CEE countries represented in this book. The chapter is based on the framework of competitiveness and economic development suggested by Porter and developed further by the Global Competitiveness Report (GCR), but also on the entrepreneurship-specific Global Entrepreneurship Monitor (GEM) and Global Entrepreneurship Index (GEI). The content of these approaches matches very well with the concept of the entrepreneurial ecosystem (e.g., Stam, 2015; Cohen, 2006; Isenberg, 2010; Foster *et al.*, 2013; Venkataraman, 2004) around the case companies. Therefore, aspects of the ecosystem are used in the comparison below.

The framework of entrepreneurship development in CEE

Stages of economic development and entrepreneurship

Porter, in his book *The Competitive Advantage of Nations* (1990), suggests four stages of evolution of national competitive development: factor-driven, investment-driven, innovation-driven, and wealth-driven (in later publications, Porter abandons the fourth stage, wealth-driven, and investment-driven is replaced with efficiency-driven). Based on that approach, Porter *et al.* (2002), suggest a division of economic development into three stages: low-, middle-, and high-income (level) stages. These stages are defined in the association of government and industry/companies with their main features and challenges within these stages. The authors mention two transitions between three stages (ibid.). They also analyze some country cases of difficulties or failures in transitioning into a higher developmental level. Later on, researchers within the framework of the Global Entrepreneurship Monitor (GEM) started to implement these three stages for a better explanation of variability of nascent entrepreneurship in different societies (Ács *et al.*, 2008). They use the concept of economic development stages for a better understanding of the U-curve, describing nascent entrepreneurship versus per capita income (Wennekers *et al.*, 2005). Deliberately, self-employment, as well as nascent entrepreneurship activity (also used as the TEA-index), is moving to decline in the transition from the factor- to the efficiency-driven economy. The competitiveness and internationalization factors in the economic development and entrepreneurship context as excerpts from the literature of both research streams are presented in Table 13.1.

The first two economic development stages are considered as being resource-based, with the third stage being knowledge-based. Although the characteristics of the stages are defined (Porter, 1990), one can find more explanation on how the process of transition can appear within stages in later publications (e.g., Porter, 2003). Mostly, the duration of the transition process depends on the sectoral structure of the economy and the region caused by (but, also causing) inequality of development. In addition, the scale of the factor's impact depends on the position of the country in the stage – just entering the stage or growing out of it (Ács *et al.*, 2008). A general conclusion for all the stages is that "some tasks are common to all governments: macroeconomic stability, provision of basic medical and healthcare, openness of the economy, and a competitive exchange rate that supports export growth" (Porter *et al.*, 2002, p. 19).

Porter (2003) discloses a microeconomic context of economic development and introduces the role of clusters and company sophistication in the economic development. Porter's model (Business Competitiveness Index – BCI), as the core of the competitiveness report of the World Economic Forum, is one of the essential tools for benchmarking countries' strengths and weaknesses. In a further development of the competitiveness framework, in 2004, the Global Competitiveness Index (GCI) was introduced (Porter *et al.*, 2008). The list of measured indicators is slightly

TABLE 13.1 Competitiveness factors, economic development, and entrepreneurship

	Type of economy/development stage/GDP per capita, USD, competitive advantage*	*Characteristics*				
		Macroeconomic context		*Microeconomic foundation of development*		*Entrepreneurship, startups*
		Pillars	*Role of government*	*Industry, companies*	*Company sophistication*	
Resource-based	Stage 1 Low-income level: < 2,000 Factor-driven Input costs	1 Institutions 2 Infrastructure 3 Macroeconomic environment 4 Health and primary education	Free market: land, labor, capital Physical infrastructure: ports, telecommunications, roads Positive attitude toward entrepreneurs Challenge: political and macroeconomic stability	Primary factors of production: land, unskilled labor Labor-intensive low-cost manufacturing – competitive advantage Simple products Limited role in the value chain Challenge: increase of efficiency	1 Competitive advantages beyond cheap inputs 2 Production process sophistication 3 Degree of customer orientation 4 Extent of marketing 5 Extent of regional sales 6 Reliance on professional management	Non-agricultural self-employment Necessity-driven entrepreneurship Orientation to primary commodities
	Transition from stage 1 to stage 2 2,000–2,999					
	Stage 2 Middle-income level: 3,000–8,999 Efficiency-driven Efficiency	5 Higher education and training 6 Goods market efficiency 7 Labor market efficiency 8 Financial market development 9 Technological readiness 10 Market size	Attraction of FDI Regulations: customs, taxation, company law Cluster development R&D Challenge: human capital, competencies	Foreign direct investment (FDI) Technology import and assimilation Inflow of capital and knowledge/technology Sophistication of products, quality Growth of companies; mergers and acquisitions Integration into international production system; standard product – competitive advantage Challenge: internationalization and technology capacity	7 Broad value chain presence 8 Control of international distribution 9 Extent of branding 10 Company spending on R&D 11 Prevalence of foreign technology licensing 12 Extent of staff training	Decline of self-employment Opportunity startups Growth of technology competence Growing spatial clustering and urbanization Innovation and IPR becomes important Growth in R&D
	Transition from stage 2 to stage 3 9,000–17,000					
Knowledge-based	Stage 3 High-income level: > 17,000 Innovation-driven Unique value	11 Business sophistication 12 Innovation	R&D and education on world technology level Entrepreneurial ecosystem Challenge: human capital (creative, entrepreneurial and innovative labor)	Social, science-based learning Ability to shift to new technologies Export orientation, increase of services sector Global integration Technology export Flexible organizational structures Challenge: generation of high rates of innovation and commercialization of new technologies	13 Capacity for innovation 14 Breadth of international markets 15 Extent of incentive compensation 16 Willingness to delegate authority	New increase in entrepreneurial activity New technologies, IP New business models Opportunity-driven new ventures Global orientation Startup seed capital

Source: Author's compilation and synthesis based on Porter (2003, 1990); Porter *et al.* (2002); Ács *et al.* (2008); Sala-i-Martín *et al.* (2015); GEDI (2014).

Note

* For economies with a high dependency on mineral resources, GDP per capita is not the sole criterion for the identification of the stage.

expanded in the course of growing availability of global data. The factors of GCI are presented as 12 pillars (Sala-i-Martín *et al.*, 2015) in Table 13.1.

The 12 pillars are grouped into sub-indexes within the stages where they have the highest importance (the result of econometric estimates by Sala-i-Martín *et al.*, 2009); these sub-indexes are *Basic requirements*, *Efficiency enhancers*, and *Innovation and sophistication factors*. The estimates (ibid.) show the decreasing share of primary factors and increasing efficiency, and innovation and sophistication factors in the course of economic development (Figure 13.1). So, we receive clear distribution patterns differentiating development stages.

Obviously, entrepreneurship as a new venture creation should follow the pattern of economic development stages. In part, some ideas come from the *Company sophistication*, as suggested by Porter (2003) in Table 13.1. Entrepreneurship researchers have made several efforts to link outcomes of the GCR and GEM studies (Coduras and Autio, 2013; Ács and Naudé, 2013; Naudé, 2011). The most popular of these efforts is the Global Entrepreneurship and Development Index (GEDI), which consists of three sub-indexes: Entrepreneurial Attitude, Activities,[1] and Aspiration (Ács and Naudé, 2013). The authors (ibid.) conclude that industrial policy should have a key focus toward entrepreneurial attitudes in the factor-driven economy, entrepreneurial activities (ability) in the efficiency-driven economy and aspirations on the stage of the innovation-driven economy. Later on, Ács *et al.* (2017) modified GEDI to make the Global Entrepreneurship Index (GEI) with some improvements of measurement. The GEI includes 14 pillars, with every pillar having its own individual and institutional component.[2] The GEDI uses seven institutional variables out of 14 originating from the GCI; others are from public sources (OECD, WB, UN, etc.); all individual-level variables come from the GEM

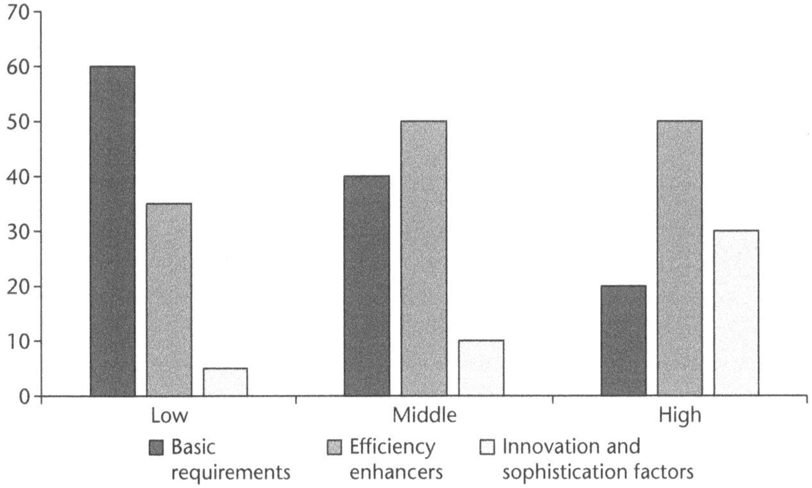

FIGURE 13.1 Weights of GCI sub-indexes depending on the development stage.

Source: Author's compilation based on Sala-i-Martín *et al.* (2009).

survey, and missing data are substituted (Ács *et al.*, 2017). Like sub-indexes of GCI, sub-indexes of GEI are also represented in all development stages. The factors behind GEI sub-indexes have different value and meaning in the particular stage, like for GCI in Figure 13.1. That means there can be an expected mutual correspondence pattern (matching) of sub-indexes of GCI and GEI to obtain a clear outline, as follows in Table 13.2.

From that approach, one can conclude that basic requirements as well as basic needs, and entrepreneurial attitudes – propensity to satisfy elementary needs via self-employment – in general, are leading economic development in the factor-driven economy stage 1 (Table 13.1). In the entrepreneurship studies, this is categorized as necessity entrepreneurship. Attitudes here mean learning startup competencies, non-fear of failure and networking by an entrepreneur, and cultural support to new venture starters by society (Ács and Naudé, 2013). Natural resources and low-cost manufacturing are the competitive advantages of companies of stage 1 on international markets. But even the poorest societies can start innovation-driven (knowledge-based) new ventures that reach global markets (aspiration: internationalization) and contribute to homeland future economic development. In

TABLE 13.2 Mutual pattern matching by sub-indexes of GCI and GEI in the economic development context

Economic development stage	*Pattern matching between GCI and GEI*	
	Global Competitiveness Index (GCI), pillars	*Global Entrepreneurship Index (GEI), pillars*
1 Factor-driven	Basic requirements: 1 Institutions 2 Infrastructure 3 Macroeconomic environment 4 Health and primary education	Attitudes sub-indexes: • Opportunity perception • Startup skills • Risk acceptance • Networking • Cultural support
2 Efficiency-driven	Efficiency enhancers: 5 Higher education and training 6 Goods market efficiency 7 Labor market efficiency 8 Financial market development 9 Technological readiness 10 Market size	Abilities sub-indexes: • Opportunity startup • Technology absorption • Human capital • Competition
3 Innovation-driven	Innovation and sophistication factors: 11 Business sophistication 12 Innovation	Aspirations sub-indexes: • Product innovation • Process innovation • High growth • Internationalization • Risk capital

Source: Author's compilation based on Ács *et al.* (2017); WEF (2017).

part, such an example could be India with its programmers running a global business, and the country still staying on the low-income level economically and having a huge digital divide (Sala-i-Martín *et al.*, 2015).

The barrier between factor- and efficiency-driven stages 1 and 2 is fragile on the scale of GDP per capita measures. Evidently, development environment and human resources become decisive factors in stage 2 (see Table 13.1). That presents higher requirements to education, technology competencies, funding, and efficient market relations (efficiency enhancers). In this stage, technology consumption and absorption anticipate technology production. Entrepreneurial abilities factors, including entrepreneurial and technology capabilities and competitive environment, meet these aspects in the best way. The productivity of manufacturing standard products and services is the main competitive advantage on international markets, initially, in this stage.

The innovation-driven knowledge economy, stage 3, including a higher level of business sophistication and innovation, creates new opportunities for entrepreneurs based on high science and technology capabilities. New ventures start as technology creators and producers. This stage is also called the entrepreneurial economy (Ács and Naudé, 2013). Starting from new product and technology ideas, entrepreneurs aspire to internationalization and fast/high growth. Particularly in the globalization era "international markets have become a substitute for domestic markets, especially for small countries" (Sala-i-Martín *et al.*, 2009: 6). There are "push" and "pull" factors for going global/international by technology/knowledge-based entrepreneurs. "Push" factor means the need to cover R&D expenses, which could not succeed in the tiny domestic market; and "pull" factor means attractiveness of foreign markets. In this stage, the growth is led by a new type of startup – opportunity-driven entrepreneurs seeking global markets from inception, also known as *born globals* (Madsen and Servais, 1997). A maturing entrepreneurial ecosystem with its support structures, including seed-funding, facilitates innovative knowledge-based and fast-growing businesses.

Comparison of entrepreneurship in the CEE countries

Trying to compare entrepreneurial ecosystems and entrepreneurship of CEE countries, one meets difficulties with finding comparable data. There exist several institutions assessing entrepreneurship, including the Global Entrepreneurship Research Association (GERA) running the Global Entrepreneurship Monitor (GEM) and measuring the Total Entrepreneurship Activity (TEA) Index, covering 61 economies in 2016. The Global Entrepreneurship Development Institute (GEDI) assesses the Global Entrepreneurship Index (GEI) in 137 countries, and the World Economic Forum (WEF) measures the Global Competitiveness Index (GCI) in 138 countries. Partly, surveys of these institutions refer to and integrate approaches and data from each other, but unfortunately, not covering our sample entirely. The only sources covering all countries, but not all entrepreneurship aspects, are the World Factbook of the CIA (2017), the World Bank (WB) and the United Nations Organization (UNO).

Therefore, the data in Table 13.3 create an incomplete comparison of the studied countries. Sources were used that provided data for most of these countries. Figures of population and GDP, given by CIA, were preferred because of the coverage of all the countries, although numbers differ slightly from official statistics of the country – for example, from the data of the national statistics of Estonia. GEM data are missing for Serbia, Ukraine, and Belarus (for Lithuania, we have the TEA index from 2014). Belarus is the only country missing data of competitiveness by the WEF.

Based on the available data, similarities can be found between the two groups of post-socialist countries: the Baltic States and Central European countries. The TEA and welfare in these countries have a growing trend; they are members of EU and NATO. Their socioeconomic developments have leveled off recently. The Baltic States are characterized by a higher TEA index. The greater role of entrepreneurship, in these countries, is also proved by a bigger share of SMEs in GDP. Partly, the major role of SMEs may also come from the Soviet legacy as the Baltic States had to rebuild their economic structure disconnecting from the Eastern market; new industries in these countries are more fragmented or less consolidated than their Western neighbors. That may partly be an indicator of moving towards an entrepreneurial and knowledge-based economy, as generalized in Table 13.1. An innovation-driven development, stage 3, is reached by Estonia; others are still in transition from stage 2 to stage 3. Estonia's case (Chapter 6) also demonstrates the controversial role of FDI in internationalization and growth of the knowledge base of a small open country's economy.

The development trajectories of former Yugoslavian republics Slovenia and Serbia are different from one another, as different as their histories are of the last 25–30 years. According to its indicators (Table 13.3) and developments (membership in EU and NATO), Slovenia is similar to the Baltic States, with slightly higher GDP, lower TEA, and a smaller share of SMEs in GDP. Slovenia is the only country, other than Estonia, in the third stage of development (WEF, 2017). Serbia, however, has remained far behind, which is explained by the long-lasting political transition (CIA, 2017); their position in development stage 2 is better than the Ukrainian position between stages 1 and 2. The competitiveness of the Serbian economy has improved by four positions in the last year, reaching 90 in 2016/2017 (WEF, 2017).

In the group of CIS countries, very little information can be found about Belarus. Although, according to some studies, the entrepreneurial environment is considered unfriendly (Ivanova, 2005), GDP per capita in Belarus is remarkably higher than in Ukraine. Also, a ranking of ease of doing (and starting) business is now even better than in some EU member states or Serbia. A low share of SMEs, in the creation of GDP, indicates undeveloped entrepreneurship in Belarus. Belarus is a unique experiment of "market socialism," with active state intervention in the economy (see Chapter 5). Ranking of competitiveness (85 among 138 economies) of Ukraine is quite low; a better sign is that the country's Innovation ranking, at 73, is much stronger. Ukraine is in transition from the factor-driven stage 1 to efficiency-driven development stage 2.

TABLE 13.3 Comparison of entrepreneurial ecosystems of CEE countries

Indicator\country	*Belarus*	*Ukraine*	*Estonia*	*Latvia*	*Lithuania*	*Hungary*	*Poland*	*Slovakia*	*Serbia*	*Slovenia*
Population, million	9.57	44.2	1.26	1.97	2.85	9.87	38.52	5.45	7.14	1.98
GDP per cap PPP, $, 2016	17,500 ↓	8,200 ↓	29,500 ↑	25,700 ↑	29,900 ↑	27,200 ↑	27,700 ↑	31,200 ↑	14,200 ↑	33,100 ↑
Exports of goods and services, %	57.2	55.9	79.2	58	72.9	94.3	50.5	94.8	50.9	79.1
GERA: TEA index, 2016	NA	NA	16.2 ↑	14.2 ↑	11.3*	7.9 ↓	10.7 ↑	9.5 ↓	NA	8.0 ↑
TEA index, opportunity**, 2016	NA	NA	12.4	11.4	9*	5.7	7.1	4.75	NA	5.8
TEA index, 2004	NA	NA	5.0	6.6★★	NA	4.3	8.8	NA	NA	2.6
The GEDI: GEI/rank, 2017	NA	26.9/66	55.5/23	43/38	49.6/28	36.3/47	46.6/31	44.1/35	23.1/79	51.5/26
SME contribution to GDP, %	21.1	NA	75	72	68.5	52	52	57	NA	63
WTO, 2017: member, year	–	2008	1999	1999	2001	1995	1995	1995	–	1995
WB, 2017: Doing business rank	37	80	12	14	21	41	24	33	47	30
Starting a business rank	31	20	14	22	29	75	107	68	47	49
WEF, 2017: GCI/rank	NA	4.0/85	4.78/30	4.45/49	4.6/35	4.2/69	4.56/36	4.28/65	3.97/90	4.4/56
Innovation and sophist./rank	NA	3.53/73	4.15/33	3.71/58	4.01/43	3.36/97	3.74/55	3.71/57	3.1/120	4.08/37
Stage of development	NA	1→2	3	2→3	2→3	2→3	2→3	2→3	2	3

Sources: Apiakun and Mets (this volume, Chapter 5); GERA (2005–2017); Lepane and Kuum (2004); WEF (2017); CIA (2017); GEDI (2017); World Bank (2017); WTO (2017); ** – author's calculations.

Notes

TEA index – Percentage of the population between the ages of 18 and 64 years who are in the process of starting a business (a nascent entrepreneur) or owner-manager of a new business less than 42 months old; TEA has the opportunity- and necessity-driven component (GERA, 2016).

↑↓ – trend of the indicator in last three years; ★★ – data 2005; * – data 2014; NA – data not available.

The Global Competitiveness Index (GCI) as well as Innovation ranking (30 and 33) are highest for Estonia. If the global competitiveness position of the sample countries is generally better than innovativeness, then Slovakia, Slovenia, and Ukraine are exceptions (Table 13.3). This may be a sign of improvement potential of their GCI. Figure 13.2 shows a good correlation between the indicators GCI and GEI, although describing two partly different sides of socioeconomic development conditions and the entrepreneurial ecosystem. One can notice some variations of similar values of indexes (e.g., Latvia and Slovakia), which remain in the confidence intervals of the method (see Ács *et al.*, 2017). One of the conclusions is that GCI characterizes, quite well, the entrepreneurial ecosystem of the sample country group.

The share of export (in percentage of GDP, Table 13.3) varies between countries, and only partly describes internationalization of firms and openness of the economy. Therefore, it is more important to understand value creation mechanisms by exporting firms. Case studies represent the palette of ways how companies of CEE create value and reach foreign markets. In this context, three cases (from Latvia, Lithuania, and Belarus, Chapters 3–5) show how entrepreneurs have reshaped traditional industries and gradually moved to international and global markets.

Some of the case studies represent the *new economy* – knowledge-based high-technology startups. Although there are different definitions of the knowledge-based and high-technology nature of the business field (Shearmur and Doloreux, 2000), usually these are "the companies which are contributing to the creation of

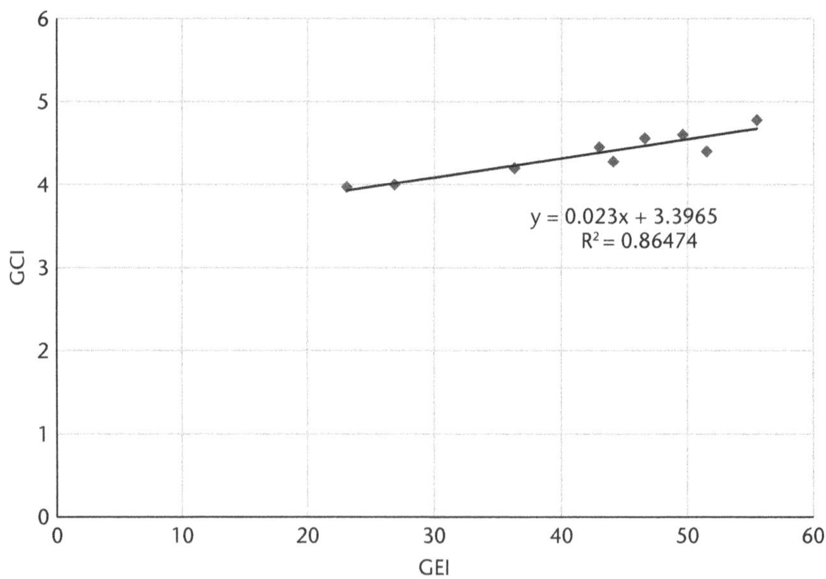

FIGURE 13.2 Correlation between GCI and GEI for the case study countries, except Belarus.

Source: Author's calculation.

high-technology new knowledge themselves, this knowledge is unique and creates a competitive advantage on the market" (Mets, 2012: 169). A group of new technology entrepreneurs (cases from Estonia, Poland, Serbia, and Slovakia, Chapters 6–9) has created startups, which, by their character, start to internationalize from inception. Another group of entrepreneurs are innovators, improving existing and creating new businesses (cases from Hungary, Slovenia, and Ukraine, Chapters 10–12), growing and widening the knowledge base of their homeland economies.

This book introduces case companies of different traditions and forms of entrepreneurship. Here, one can find cases representing firms of the same age as the transition process of their home countries (Chapter 4: Vičiūnai Group, Lithuania; Chapter 12: Apollonia, Ukraine). This suggests that the entrepreneurs just needed the starting point of economic freedom in their countries of origin to kick off their business. Another group comprises cases of corporate entrepreneurship based on the example of companies (Chapter 3: Laima, Latvia; Chapter 10: Richter Gedeon, Hungary; Chapter 11: Hidria, Slovenia) which were privatized during reforms or which were directly impacted by existing industries during socialist times. To some extent, Telegrafia, Slovakia, can be considered to be in this group (Chapter 9), inheriting the background of the business started in 1919. But, certainly, newly founded firm Vičiūnai Group (Lithuania) belongs with the examples of corporate entrepreneurs: growing fast, it started to merge businesses from outside its homeland and widened its field as a corporation.

Discussion and conclusion

A general overview of the entrepreneurial ecosystem in CEE demonstrates the strong influence of political and socioeconomic agendas on the development of these countries. Trying to understand the different developmental levels of the countries with similar historical backgrounds, one can notice how political decision and volition to implement reforms, but also choice of partners by governments, has played a very decisive role. Comparative analysis of political, cultural, and historical path-dependence of development trajectories could be a topic of further study. But one is clear, internationalization of businesses and countries is a part of entrepreneurship and socioeconomic development.

Entrepreneurship in CEE developed in synchronism with economic and democratic reforms in the 1990s. Almost all countries started with the privatization of industry and creating a physical and legislative environment of the market economy. An exception here is Belarus, declaring "market socialism" as its socioeconomic development doctrine. The case studies, as well as comparable data of their country of origin above, create a better understanding of the internationalization and entrepreneurship development processes in these countries. These processes are reciprocally interdependent and could be generalized in the following way:

- Openness and internationalization of the entrepreneurial ecosystem are the keys to competitiveness, entrepreneurship, and socioeconomic development of small CEE countries. The best successors of the transition have been the Baltic and Central European countries, and Slovenia, which started the market economy and democratic reforms in the early 1990s. One of the first steps to internationalization by these countries was an accession to the WTO (www.wto.org). These countries oriented to the Western markets and collaborated with the EU. Established benchmarks and direct support by the EU helped them, at a faster pace, build up the basis of the macroeconomic "pillars" and environment. CIS countries oriented to Russia and former Soviet republics, and globalization by joining the WTO occurred much later or is still in the application phase (Belarus).

- Opportunities for entrepreneurs depend on the developmental stage of the society following the logic of the companies' business sophistication and macroeconomic environment of the country. Most of the CEE countries are in the stage where development is led by opportunity-driven entrepreneurship where the growing success factor is the entrepreneurial ecosystem with its national and international context. That is also the challenge of their governments, deciding which strategic key factors should be considered, and how to follow the strategy.
- Internationalization aspirations of new ventures/businesses grow with the level of economic development, particularly for innovative knowledge- and technology-based startups of small country origin.
- The role and state of entrepreneurship and internationalization in a particular country is an outcome as well as an engine of transition process, depending on the political choices by the CEE countries. There are similarities and diversity between development trajectories of post-Soviet, former "democratic" and Yugoslavian republics. Starting with revolutionary decisions 25 years ago, inequality inside the particular country groups with similar legacies was smaller than that which can be seen now.

The countries of CEE are not homogeneous; they differ by size, history, welfare, and entrepreneurial orientation. Also, the need for internationalization is different. That is reflected in the indicators of foreign direct investment and export. Therefore, because of smaller domestic sales, smaller countries need more international trade to compensate their own tiny home market with exports and cover the needs with imports. Therefore, for example, the figure of roughly 50 percent of exports by Poland is not exactly comparable to the similar number by Serbia. The first of these is a much bigger market, with twice as much purchasing power per capita than the other. But even figures of export and the size of the country are not the full "truth." From the country case studies, the structure of value creation in exports is showing growing importance of the knowledge economy in small Estonia and much bigger Poland. That means an opportunity for further study into how entrepreneurial and knowledge-based the economies of all the CEE countries are.

In conclusion, the Eastern European countries started their transition from a closed and entrepreneurship-hostile Soviet system, and the Central and South

European countries from less hostile environments 25 years ago. Now they are reaching different positions in the global society in various ways. Some countries, among them Belarus, Ukraine, and Serbia, are still in transition. Other countries are in a post-transitional period. The role of entrepreneurs has been invaluable in reaching that point. Entrepreneurship and internationalization are two sides of the same coin in this process.

Notes

1 In the GEDI report, the sub-index (term) *Entrepreneurial Ability* describes the same dimension.
2 For a detailed description, please read Ács *et al.* (2017).

References

Ács, Z.J. and Naudé, W., 2013, "Entrepreneurship, stages of development, and industrialization," in A. Szirmai, W. Naudé, and L. Alcorta, eds., *Pathways to Industrialization in the Twenty-first Century*, Oxford: Oxford University Press, pp. 373–392.

Acs, Z.J., Desai, S., and Hessels, J., 2008, "Entrepreneurship, economic development and institutions," *Small Business Economics*, 31 (3), pp. 219–234.

Ács, Z.J., Szerb, L., Autio, E., and Lloyd, A., 2017, *The Global Entrepreneurship Index 2017*, Washington, D.C.: The Global Entrepreneurship and Development Institute.

CIA, 2017, *The World Factbook*. Available at www.cia.gov/library/publications/resources/the-world-factbook/index.html. Accessed May 17, 2017.

Coduras, A. and Autio, E., 2013, "Comparing subjective and objective indicators to describe the national entrepreneurial context: The Global Entrepreneurship Monitor and the Global Competitiveness Index contributions," *Investigaciones Regionales*, 26, pp. 47–74.

Cohen, B., 2006, "Sustainable valley entrepreneurial ecosystems," *Business Strategy and the Environment*, 15, pp. 1–14.

Filatotchev, I., Wright, M., Buck, T., and Zhukov, V., 1999, "Corporate entrepreneurs and privatized firms in Russia, Ukraine, and Belarus," *Journal of Business Venturing*, 14, pp. 475–492.

Foster, G., Shimizu, C., Ciesinski, S., Davila, A., Hassan, S., Jia, N., and Morris, R., 2013, *Entrepreneurial Ecosystems around the Globe and Company Growth Dynamics. Report Summary for the Annual Meeting of the New Champions 2013*, Geneva: World Economic Forum.

GEDI, 2017, *The Global Entrepreneurship Index*. Washington, DC: The Global Entrepreneurship and Development Institute.

GERA (Global Entrepreneurship Research Association), 2005–2017, *Global Entrepreneurship Monitor: Global Report*. London: GERA.

Isenberg, D.J., 2010, "How to start an entrepreneurial revolution," *Harvard Business Review*, June, pp. 41–49.

Ivanova, Y.V., 2005, "Belarus: Entrepreneurial activities in an unfriendly environment," *Journal of East-West Business*, 10 (4), pp. 29–54.

Jones, E. and Whitworth, A., 2014, "The unintended consequences of European sanctions on Russia," *Survival*, 56 (5), pp. 21–30.

Karatnycky, A., 2005, "Ukraine's orange revolution," *Foreign Affairs*, 84 (2), pp. 35–52.

Lepane, L. and Kuum, L., 2004, *Enterprise of Estonian Population*, Tallinn: Estonian Institute of Economic Research (in Estonian).

Madsen, T.K. and Servais, P., 1997, "The internationalization of born globals: An evolutionary process?" *International Business Review*, 6 (6), pp. 561–583.

Mets, T., 2012, "Creative business model innovation for globalizing SMEs," in T. Burger-Helmchen, ed., *Entrepreneurship – Creativity and Innovative Business Models*, Rijeka, Croatia: InTech, pp. 169–190.

Naudé, W.A., 2011, "Entrepreneurship is not a binding constraint on growth and development in the poorest countries," *World Development*, 39 (1), pp. 33–44.

Porter, M.E., 1990, *The Competitive Advantage of Nations*, New York: Macmillan.

Porter, M.E., 2003, "Building the microeconomic foundations of prosperity: Findings from the Microeconomic Competitiveness Index." Available at http://citeseerx.ist.psu.edu/viewdoc/download?doi=10.1.1.194.4526&rep=rep1&type=pdf. Accessed July 5, 2017.

Porter, M.E., Delgado, M., Ketels, C., and Stern, S., 2008, "Moving to a new Global Competitiveness Index," in M.E. Porter and K. Schwab, eds., *The Global Competitiveness Report 2008–2009*, Geneva: World Economic Forum, pp. 43–63.

Porter, M.E., Sachs, J.D., and McArthur, J.W., 2002, "Executive summary: Competitiveness and stages of economic development," in M.E. Porter, J.D. Sachs, P.K. Cornelius, J.W. McArthur, and K. Schwab, eds., *The Global Competitiveness Report 2001–2002*, New York: Oxford University Press, pp. 16–25.

Sala-i-Martín, X., Blanke, J., Drzeniek Hanouz, M., Geiger, T., and Mia, I., 2009, "The Global Competitiveness Index 2009–2010: Contributing to long-term prosperity amid the global economic crisis," in K. Schwab, ed., *The Global Competitiveness Report 2009–2010*, Geneva: World Economic Forum, pp. 3–47.

Sala-i-Martín, X., Crotti, R., Di Battista, A., Hanouz, M.D., Galvan, C., Geiger, T., and Marti, G., 2015, *Reaching Beyond the New Normal: Findings from the Global Competitiveness Index 2015–2016. World Economic Forum*, New York: Oxford University Press.

Shearmur, R. and Doloreux, D., 2000, "Science parks: Actors or reactors? Canadian science parks in their urban context," *Environment and Planning*, 32 (6), pp. 1065–1082.

Smallbone, D. and Welter, F., 2001, "The distinctiveness of entrepreneurship in transition economies," *Small Business Economics*, 16 (4), pp. 249–262.

Stam, E., 2015, "Entrepreneurial ecosystems and regional policy: A sympathetic critique," *European Planning Studies*, 23 (9), pp. 1759–1769.

Varblane, U. and Mets, T., 2010, "Entrepreneurship education in the higher education institutions (HEIs) of post-communist European countries," *Journal of Enterprising Communities: People and Places in the Global Economy*, 4 (3), pp. 204–219.

Venkataraman, S., 2004, "Regional transformation through technical entrepreneurship," *Journal of Business Venturing*, 19, pp. 153–167.

WEF, 2017, *The Global Competitiveness Report 2016–2017*, Geneva: World Economic Forum.

Wennekers, S., van Stel, A., Thurik, A.R., and Reynolds, P., 2005, "Nascent entrepreneurship and the level of economic development," *Small Business Economics*, 24 (3), pp. 293–309.

World Bank, 2017, *Doing Business*. Available at www.doingbusiness.org/data. Accessed August 8, 2017.

WTO (World Trade Organization), 2017, *WTO Membership*. Available at www.wto.org/english/thewto_e/whatis_e/tif_e/org6_e.htm. Accessed July 6, 2017.

INDEX

Page numbers in **bold** denote tables, those in *italics* denote figures.